ROAD TO SUCC.

A Guide for Doctoral Students
and Junior Faculty Members
in the Behavioral and Social Sciences

Dr. Viswanath Venkatesh
vvenkatesh@vvenkatesh.us
http://vvenkatesh.com

This edition published by
Dog Ear Publishing
4010 W. 86th Street, Ste H
Indianapolis, IN 46268

www.dogearpublishing.net

ISBN: 978-145750-405-1

This book is printed on acid-free paper.

Printed in the United States of America

Table of Contents

SECTION 4: TEACHING AND SERVICE

SECTION 5: GENERAL ADVICE

ENDNOTES

FOREWORD

The problem with being a successful researcher, a productive academic and a balanced person is that very important lessons are often not taught or not taught in a formal way. Important hints for success frequently come by personal observation and hints from colleagues. Sometimes, they come too late; one often wishes the counsel and advice could have come during early career struggles and mid-career decision making. Of course, one can always seek advice from valued colleagues, but wouldn't it be great also to read some advice from those who have been successful (but have been through trials, tribulations and tough decisions)? Their experiences cannot answer all questions but they can help your quest for understanding how to succeed. They can suggest questions as well as possible answers and enrich your search for the right path for you.

This book is a guide that helps fill the need for guidance, hints and good advice. I have known Viswanath Venkatesh (Venki) since he was a doctoral student at Minnesota. I have seen him become a very productive researcher and faculty member. He has listened to advice during his career. He has also observed himself, observed others, learned from his successes and mistakes, and learned from the successes and mistakes of others. He is well-positioned to share what he has learned. He has also included some interesting, relevant essays from others.

I commend Venki for preparing this book and recommend it to those who are beginning a research career, those who are in the early years as an academic, and those who are examining their current state and wondering how they should deal with important issues. I also recommend this book to senior researchers for valuable tips and tools that will undoubtedly aid their advising of doctoral students and junior faculty members. The book thus will be a great resource for those seeking to pave their road to success in academia and also for those seeking to help others pave the road to success in academia.

Gordon B. Davis
Honeywell Professor of Management Information Systems, Emeritus
Carlson School of Management, University of Minnesota

Book Overview

This book provides guidance and tools to help PhD students and junior faculty members successfully navigate and mature through the various stages of an academic career. Senior faculty members can use this book as a source of ideas to advise their PhD students and junior colleagues. This book presents knowledge that is seldom imparted in PhD programs, and organizes the same as advice and tools related to achieving success at research, teaching and service, all while maintaining work-life balance. The advice and tools provided are based on years of experience of the author and guest contributors, who have successfully navigated many of the same challenges and mentored many PhD students and junior faculty members. This book is suitable both for those who seek careers in research universities or universities that promote greater balance across research, teaching and service.

Life in academia is like life in no other profession. The intellectual freedom in conducting research coupled with the ability to positively impact the lives of students through teaching makes it exciting and noble. The road to success in making a difference through knowledge creation (research), knowledge dissemination (teaching) and activities related to both (service) is riddled with many challenges. While PhD programs are designed to teach students the nitty gritty details of conducting research, few focus on the broad issues of how to build a successful research program, how to build an effective teaching portfolio and how to do deal with the many other challenges encountered. Navigating the broader challenges of academia is often accomplished by trial-and-error or ad-hoc mentoring one may receive. This book, which provides advice and tools, seeks to help researchers achieve success by navigating through these very challenges. The book comprises 20 chapters that are organized into five major sections:

1. Research
2. Managing the PhD program
3. Life after the PhD
4. Teaching and service
5. Broader advice

In addition to the author, both junior and senior scholars have provided contributions to share their own experiences and observations of others who have been successful.

The most important component of the book is the various tools (e.g., how-to advice, checklists) that are provided to help junior researchers head up the road to success and to arm senior researchers to guide junior researchers along the way. The various tools target the following six areas:

1. Building and sustaining a research program
2. Writing a paper
3. Responding to reviews

4. Planning and monitoring through various stages of the PhD program
5. Becoming an effective teacher
6. Achieving work-life balance

AUTHOR BIOGRAPHY

Dr. Viswanath Venkatesh has published numerous articles in leading journals in the fields of organizational behavior, psychology, marketing, operations management, information systems (IS) and human-computer interaction. His articles have been cited about 14,000 times per Google Scholar and 5,000 times per Web of Science, with many of his articles being among the most cited in various journals. In 2009, one of his articles was identified by *Science Watch* (a Thompson Reuters' service) as the most influential in one of the four *Research Front Maps* in business and economics. He has worked with many junior faculty members and PhD students and mentored them in the art and science of publishing research. His work and the work of his students, which have received over $10M in funding from various corporate and government sources, has been presented across the world at leading conferences, universities, corporations and non-profit organizations, including the United Nations.

He completed his PhD at the University of Minnesota in 1997. He is a Distinguished Professor and the first holder of the George and Boyce Billingsley Chair in information systems at the Sam M. Walton College of Business, University of Arkansas, where he has been since June 2004. Prior to joining Arkansas, he was on the faculty at the University of Maryland. In addition to presenting his work at universities across the world, he has held many visiting appointments—e.g., Australian National University, Helsinki School of Economics, Hong Kong University of Science and Technology, Indian School of Business, MIT and University of Hawaii. He has taught a wide variety of undergraduate, MBA, exec MBA, PhD, and executive courses. Students have rated him to be among the best instructors at the various institutions where he has served and he has received teaching awards at the school and university levels.

He has performed extensive administration and service. At Arkansas, from 2004 to 2009, he was the director of the information systems PhD program. When he was the director of the information systems PhD program at Arkansas (2004-'09), he led large-scale program revision efforts that transformed the program to produce highly productive doctoral students and graduates. At Maryland, he was the director of the MBA consulting program and led undergraduate curriculum revision efforts. In 2009, he launched the IS research rankings web site (http://www.vvenkatesh.com/ISRanking), which has received many accolades from the academic community and is now affiliated with the Association for Information Systems (AIS). He has served or is serving on the editorial board of several journals: *Information Systems Research, AIS Transactions on Human-Computer Interaction. Decision Sciences, MIS Quarterly, Management Science, Organizational Behavior and Human Decision Processes,* and *Production and Operations Management.* He has been named to *Marquis' Who's Who in the World, America, and/or Science and Technology* each year since 2007.

His research focuses on understanding the diffusion of technologies in organizations and society. For over a decade, he has worked with several companies and government agencies in different capacities ranging from a systems engineer to a special consultant to the Vice-President, and has rigorously studied real world phenomena. Recently, he served on an expert panel at the United Nations on the advancement of women. His work has appeared in several journals including *Management Science, MIS Quarterly (MISQ), Information Systems Research (ISR), Communications of the ACM, Organizational Behavior and Human Decision Processes (OBHDP), Journal of Marketing, Personnel Psychology, Production and Operations Management (POM), Journal of the American Medical Informatics Association, Decision Sciences Journal (DSJ),* and *International Journal of Human-Computer Studies.* Some of his papers are among the most cited papers published in the respective journals: his *ISR* (2000) is the 2nd most cited paper, his *DSJ* (1996) is the 1st most cited paper, his *MISQ* (2003) is the 2nd most cited paper, and his *Management Science* (2000) is the 5th most cited paper.

More information about Dr. Venkatesh, his publications, past research and ongoing work is available at: http://vvenkatesh.com.

GUEST CONTRIBUTOR BIOGRAPHIES

Dr. Likoebe M. Maruping is an associate professor of Computer Information Systems in the College of Business at the University of Louisville. His research is primarily focused on the team design configurations and team processes through which software development teams improve software project outcomes under dynamic and/or uncertain project conditions. He also enjoys conducting research on virtual teams and the implementation of new technologies in organizations. Likoebe's current research interests are in the multilevel mechanisms through which information systems phenomena unfold in team contexts. His research has been published or is forthcoming in premier information systems, organizational behavior, and psychology journals including *MIS Quarterly, Information Systems Research*, *Organization Science, Journal of Applied Psychology*, and *Organizational Behavior and Human Decision Processes*. Likoebe currently serves as Associate Editor for *MIS Quarterly* and is on the editorial board of *IEEE Transactions on Engineering Management. MIS Quarterly* named him "Reviewer of the Year" in 2009.

Dr. Tracy Ann Sykes completed her PhD in information systems at the University of Arkansas in 2009. She worked at the National Science Foundation and the Australian National University before returning to join the University of Arkansas as an assistant professor in Fall 2011. Her research focuses on leveraging social network theory, methods and analyses to understand technology-related phenomena. Dr. Sykes is also working on several projects in the context of organizational and societal diffusion of technologies in developing countries, particularly in India. Her work has been published or is forthcoming in leading journals, such as *MIS Quarterly*, *Information Systems Research*, *Production and Operations Management*, and *Journal of the American Medical Informatics Association*. Her work has also been presented at various conferences, such as the *International Conference on Information Systems, Hawai'i International Conference on Systems Sciences, Decision Sciences International* and *Academy of Management Conference.*

Dr. Varun Grover is the William S. Lee (Duke Energy) Distinguished Professor of Information Systems at Clemson University. He has published extensively in the information systems field, with over 200 publications in major refereed journals. Nine recent articles have ranked him among the top four researchers based on number of publications in the top Information Systems journals, as well as citation impact (h-index). Dr. Grover is Senior Editor (Emeritus) for *MIS Quarterly, Journal of the AIS* and *Database*. He is currently working in the areas of IT value, individual and strategic impacts of IT and process transformation, and recently released his third book (with M. Lynne Markus) on process change. He is recipient of numerous awards from USC, Clemson, AIS, DSI, AoM, Anbar, PriceWaterhouse, etc. for his research and teaching and is a Fellow of the Association for Information Systems.

Dr. Susan A. Brown is a McCoy Rogers Fellow and associate professor of Management Information Systems in the University of Arizona's Eller College of Management. She received her PhD from the University of Minnesota and an MBA from Syracuse University. Her research interests include technology implementation, individual adoption, computer-mediated communication, technology-mediated learning and related topics. Her research has been published in *MIS Quarterly, Organizational Behavior and Human Decision Processes, Information Systems Research, Journal of MIS, IEEE Transactions on Engineering Management, Communications of the ACM,* and *Journal of the AIS,* among others. Her research has been funded by the National Science Foundation. She has received more than 20 citations and awards for her teaching. She has served or is currently serving as an associate editor for *MIS Quarterly, Information Systems Research, Journal of the AIS* and *Decision Sciences.*

Dr. Andrew Burton-Jones is an assistant professor at the Sauder School of Business at the University of British Columbia. He holds a B. Comm. and M. Inf. Sys. from the University of Queensland and a PhD from Georgia State University. He has three research streams. His first stream seeks a deeper understanding of how information systems are used in organizations, and how they could be used more effectively. His second stream focuses on improving methods used to analyze and design information systems. His final research stream centers on improving theories and research methods used in the information systems field. He has published in *Journal of the Association for Information Systems, Information Systems Research, MIS Quarterly,* and other outlets, and has received several awards for his research, teaching, and service. Prior to his academic career, he was a senior consultant in a Big-4 consulting firm.

Dr. Gordon B. Davis is the Honeywell Professor of Management Information Systems Emeritus in the Carlson School of Management at the University of Minnesota. He is recognized as one of the founders of the academic discipline of management information systems (MIS). In 1967, he, along with two colleagues at the University of Minnesota, started the first formal academic degree program in MIS. This program achieved a consistent ranking as one of the top programs. He headed the PhD program in MIS at Minnesota 1968 through 1993 and served as advisor, co-advisor, or committee member to over 100 doctoral students. He has lectured in 25 countries, published 23 books, with translations in several languages, and written over 150 articles, monographs and book chapters. His book, *Management Information Systems: Conceptual Foundations, Structure, and Development,* has been recognized as a classic foundational text in MIS. His monograph, *Writing the Doctoral Dissertation,* has been used by more than 60,000 doctoral students around the world.

ACKNOWLEDGMENTS

There have been many who have influenced my thinking and contributed greatly to my success over the years and the ideas I share here reflect their exceptional contributions to my own development in the past and each and every day.

My deepest gratitude is owed to my parents, Subhalakshmi Viswanath and Hariharan Viswanath, for their tough love in my formative years and for all their advice and patience for many, many more years. Also, many thanks to my brother, Kaartik Viswanath, for always being there not only to argue and fight with, but also as a friend.

Professors Fred Davis and Gordon Davis, my advisors in the PhD program at Minnesota, have been very influential in my development not only as a researcher but also as a person. I am thrilled that Gordon contributed the foreword and a chapter to this book.

Many others at the University of Minnesota, especially Gerry DeSanctis—whose comments on my first paper, written in the first quarter of my PhD program, "Keep working on this, you are on to something big!" is something I consider one of my greatest achievements and motivators—have been very instrumental in my development as an academic.

Professors Sue Brown, Mike Morris and Cheri Speier, who have been my partners-in-crime on several papers and great friends for over a decade now, taught me more than they could ever know. I owe a great deal of the advice that is shared in this book to what I learned from them and from working with them. I am delighted that Sue has contributed three tightly related chapters to this book.

Other collaborators in recent years, especially Professor Arun Rai, have provided me enormous advice and extended their friendship that I will always treasure. Many others all over the world, but especially from Arkansas and Maryland, where I have been a full-time faculty member since I graduated, and Hong Kong University of Science and Technology and Australian National University, where I have visited frequently and spent extended periods of time, have shared in my journey in academia and contributed positively either through advice or through their friendship—there are far too many to name. Others, both within and outside academia, have extended their friendship to celebrate the good times and support me during the bad times.

Several PhD students in the Maryland and Arkansas programs have knowingly or unknowingly contributed to my development as a mentor. Some students have even contributed to this book by being bad!

I owe a great debt to the contributors of various chapters. What each of them has contributed has enriched the book in ways beyond my wildest imagination. I know that each of them is very busy, with many competing demands on their time, so first and foremost, I appreciate that they took the time to share their ideas for this labor of love. Three junior scholars, Likoebe Maruping, Tracy Sykes and Andrew Burton-Jones, and three senior scholars, Varun Grover, Sue Brown and Gordon Davis, have contributed great insights. Likoebe Maruping is an immensely successful junior scholar, a former PhD student of mine of whom I am very proud. I thank him for sharing his thoughts and experiences related to developing a research program, especially framed around the timeframe within which papers are moved forward—if only I had read this chapter when I was a student, maybe I too would have graduated with a top journal publication! Tracy Sykes, another former PhD student of mine of whom I am very proud, has a million ideas a minute and has put a fair bit of them into papers to build a very strong record within just 2 years of graduation. I thank her for sharing what worked for her and things she'd have done differently in her program—I only wish I had read about her experiences when I was a student! Andrew Burton-Jones is another successful junior scholar who has also made many excellent research contributions. I thank him for sharing the keywords and phrases he works by—I learned a lot from them and I hope I too can work by them. While Sue Brown could have written on just about anything given how effectively she balances research, teaching and service, I am thankful that she placated me and wrote three chapters about various aspects related to teaching. No one else I know cares more about students or has a more holistic view of teaching than she does. Despite having been teaching for over a decade and a half, I must admit to not knowing or doing more than half the things she describes in her chapters—after having read her chapters, I know I will now be a more effective teacher. I am greatly appreciative that Varun Grover, a highly accomplished scholar, who has written very many articles advising PhD students, agreed to integrate four of his essays (which previously appeared in *Decision Line*) related to PhD education into a chapter for this book. Finally, I am very thankful and indebted to Gordon Davis, who is widely regarded as the father of the field of information systems, not only for the chapter he contributed, which will undoubtedly help PhD students and junior faculty members (and just about any working professional really) ensure that they achieve balance in life, but also for his encouragement and guidance throughout the writing and publication process of this book.

I owe thanks to Tracy Sykes and Hillol Bala for reading many of the early drafts of various chapters and giving me feedback both from the perspective of a student and a junior scholar. The chapters are all better for their feedback. My very special thanks to Tracy for her extremely patient and careful editing of several versions of each chapter, both from content and style perspectives, that has greatly improved the readability of all chapters. Many PhD students in various courses in different universities have read specific chapters and provided useful feedback that has helped shape and tighten the content of this book. Still others, Supreet Joglekar and Rinkesh Pati, have performed the painstaking task of dealing with the references and other none too trivial details. I would also like to thank Frank Chan and Xiaojun Zhang for their efforts in getting the website for the book and its sale fully functional and integrated with my website. As the book went to print from its draft form and as all the "big name" publishers were dropped, my thanks go to Jaime Newell, who has been very helpful in managing the many activities, including helping create chapter summaries, design graphics and interface extensively with the publisher, that brought this book to print. Finally, the team at Dog Ear Publishing has been helpful and patient through all stages of the production process.

CHAPTER 1

INTRODUCTION

This book is a synthesis not only of my experiences as a PhD student, faculty member and mentor, but also of my observations of several PhD students, some of whom I've worked with closely as the supervisor of their dissertation work. Serving as the director of a PhD program exposed me to many students over the years, their challenges and some solutions that either I developed to help them or emerged as a result of discussions with the students themselves. This book presents advice and tools that I have assembled from these varied experiences. I am delighted that some of those I've imposed upon have contributed their expertise and provided insightful chapters that are sure to help this book achieve its goal of helping junior academics chart a holistic course to success in the behavioral and social sciences. I should note that my experiences have been primarily in North America but, based on experiences I've had on extended visits to universities around the world, and interactions and conversations I've had with scholars in other countries, I believe much of the advice provided in this book will work in most settings. However, some practices (e.g., coursework, tenure) will vary across countries. This may, in turn, necessitate altering how the advice is used to fit the specific context.

Roadmap Through The Chapters

Eighteen of the book's twenty chapters, i.e., besides this one and the conclusions, are organized into 5 sections:

1. *Research:* This section provides advice and tools on how to build a successful research program, and how to write papers for scholarly journals, including how to manage the review process, in the social and behavioral sciences.

2. *Managing the PhD program:* This section provides advice on how to manage the PhD program, and presents advice on how to navigate the various stages in the program and transitions across these stages.

3. *Life after the PhD:* This section provides advice on how to manage life as an assistant professor, with a focus on strategies to make tenure.

4. *Teaching and service:* This section provides advice on two key things academics do besides research—i.e., teaching and service—and how to perform both effectively to achieve synergies and benefits from these activities.

5. *Broader advice:* This section provides advice that cuts across all phases of a student's and junior scholar's academic life.

Given that there are a few guest contributions, there is some overlap in the ideas and the messages across some of the chapters, including some of my chapters, but often while the message is consistent, the perspectives taken are different. I see this as valuable, particularly because it reinforces the key points that pave the road to success in academia.

With regard to the question of the sequence in which one should read the sections and chapters, I would say it is, of course, a reader's choice depending on his or her own interests. But, I offer the following broad guidance:

1. *PhD students:* Read section 2—i.e., chapters 8 to 11—first, followed by other sections in sequence (1, 3, 4 and 5)—i.e., chapters 1 to 7 and 12 to 20.
2. *Junior faculty members:* Read the chapters in order.
3. *Senior faculty members:* Read the chapters in order.

Choice Of Publisher

Many of my friends in the academy have told me that writing a book is a *labor of love*. I didn't know how much of a labor of love it would truly end up being until I started talking to publishers about getting this book published at as low a price as possible in order to make it available to as broad an array of readers as possible. I have interacted with several leading publishers over the past couple of years in an effort to complete this book and came away with responses from limited interest in the book due to topical misalignment to their current goals to exorbitant pricing for the book in order to, I assume, meet certain financial goals. Therefore, I decided that the best way to publish this book would be to turn this into even more of a *labor of love* by publishing the book at my own expense through a publishing house that will allow me to keep the sale price of the book as low as possible. The current price of the book seeks to achieve recuperation of my out-of-pocket costs over a few years of book sales. My goal is to re-evaluate the price at that point so as to lower it further (assuming no new editions, of course). For this reason, I further appreciate the generous contributions of the guest authors who share the same goal of helping the next generations of academics.

Chapter 2

Building and Sustaining a Research Program

***Note:* As noted in chapter 1, I suggest the student reader begin with section 2 (chapter 8).**

A research program is the careful and programmatic pursuit over several years of research in a few defined topic areas. There are many successful scholars in different fields from whom much can be learned about successfully building and sustaining a research program. Most successful scholars have surely taken a systematic approach to their research. The crux of a successful *research program strategy* is the emphasis of depth over breadth. This strategy comprises several elements. Some of these elements drive not only project and co-author selection, but also day-to-day planning and behaviors. First, I will discuss some of the major aspects of this strategy. Then, I will present the principles that have worked for me in the pursuit of my research program. Finally, I will elaborate on these principles and illustrate them with examples from my work. In this discussion, I will primarily focus on my own first few years as a researcher.

As I have often told PhD students, most dissertations aim to achieve *world peace*. By this, I mean the proposed research projects are overambitious, far too expansive and try to do far too much—i.e., attempt to achieve *world peace.* They are very grandiose and sprawling in scope. This is both bad and good. It is bad in that no dissertation can truly achieve the goal of *world peace* or any sizeable fraction of it. The dissertation typically needs to be scoped down. However, the good news is that when a thorough topic analysis is done and the gaps are identified, the early ideas do tend to have the makings of a solid research program for several years to come. I almost always see committee members leaving proposal-related meetings or discussions saying: "That is too much for a dissertation, it needs to be scoped down further." Typically, students' initial attempts at a dissertation tend to be many (usually 5-10) years of work, rather than just a dissertation.

Gordon Davis used to have students write a paper along the lines of "World Class Scholarship in [topic]: My Ten-year Plan." My paper, for example, was titled: "World Class Scholarship in Technology Adoption: My Ten-year Plan." It was one of the exercises that had a great impact on me and on the choices I made regarding how to pursue my research career. What topic a student chooses to write about is itself not the most important thing in the grand scheme of things. The paper got me thinking about scholarship in terms of a program of research and being a successful scholar in a 10-year time frame. Such a focused research program emphasizing depth was also reinforced to me by Fred Davis, who would frequently say: "try to be known for something." I also heard Jay Nunamaker, Joe Valacich and Brad Wheeler [academic grandfather, father, and son] at a panel at the AIS conference in Baltimore in 1997 giving the very same advice. In the PhD program at Arkansas, we have used this exercise, borrowed from Gordon Davis' idea, in the introductory PhD seminar on IS research and, if nothing else, it gets people tuned into the idea of a research program that is committed to building depth over the long-term, and that it is a long-term journey (marathon) and not a short-term assignment (sprint).

I will now discuss what I have learned in the pursuit of my research program. I will provide specific examples from my research program as a way to illustrate more general lessons learned.

I found developing and maintaining a solid pipeline to be essential to building and sustaining a research program. While creating and managing a pipeline is one of the most important aspects of building a successful and tenureable portfolio of publications, most people find it one of the hardest things to do. A pipeline, broadly speaking, is the series of research projects and/or papers that a researcher has at various stages of completion—i.e., idea formulation, model development, data collection, data analysis, writing (initial submission or revision) and under review (initial review or advanced round of review)—such that there will [hopefully] be a steady stream of publications over time. Unfortunately, cycle time, number of revisions, complexity of revisions and the luck of the draw (i.e., randomness in the review process), among other things, vary so much that it is nearly impossible to keep the pipeline steady and smooth. For instance, I was fortunate enough to have several articles be accepted in 1999-'00 such that six of them appeared in 2000, compared to years when I had only one paper appear.

Despite our best efforts to manage the pipeline, things may not work out exactly as we plan. However, if we don't bother to plan, it is certain to be difficult to keep a steady stream of publications flowing. Managing a pipeline is not just working on many papers at a given time or working on papers in some ad-hoc fashion such that there are many papers in play, rather it is having research projects in all phases of the research process going at any given time. There are a few basic strategies that I employed early in my career in order to manage my pipeline. I have organized my thinking about managing a pipeline into five areas:
1. Streams of research
2. Getting practical about streams
3. Research project versus research study
4. Populating your pipeline
5. Plan, plan, plan

In the remainder of this chapter, I will elaborate on each of these ideas and the underlying principles with illustrations from my experiences.

1. Streams Of Research

A research stream is work within a particular topic area and the word "stream" is used specifically to refer to the idea that it is ongoing. One of the essential elements of my research strategy was to work within a few (I worked on two—two or three are fine—more on this later) well-defined streams of research. Each research stream should have an overarching research question. An overarching research question should not be confused with a topic area. A topic area is much broader. For example, "employee job outcomes" is a topic area and "what are the drivers and consequences of employee job satisfaction?" is an overarching question within this topic area. It is important to relentlessly pursue various aspects of the chosen overarching research question. This sometimes requires turning down research projects that will not contribute to answering the chosen research question.

At the start of my career as an assistant professor, my primary stream was "technology in organizations," with much of the focus being on individual-level technology adoption. In this stream of work, my overarching research question was: "What are the drivers of technology adoption and use?" A fairly broad research question. My work included the pursuit of determinants of technology adoption, various contingencies and usability. I drew from a diverse base of psychology and organizational behavior theories. Restricting myself to this research stream and the overarching research question helped keep me focused. There were several projects I did not pursue because they did not fit with my research question.

One possible positive side effect of the pursuit of a single overarching research question is that there is the potential to be known for something. There is the potential to be one of the handful of experts in a particular topic area, and if you are lucky, within a short period of time. Both Fred Davis and Joe Valacich gained reputations for being leading scholars within a fairly short period of time due to their expertise and successful publication records in a particular topic area. I have discussed this issue of depth vs. breadth with others. While people favor one side or the other, seldom do they dismiss the other side. A risk of favoring depth over breadth is that external evaluators at the time of tenure[1] may say, "Person X is narrow [or too focused]." However, it is likely that if *that* is the most damning thing said about a tenure case, the tenure case should be alright. Another risk is the possibility that the person is seen as being interchangeable with (read: clone of) his or her advisor—a risk that is particularly substantial if your advisor is a well-established scholar and your dissertation is in the substantive area in which your advisor is already well-established and well-known. This is a matter I will delve into in greater detail later. But, for the moment, I will say this: it is imperative to demonstrate one's ability in doing high-quality research without one's advisor, regardless of the topic area of the dissertation or the research pursued after the dissertation.

It is interesting that, although I began my research hoping to be known for "individual-level research on technology implementations in organizations" or even "technology adoption and use," at almost every university I have visited to give a talk, I have been introduced as a "TAM researcher."[2] While I always try to set the record straight with what I think I really study—i.e., technology implementations in organizations—I have come to realize that it doesn't matter. But, one thing is certain to me, it is still better than being introduced as someone who does research such that no one really knows what one does.

2. Getting Practical About Streams

I am reminded of an essay I wrote in an exam in my high school French class. The essay was supposed to be about "a cow." I had prepared *a priori* by writing essays on many different simple topics but nothing about a cow (or even something remotely close). Eventually, after some deliberation, I recalled that I had prepared an essay about a tree—there was an old and famous tree in the city where I grew up. So, I went ahead and wrote that essay and concluded with something to the effect: "The cow is tied to the tree." Much like the cow is tied to the tree, almost any study can be forced to fit into a broad research question in a carefully crafted research statement [for tenure, for example]. While it may appear like I am suggesting that it should be fine to pursue pretty much any topic as there will be a way to make it fit into a theme, actually, my recommendation is quite the opposite so as to not have to be stuck like I was in my French exam. My recommendation is to carefully articulate a few specific questions early in one's research career and to pursue those questions. What does it mean to pursue those questions? I am not talking about only trying to answer those questions, but also investing time in reading and tracking the *relevant* literature in different fields that addresses those questions.

For me, the specific research questions/issues that related to my first stream of research on "technology in organizations" were:
i.   What factors influence employee adoption and use decisions?
ii. How can employee adoption and use be enhanced?
iii. What are the consequences (impacts) of employee adoption and use decisions?

The questions are not set in stone. They are still fairly broad. They evolve. The questions tend to get tweaked or changed over the years to fit with what sounds current, to be in step with how papers and ideas evolve. Regardless, having questions and pursuing those questions is important. It circumscribes many things. It prevents the infamous "opportunities of a life time that come by twice a day"—a term that I use to refer to absolutely can't-miss projects that people come to you to discuss just about twice a day—from derailing a set path. It prevents the need to ramp up on completely new topics with an indeterminate payoff. It prevents going down a path [topic] that you may later find uninteresting when compared to a path that you have chosen and that you like.

The third question in my set of specific research questions evolved. When I was in the PhD program, I had thought about: "What are the consequences (outcomes) of employee adoption and use decisions?" It grew into: "What are the broader outcomes of system use?" It further changed to: "How are job outcomes affected by technology use?" After a couple of promotions and about a decade as a faculty member, I stopped worrying about this question so much, which is why it is not even a question anymore but a statement: "Broader issues: (a) impact on outcomes, (b) IT personnel, (c) performance, etc." However, it was always there. It helped me move into other areas rooted in psychology and organizational behavior. I made a significant investment in theories related to personality and job outcomes, such as job satisfaction. I built on my knowledge of psychology theories and literature (e.g., literature related to the theory of planned behavior) and motivation theories, and invested time in reading the literature in these related yet distinct domains.

The basic idea underlying my research program was represented graphically (see Figure 2-1) in my 2003 *MIS Quarterly* paper[3] (co-authored with Mike Morris, Gordon Davis and Fred Davis) that reviewed and synthesized prior technology adoption research.

Figure 2-1. Overview Of My Research Program

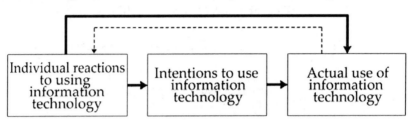

A key outcome of having an overarching research question, a few specific questions within the broad question, and pursuing research within the scope of these questions is that it is sure to lead to a focused stream of work. Whether intended or not, most doctoral students start with a focal stream of research. It is, after all, what sends students down the path of the dissertation. Even if PhD students are actively collaborating with faculty members on other research, most PhD students should have the dissertation-related research as their first original stream of research. The dissertation research topic requires a substantial investment in time, energy and most importantly, acquisition of knowledge and expertise in a domain. As this is always the case, it is good to have this stream be the focal stream.

I have seen many reasons for assistant professors to not have published their dissertation work. Some of these reasons include rejections at a journal or three, inability to craft strong papers out of the dissertation, a lack of desire to continue to work with the advisor and being involved with other interesting research projects at one's place of employment. Not publishing from one's dissertation is essentially throwing away years of work and losing traction in what could be a productive stream. Soon after traction is lost in the dissertation work itself, the assistant professor may lose interest in the general area and move on to other areas that are of greater interest. While it is not my place to question someone's interest, I do think it is important to recognize what an assistant professor is throwing away because of this. Most of us consider it great fortune when a paper we write makes it through the review process at a premier journal, given that acceptance rates at such journals are usually in the neighborhood of 10%. But the process takes time. Therefore, giving up too early on a paper or series of papers because of a rejection is not a good idea. Even worse is giving up entirely on the dissertation research stream and the substantial time investment it represents.

While Figure 2-1 captures an overview of my research, as presented in the *MIS Quarterly* (2003)[4] paper, my work in the first stream of research was quite a bit more specific (and will be discussed later). The focus of my dissertation research is shown in Figure 2-2—these and subsequent figures about my streams of research are conceptual diagrams meant to provide an overview, and it should be noted that they are not research models. The focus of the work was on understanding the determinants of technology adoption and use. In my case, I worked on a fairly mature topic which, even at the time I started working on my dissertation, was declared to be dead: technology adoption. I wrote my dissertation as a series of essays and published three of them [in substantially revised forms, of course] in *Information Systems Research* (2000),[5] *Management Science* (2000)[6] and *MIS Quarterly* (2003).[7]

Figure 2-2. Stream #1: Dissertation Research

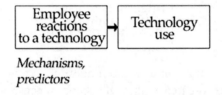

Beyond my dissertation, I examined various contingencies related to technology adoption and use decisions, shown in Figure 2-3. While the various contingencies were incorporated in the *MISQ* (2003)[8] article mentioned in conjunction with Figure 2-2, the original work theorizing about each of the contingencies appeared in a series of papers, including papers in *MIS Quarterly* (2000),[9] *Organizational Behavior and Human Decision Processes* (2000)[10] and *Personnel Psychology* (2000).[11]

Figure 2-3. Stream #1: Contingencies

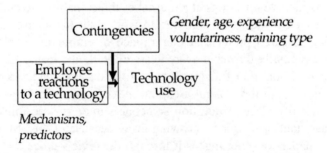

In continuing work on the broad topic of technology adoption, I focused on aspects that would help enhance adoption and use, as shown in Figure 2-4. I studied and compared training interventions. I studied and compared different system designs. Some of my more recent work in this area, spearheaded by a recent PhD student/graduate, Dr. Tracy Ann Sykes (author of chapter 10), has focused on the role of social networks. These investigations have led to papers published or forthcoming in IS and psychology journals, including *MIS Quarterly* (1999, 2009),[12,13] *Organizational Behavior and Human Decision Processes* (1999)[14] and *Personnel Psychology* (2002).[15]

Figure 2-4. Stream #1: Enhancing Adoption And Use

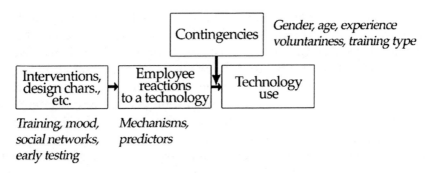

To this day, I am interested in the topic of technology in organizations, with a focus of some of my recent work being on the impacts of technology use on job outcomes, such as job characteristics, job satisfaction and job performance. A paper studying job characteristics in the context of an information system implementation appeared in *MIS Quarterly* (2010).[16] Figure 2-5 captures the evolved focus of my work, illustrating past and future work.

Figure 2-5. Stream #1: Consequences

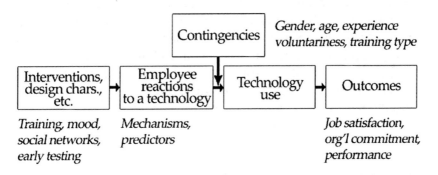

Having a second stream of research is important because it demonstrates that you have branched out beyond your dissertation. There are at least two other compelling reasons to have a second stream. The first reason is that having a second stream (i.e., one that is distinct from the dissertation stream) tends to be an important factor in the minds of many external letter-writers in their promotion and tenure evaluation (and, of course, it is also important to the powers-that-be who vote on promotion and tenure cases). It is important for an assistant professor to demonstrate that he or she has been able to do independent research that is not tied as strongly to one's advisor and to the advisors' work. This second stream of research is particularly important if the dissertation work is in the advisor's primary research area. The second reason is related to the first. The more prolific one's advisor is, the greater the need for a strong second stream and perhaps, success in the second stream. I will elaborate on the two reasons below, and touch on some of the other benefits of having a second stream.

In order to most effectively capitalize on the time and effort that went into your dissertation, it will be nice to leverage your knowledge in that stream to a second stream. There are a few different ways to achieve this. One way is to conduct research on a topic that uses the theory bases with which you are familiar from working on your dissertation. Another way is for you to collaborate with others in your new place of employment to fashion a second stream where you bring to the table your expertise in the first stream. Still another way is to collaborate with former PhD student colleagues. In my case, my second stream began with collaborations with Sue Brown (currently at the University of Arizona)—we overlapped as PhD students at the University of Minnesota. We started by working on adoption and use of personal computers in homes. It was an interesting and fruitful second stream for me, even though it was extremely challenging, especially in the early stages. It allowed me to leverage my knowledge of social psychology theories and research on technology adoption. While building on my knowledge base from my work on technology adoption in organizations, this second stream helped me delve into the marketing literature and some psychology literature that I had not previously encountered. Interestingly, this second stream also dragged me kicking and screaming into qualitative approaches. The novelty of working with qualitative data [at least for me] and learning by trial and error made it much harder to publish the first paper in this stream, which eventually appeared in *MIS Quarterly* in 2001.[17] The stream has really evolved and become a lot broader: going from "PCs in homes" to "technologies in homes" to "technologies in society." Besides the work with Sue, I became interested in the usability of web sites, usability of wireless sites, consumer e-commerce adoption and more recently, the digital divide [particularly in India]. The specific research questions in my second stream, "technology in society," in the early stages of formation are shown below:
i.   What factors influence consumer adoption and use decisions?
ii. How can consumer adoption and use be enhanced?
iii. What are outcomes of technology use among consumers?

The evolution of this, my second, stream of research took different twists and turns. The summary picture that captures the first few years of my work in this stream is shown in Figure 2-6.

The topic area, the overarching research question and the various pictures illustrating my research helped me stay focused. There was one final tool that I used to complement what I have already described: a spreadsheet that I constantly updated. A snapshot of my spreadsheet, as it appeared sometime in 2003, is shown in Table 2-1—note that references are shown only to the published papers in the table.[18] The spreadsheet complements the questions and figures discussed thus far. The purpose of the spreadsheet was to serve as a monitoring tool. If I started any new project, it became an entry in the spreadsheet. The spreadsheet also helped me determine if I should take on a new project. If a project could not be easily fit into the spreadsheet—in terms of content, not just blank space—the answer was a definite no. If there were many pending projects in the spreadsheet, it meant I needed to devote more time to moving other projects forward rather than taking on new ones. Thus, the spreadsheet served as a gating, planning and monitoring tool. I use it to this day (although in a far less hard-nosed manner) with considerable success to keep me focused.

Figure 2-6. Stream #2: Technology In Society

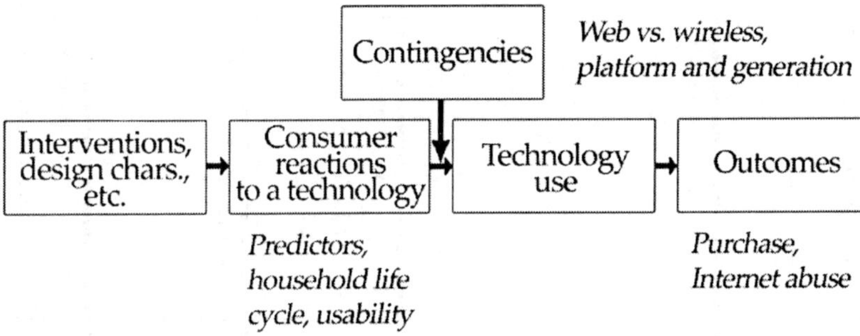

Returning to the first stream, how does one go about managing the first stream effectively? The following presents my thoughts and experiences:

I was fortunate to have a committee that comprised Fred Davis, Gordon Davis, Shawn Curley, Phil Ackerman and Ruth Kanfer. Although Fred had left for Maryland after my second year in the PhD program, he continued to serve on my committee with a general understanding that he was going to be the content advisor, while Gordon's role was to supervise the process and ensure that I did not drop the ball! They were both great mentors. Gordon provided process guidance, was someone who allowed me to bounce ideas off him, and provided suggestions on how reviewers and editors would react to various ideas and papers. Fred served as a sounding board for theory and research design issues. The benefit of having both of them on my committee was that they were both very well-established scholars. However, by the time I graduated, Fred was synonymous with technology adoption research and thus, perhaps a key downside of the famous advisor came into play. A PhD student is likely to get a lot less credit [deservingly or undeservingly] for publications with such a prolific and famous advisor. Interestingly, Fred tells the story of a similar challenge he faced when he wrote early papers with Rick Bagozzi and Paul Warshaw. I took many steps to proactively manage the risk of letter-writers in particular, and researchers in general, undervaluing my contributions. More importantly, I had to take these steps to build confidence in my own skills, showing that I had,

Table 2-1. A Spreadsheet View Of My Research Program

Research Papers '96 to '03		Published Works	Present (Under Review)	Current/Future Projects
Stream 1: Technology in Organizations	What are the factors influencing employee adoption and use decisions?	Determinants of percd. usefulness (MSci 2000); Determinants of percd. ease of use (ISR 2000); Computer self-efficacy (Deci Sci 1996); Measures (IJHCS 1996); Distance education (IJHCS 2002); Model unification (MISQ 2003)	Role of time and behavioral expectation (OBHDP); Expectation disconfirmation (OBHDP)	Predictive validity; Habit
	How can employee acceptance and use be enhanced?	Game-based training (MISQ 1999; IJHCS 2000); Mood (OBHDP 1999); Gender effects (MISQ 2000; OBHDP 2000); Age effects (PPsyc 2000); Telecommuting (PPsyc 2002); Pre-prototype testing (IEEE forthcoming); Gender, a psyc view (JASP forthcoming); User acceptance enablers (Deci Sci 2002)	Networks and organizations (AMJ); Gender and age effects (IEEE)	Training and overconfidence
	Broader issues: (a) impacts (b) IT personnel (c) performance, etc.	SFA implementation (JM 2002)	Job scope and job satisfaction (OBHDP); Gender and IT personnel (JAP, 2 MISQ); Technology use, job satisfaction, org commitment and performance (ISR)	Business process; ERP systems; IT in developing; Performance (self /other)
Stream 2: Technology in Society	What are the factors influencing consumer adoption and use decisions?	Home PC adoption; qualitative study (MISQ 2001); Late adopters and laggards (CACM 2003)	and household life cyle (MISQ)	Inter-channel comparison; Online consumer behavior
	How can consumer adoption and use be enhanced?	Web site usability (ISR 2002); Usability: web vs. wireless (CACM)	Web vs. wireless site usability (MISQ); Usability, use and purchase (MSci)	Integrating adoption research and communication theories
	What are the outcomes of technology use?			Internet addiction

in fact, learned the trade and could, in fact, publish papers and make substantial contributions on my own. The three key steps, the first two of which are intertwined, were:

i. I had an essay in the dissertation designed to be a solo paper—this paper appeared in *Information Systems Research* in 2000.[19] Fred Davis advised me to pursue an essay as a solo paper and it was determined that the determinants of ease of use would be an ideal candidate for that—I was far more interested in the ease of use construct [from TAM] than he was; I also believed in the potential impact that determinants of ease of use could have far more than he did. It was a natural fit. I give very similar advice to the PhD students I advise [on their dissertation].[20] By writing a solo paper, a junior scholar can mitigate the belief that the advisor carried the paper over the finish line. Many PhD students never publish a single paper in a premier journal besides the one or two they publish with their advisor. So, even if you get wings, until you show that you can fly solo, you get less credit.

ii. I started working on a solo research project outside my dissertation early in my career, with a hope of seeing it to fruition before I was up for promotion. I was fortunate that this paper appeared in *MIS Quarterly* in 1999.[21] This project was related to, yet distinct from, my dissertation and focused on training interventions. Training interventions just happened to be of great interest to one of the companies I was collecting data from as part of my dissertation. I pursued this project alone and ended up with two fairly solid studies. Pursuing the publication of the *MIS Quarterly* (1999) paper as a sole author taught me a lot—I learned a lot about all phases of a research project and paper. I even ended up having to do two studies [experiments] as a result of not doing some things right in the first experiment. The two solo papers—i.e., *MIS Quarterly* (1999) and *Information Systems Research* (2000)[22]—helped me in establishing an identity and reputation distinct from my advisor's and that of other senior collaborators.

iii. I found collaboration with peers to be an effective third strategy for building a research portfolio to combat potential concerns about publishing papers only with a senior scholar/advisor—i.e., Fred Davis. I collaborated with peers where the credit would be fairly equal. I had the good fortune of working with Sue Brown, Mike Morris (currently at the University of Virginia) and Cheri Speier (currently at Michigan State University). All three of these collaborators were peers and thus, credit was more likely to be fairly evenly shared. While Sue and I met while in the PhD program, I met Mike through an introduction from Joe Valacich (Mike's advisor at Indiana University) and I met Cheri when I interviewed at Oklahoma University for a job as a rookie assistant professor. In each of these three cases, I collaborated with them due to overlapping interests. I never really steered far from my overarching question or my major streams of research—this approach helped me a great deal. I will elaborate in greater detail on building and sustaining effective collaborations in chapter 7. Dr. Maruping's chapter (chapter 3) also discusses different types of collaboration and provides advice on structuring collaborations.

3. Research Project Versus Research Study

Although I have heard the terms "research project" and "research study" used interchangeably, to me, there is a big distinction between the two. I view a research project as larger in scope, involving a research design that can answer several interrelated questions and potentially, including more than one research study. A research project thus involves collecting data for more than one paper and considers additional constructs related to each paper such that alternative explanations and models can be probed. This is in contrast to more traditional thinking where a research study is much more focused. Although, to some extent, this is semantics, focusing your thinking on a research project, as described above, allows you to think big and design better and more comprehensive studies. In essence, the focus on a broad research project provides for multiple papers and having more than one plan of attack—instead of only a plan A, it can create potential plans B, C and even D. One added advantage of thinking about a research project in such a manner is that you can engage in few high-quality data collection efforts. Another benefit of such an approach is that it may allow the pursuit of longitudinal data that in turn allows you to understand phenomena as they unfold over time and to craft better papers as a result.

Perhaps one of best decisions I made early in my career was to always think in terms of research projects, as described above. This decision was partly driven by the fact that I started doing field research. Working with organizations made me realize how difficult it is to get an organization to fully commit to a research project. It, therefore, immediately made sense to me to think about collecting data such that a series of papers could be written rather than simply conducting a research study that was narrow in scope and going to be embedded in one paper at most. Further, if the core idea related to a narrowly conceptualized research study is unappealing to the reviewers [at multiple premier journals], the paper and all the effort that went into the study ends up in a second-tier journal. In contrast, in a more broadly conceptualized research project, there will likely be avenues for the addition of other constructs and the consequent revision of a paper such that it will be more appealing to premier journals.

My dissertation focused on five related, yet distinct, questions that fueled five essays:
i. What are the determinants of perceived usefulness?
ii. What are the determinants of perceived ease of use?
iii. Of the various technology adoption models, which one possesses the greatest predictive validity?
iv. Do the various technology adoption models accurately predict self-reported behavior only or actual behavior also?
v. What is the role of habit in intention models?

It was clear to me that successful papers related to the above questions could greatly help my tenure case.[23] As I started having conversations with organizations, I discovered that they were facing many problems that prevented successful deployment of information systems, typically with users resisting new information systems. I soon talked a few organizations into allowing me to collect longitudinal data. The best part of thinking about these questions and focusing on a broad research project when I collected data from organizations was that I was able to design my data collection such that I would be able to answer the above five questions within the scope of one research project and with other constructs that allowed for substantial revision of the papers via the addition of constructs to the model/paper during the revision process. My data collection was designed as shown in Figure 2-7.

Figure 2-7. Dissertation Data Collection

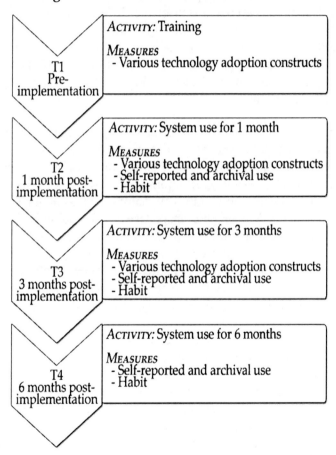

The questionnaires at various stages of data collection included questions for essays 1 through 3. In the later stages of data collection, system use and habit data were obtained. In a small number of companies, both self-reported and actual use data were collected that related to essay 4. Each of the first three essays led to a published paper that leveraged longitudinal data collected in multiple companies, although I used different slices of the data set for each of the papers. I have yet to actually get around to sending out papers related to essays 4 and 5, mostly because I became interested in several other related yet distinct issues that emerged as I was working on the dissertation. There were several positive consequences of this strategy that have worked well for me. For example, one of the companies wanted to know if there was something they could do to foster adoption and use rather than simply gaining a better understanding. Think intervention! You may recall this was, in fact, one of my areas of interest. This allowed me to study innovative training interventions that led to the paper in *MIS Quarterly* in 1999[24] that I discussed earlier. Another organization was interested in examining different user interface designs and their impacts. I pursued that aspect also within the scope of my dissertation data collection and a comparison of the different user interface designs led to a paper in *Personnel Psychology* in 2002.[25] While a narrowly focused research study or two may have helped me keep the blinders on what I was investigating, the broader thinking in terms of the research project enabled me to be flexible and agile in pursuit of opportunities that helped further my research program that was, of course, driven by the overarching research question and consequent specific questions.

In my dissertation research project, various demographic characteristics were collected because, at that time, little prior research had focused on demographic characteristics and technology adoption. Unlike psychology and organizational behavior journal articles, at the time of my early work (over a decade ago), information systems journals tended not to have a baseline model that incorporated only control variables, say demographic characteristics, as predictors. Thus, a focus on demographic characteristics for possible direct and moderating effects on key dependent variables presented an additional focus made possible by broader thinking. I also found that the reference disciplines of psychology and organizational behavior were interested in gender and age differences related to a variety of phenomena. This prompted me to work on a series of papers on gender and age differences in both information systems and psychology/organizational behavior journals: *MIS Quarterly* (2000),[26] *Organizational Behavior and Human Decision Processes* (2000),[27] *Personnel Psychology* (2000),[28] *Journal of Applied Social Psychology* (2004)[29] and *IEEE Transactions on Engineering Management* (2005)[30]— articles that were possible simply by thinking more broadly and collecting a more comprehensive dataset. It was also, of course, a stroke of luck that the demographic characteristics that almost everyone collects as a matter of routine led to a series of papers. However, it is possible to manage this process proactively by examining the literature, including in reference disciplines, in order to identify a few constructs and scales that may lead to an increase in the survey length by 20-30 questions and feed into an interesting paper targeting reference discipline journals. A related approach would be to find interesting areas that could tie to the main question(s) being investigated that in turn could drive the selection of constructs from the reference discipline to be included as part of the data collection process.

A key question is how do you know what data to collect? One way that I think about it is to delve into related concepts, competing theories, and higher- or lower-level concepts and constructs, including additional dependent variables. By doing so, you are likely to be able to develop additional papers, comprehensive models and competing models.

4. Populate Your Pipeline

In order to understand the importance of populating your pipeline, one must first appreciate the various stages of the research process and what it means to have papers at various stages. This is perhaps more important in the first 3 years of one's life as an assistant professor than at any other time in one's career [later you get in your career, assuming you are actually working on research, your research pipeline tends to be full all the time]. The basic idea of the various phases of an empirical research project is depicted in Figure 2-8. The figure presents a simplified version of the phases of an empirical research project from the generation of the idea(s) to the publication of the paper. This simplified illustration does not show iterations across phases.

Figure 2-8. A Simplified View Of The Stages Of The Research And Publication Process

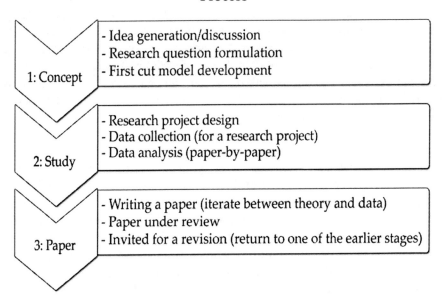

1: Concept
- Idea generation/discussion
- Research question formulation
- First cut model development

2: Study
- Research project design
- Data collection (for a research project)
- Data analysis (paper-by-paper)

3: Paper
- Writing a paper (iterate between theory and data)
- Paper under review
- Invited for a revision (return to one of the earlier stages)

All too often, I have seen junior faculty members complete a paper, submit it and then wonder what they are going to study next. When I have asked them about working on a paper for which they have already completed the data analysis, the reply is often "I don't have such a paper." For most people, this situation is usually rectified by the end of their third or fourth year as an assistant professor. But, in the early stages, the pipeline is not typically well-populated. It is the difference between a steady flowing stream (a well-filled pipeline) and a blast of water followed by nothing like a clogged drain (a poorly managed pipeline).

The main point, here, is that you should always have papers in various stages of the above research process. Of course, it is easier said than done, but I will share below some ideas on how it can be accomplished.

The notion of a research project (vs. a research study) can help in populating and sustaining a pipeline. One of the critical elements of a research project, as I discussed earlier, is collecting data to fuel several related papers. With the additional data, it will be easier to write more papers and to have papers in various stages of the process so as to keep the pipeline healthy and populated.

A junior faculty member should work within the framework of an overarching question and identify a few specific questions—ideally, these two steps are already done from the days of your dissertation. You should further identify a few selected researchable questions within the specific question(s). These researchable questions are akin to research questions in a paper. Your research design should be in keeping with the research project that I described earlier that allows you to collect data to feed into several papers. Start analyzing data. You will almost always have several interesting findings when you have an extensive data set. As the iteration between theory and data unfolds, there may be more papers than you had previously envisioned. As you complete one paper and push it out the door, you will not wonder what to do next, but rather you will be able to pursue papers that focus on other interesting findings from the dataset. Overall, the successful completion of each broader research project gives you many papers, both planned and unplanned, on which you can work, that in turn allows you to wait for the right opportunities for data collection rather than being forced to settle for less-than-ideal data collection opportunities.

Another way you could populate your pipeline [with papers] is by collaborating with your colleagues. Many lunches and coffees with your colleagues will frequently involve conversations about research ideas. Some of these conversations may even have sufficient merit to move to the next stage of the research process where specific research questions and models are formulated. If you pursued your dissertation as a broad research project wherein data were collected to answer questions beyond the dissertation itself, you can take your time discussing ideas, formulating next steps, and building collaborations that help you stay within your primary research streams and leverage your knowledge base rather than rushing into research projects and/or collaborations. If your dissertation does not have much room for additional papers, there should be a sense of urgency in carving out new project ideas so that your pipeline can be populated. In all cases, if the ideas, research questions identified and models are many and interrelated, the research design will be broad enough that after data collection is completed, there will be a lot of data analysis to be done, models to be tweaked and a healthy number of papers that can be written. After my dissertation was completed, I was very selective in building collaborations and designing research projects. One example of a now mature project from which I published three papers focused on usability. One elaborate study was conducted wherein I began construct and instrument development [related to usability] in a course I was teaching on web application development—this led to two papers with Ritu Agarwal, one in *Information Systems Research* (2002)[31] on the construct and measure development and empirical validation, and one that developed and tested a model of online purchase behavior in *Management Science* (2006).[32] The third paper was an off-shoot on which I worked with V. Ramesh (Indiana University): using the usability construct and instrument developed in earlier work to compare web and wireless site usability—the paper appeared in *MIS Quarterly* (2006).[33] Similarly, I have ongoing major projects with Sue Brown, Mike Morris and Cheri Speier that began years ago, and all of which have led to papers and have left plenty of data yet to be analyzed and crafted into more papers. Slowly but surely, the more years that have elapsed since the completion of my PhD, the more research projects I have conducted and completed. Some of these have led to meaningful research sites for my PhD students to pursue dissertations (or other research) or for me to broaden my own research. However, in the early stages of my career, rather than creating too many collaborations, studies and papers, I was very proactive and mindful about having a few collaborations, a few elaborate research projects and having something at various stages of development in the pipeline that were within the scope of the few research projects.

5. Plan, Plan, Plan

The process of planning is critical to the successful execution of all the other ideas discussed thus far. Earlier, I had presented my spreadsheet view of a research program. In addition to serving the function of helping me choose projects, the spreadsheet also helped me keep track of my projects and papers. It helped me plan and monitor.

After the merger of the Information Systems department with the Management Science and Statistics department at the University of Maryland, an informal mentoring program was instituted. As an aside, I believe this is an excellent idea and if such a thing does not exist, you should talk to senior faculty members to make such a thing happen. I was lucky to have Michael Fu, a professor in management science, as my mentor. Michael was great—he was easy to talk to, he was accessible, and he always shared his views on do's and don't's. Although Michael was not familiar with information systems research or the journals that I targeted, he always gave me great advice about how faculty members in other departments would see various aspects of a portfolio. When the mentoring program began, I decided it was best to have a plan for my first meeting with my mentor and soon after, a reflection of what I had done during the past semester. It was a very simple but powerful idea, and I believe by using this approach junior faculty members can benefit immensely. It was very useful in helping me focus on the big picture. It also helped me keep my plate from overflowing. Even now, I use a planning document each semester to help give me a sense for what I need to do and when. It is slightly different from a yearly or daily planner in that the plan I suggest focuses on research projects and papers. This plan in turn feeds your to-do lists on a monthly, weekly or even daily basis, and helps you monitor your progress towards your research goals. Table 2-2 is an example of a review and planning document that I used in 2000. The focus of the document is to assess the status of key outcomes related to research (how many papers and in what sorts of journals), reflect on past activities, and plan for the upcoming semester. Such a tool can help junior faculty member and mentors identify potential problem areas. Further, such a tool can help provide the junior faculty member the necessary guidance to perform a course correction or consideration to reduce or manage teaching and service. It will also alert senior faculty members and the department chair of excessive activities on either front and thus, quite likely promote corrective action. One final lesson in all this is for junior faculty members should clamor for mentoring—it will be beneficial both from the perspective of research progress and politics (I realize I haven't mentioned politics before—but let me note here that by seeking mentoring, a junior faculty member demonstrates enthusiasm and interest, both of which will stand him or her in good stead from a political perspective come time for the promotion evaluation).

Table 2-2. A Planning Document Illustration

January 2000 Meeting

Review of Fall 1999 and Plan for Spring 2000

Junior Faculty Member: Viswanath Venkatesh

Mentor: Michael Fu

Dept Chair: Arjang Assad

Status of Publications in Sep 1999	Current Status (Jan 2000)
8 journal publications in top-third; of these, 5 are "A+" journals (1 at Management Science, 2 at OBHDP, 2 at MISQ) 4 conference proceedings (2 at ICIS—about 20% acceptance rate) 14 "in preparation"	10 journal publications in top-third; of these, 7 are "A+" journals (1 at Management Science, 2 at OBHDP, 2 at MISQ, 1 at ISR, 1 at PPsyc) 4 conference proceedings (2 at ICIS—about 20% acceptance rate) 2 "A" journal articles in "revise and resubmit" status 14 "in preparation"
Goals Set in Sep 1999	**What was Actually Done?**
Final editing called for on all accepted papers	Final edits done on Management Science, OBHDP (additional revision)

Table 2-2 *Continued.* A Planning Document Illustration

Resubmit papers in revise-and-resubmit status, currently on authors' desk: MISQ, PPsyc, ISR	Done
New submissions: MS (gender differences research), JMIS (ERP), JCR (electronic commerce)	(a) Gender differences draft completed—submitted to the Academy of Management Conference (b) ERP project begun with Ritu (c) E-commerce paper draft completed—pending org approval
Major data collection in Europe in Nov/Dec (includes travel to Europe, may hinder new submission goals)	Done on 2 new projects
Developing new course for delivery in Spring 2000	Developed MBA and UG electives in e-commerce
	Started new project with Samba on adoption of technology in a bank in India

Summary of Research, Teaching, and Service (Since Sep 1999)

Research
- Final edits done
- 2 new paper drafts completed
- Begun 2 new research projects
- Collected data on 2 other projects

Teaching
- Taught BMGT302—evaluations of 4.69 and 4.66
- Developed new MBA and UG electives on e-commerce

Service
- Faculty search committee
- Faculty advisor, Information Systems Society (UG)—going through major revamping UG curriculum revision—including helping Dept Chair seek approval for new course (BMGT406)

Goals for Spring 2000	**Comments**
Proof-reading final versions of papers going to print: ISR, PPsyc	

Table 2-2 *Continued*. A Planning Document Illustration

Submit 2 new papers for review (drafts completed, gender and e-commerce)	
Revise and resubmit paper on authors' desk: Journal of Marketing	
More progress on usability research with Ritu	
Collect data in India on bank project with Samba	
Teach new electives	

Concluding Thoughts

The research program that I discussed in this chapter emphasizes depth over breadth. Such a research program takes a multi-year view that aims to develop and pursue research projects that probe deeply into a particular area. Such a research program ultimately aims to make the *whole* of a researcher's contributions greater than the sum of its parts (individual papers). I hope the strategies that were presented in this chapter help you on your road to becoming a successful researcher.

Key Takeaways

1. Emphasize depth
2. Think about research to be conducted over the next 5-10 years
3. Try to be known for something
4. Streams of research
   i. Work within a few (2-3) well-defined streams of research, wherein each stream should have an overarching question that guides the selection of new projects
   ii. A research question is not to be confused with a topic area—a topic area is much broader
   iii. Focus and exclude—there may be several projects that you do not pursue because they do not fit within your topic and research questions
5. Getting practical about streams
   i. Carefully articulate a few specific research questions early in your career and pursue those questions
   ii. Research questions evolve
   iii. Watch out for "opportunities of a lifetime that come by twice a day"
   iv. Have a graphical depiction of your research program (see Figure 2-1 for an example)
   v. Caution: Not publishing from the dissertation is essentially throwing away years of work and losing traction in what could be a productive stream
   vi. Having a second stream is important because it demonstrates that you have branched out beyond your dissertation

      vii. Leverage the knowledge from your dissertation stream into a second stream by conducting research in a topic area that could use the theory bases with which you are familiar from working on your dissertation

      viii. To establish independence as a researcher, consider:

         a. Designing a solo paper as part of your dissertation

         b. Working on a solo paper outside your dissertation

         c. Collaborating with peers

6. Research project versus research study

    i. A research project is larger in scope involving a research design that can answer several interrelated questions and potentially includes more than one research study, thus a research project thus helps fuel more than one paper

    ii. Advantages of thinking in terms of research projects:

       a. You can engage in fewer but higher quality data collection efforts

       b. Allows for the pursuit of longitudinal data that in turn allows you to understand phenomena as they unfold over time and to craft better papers as a result

    iii. What additional data should you collect? Collect data about related concepts, competing theories, and higher- or lower-level concepts and constructs, including additional dependent variables—this will lead to additional papers, comprehensive models and competing models

7. Populate your pipeline

    i. You should always have papers in various stages of the research process

    ii. The notion of a research project (vs. a research study) can help in populating and sustaining a pipeline

    iii. One of the critical elements of a research project, discussed earlier, is collecting data to fuel several related papers

    iv. A junior faculty member should work within the framework of an overarching question and identify a few specific questions—ideally, these two steps are already done from the days of the dissertation

    v. Another way you could populate your pipeline with papers is by collaborating with your colleagues

8. Plan, plan, plan

    i. The process of planning is critical to the successful execution of all the other ideas discussed in this chapter

    ii. Use the planning document tool shown in Table 2-2

    iii. Clamor for mentoring

CHAPTER 3

WHEN A PLAN COMES TOGETHER:
STRATEGIES FOR DEVELOPING A HEALTHY PIPELINE
Dr. Likoebe M. Maruping

Associate Professor
College of Business
University of Louisville
Louisville, KY
Likoebe.maruping@louisville.edu

Shortly before I began my doctoral studies in information systems at the University of Maryland, I attended one of the information systems field's major conferences—the *International Conference on Information Systems* (ICIS). Having turned down a job offer as a programmer, I was in need of some reassurance that my decision, to pursue a doctoral degree, was a good one. Especially because I was foregoing a "steady" job and comfortable salary in exchange for an uncertain future. I was not disappointed. The information systems field was at its height, with companies hiring college graduates as quickly as they could get them. At the conference, I was amazed at how aggressively universities were hiring information systems faculty members. I recall hearing stories about recruiters chasing down soon-to-be PhD graduates for interviews. It was every job candidate's dream. However, as with all things cyclical, the job market entered into a downturn. Over the span of a few short years, it became increasingly difficult for candidates to find good jobs. The number of jobs per candidate rapidly decreased. Soon, there were more candidates on the market than there were jobs available. Naturally, as the market for jobs became more competitive, recruiters' standards for interviewing and eventually extending offers to candidates increased.

Entrants into academia who are vying for positions at research universities face tremendous pressure at two points: (1) securing the first job; and (2) getting tenure at that institution. Journal publications have proven to be the common driver of success in achieving both of these ends. In the case of doctoral graduates, although hiring decisions are driven by a variety of factors, including teaching needs and departmental strategic objectives, it is clear that one's publication record is a core differentiator between those who are successful at securing a job and those who are less successful. This is especially true in tight job markets where departments are under pressure to hire candidates who have a good chance of making tenure. Hence, whereas a successfully defended dissertation proposal and a conference proceeding or two were enough to get a candidate a job at a good research university at the height of the market, in recent years, it has become increasingly necessary for candidates to have at least one publication to even be considered for a job. In the case of junior faculty members, the old adage "publish or perish" continues to ring true. As research universities continue to enhance their standing as institutions of excellence in research, the standards for achieving tenure at these institutions continue to increase and consequently, junior faculty members are under constant pressure to produce publications in top journals.

With these pressures ever present, what is a junior academic to do? How are they to manage? The pressures identified above underscore the need for new entrants into academia to have a carefully crafted plan for successfully landing a job and subsequently, making tenure at a research university. My objective in this chapter is to outline some strategies for achieving these two goals through journal publications. These strategies are based on personal experiences as well as observations of colleagues in different fields. I will approach this discussion from the perspective of managing research projects aimed at producing journal publications. I fully recognize that there are many other factors that influence success at landing a job (e.g., reputation of the candidate's advisor, institution and/or department; the novelty and need for the candidate's research area) and making tenure (e.g., collegiality and service to the institution). Similarly, I recognize that different tiers of institutions place different emphases on journal publications. Some institutions place greater emphasis on the number of publications and less on the quality; others emphasize quality while placing less emphasis on quantity; and still others emphasize impact and thought leadership (think Harvard, Stanford). Given my own experience and observations, I restrict my focus to academics aiming to secure jobs and make tenure at research universities that emphasize a balance between quantity and quality of publications. I discuss the following strategies:

1. The challenge for doctoral students
2. Strategies for doctoral students
   i. Strategy 1: From seed to blossoming flower
   ii. Strategy 2: Building a house one brick at a time
   iii. Strategy 3: Learning from those who know
3. The challenge for junior faculty members
4. Strategies for junior faculty members
   i. Strategy 1: The loner
   ii. Strategy 2: The managed program
   iii. Strategy 3: The opportunist

1. The Challenge For Doctoral Students

Before identifying and discussing various strategies for managing the journey toward landing the first job and making tenure, it is important to take a step back and paint a clearer picture of the timelines along which entrants to academia must operate. Figures 3-1 and 3-2 below illustrate: (1) the timeline for doctoral students progressing through their doctoral programs; and (2) a fairly liberal timeline for moving a paper from initial idea to final publication.

As shown in Figure 3-1, I assume that the average doctoral student takes five years to complete their program. Although four years has typically been the standard amount of time to complete a doctoral program, in recent years, programs are increasingly encouraging their students to stay an extra year to enhance their journal publication record.

Figure 3-1. Timeline For Progression Through Doctoral Programs

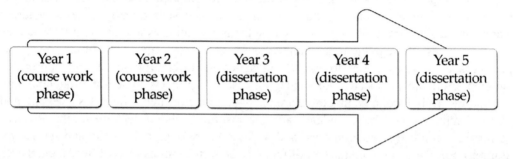

Figure 3-2 shows a simplified timeline for taking an idea and transforming it into a journal publication. As illustrated, it can take a year to conceptualize an idea, vet the idea with colleagues, perhaps conduct a pilot study and then, orchestrate the data collection to test the idea. Once data collection has been completed, it can take up to a year to format, clean and analyze the data, and then write the paper in preparation for the initial submission. The review process itself can take two or more years before a paper is accepted. If you juxtapose the timelines presented in the two figures, it is clear that doctoral students need to hit the ground running if they are to have any chance at success. Time is working against students from the moment they begin their doctoral studies. This seems rather unfair given the lack of familiarity incoming doctoral students have with conducting academic research and publishing in academic journals, not to mention a general lack of knowledge regarding the various topic areas in their chosen field of study. However, the reality is that the market values doctoral students with top-tier publications and these are the candidates who secure jobs even during tight markets. Therefore, doctoral students should turn time into an ally and put themselves in an advantageous position on the market by engaging in research *early* in their doctoral programs. I will discuss a couple of strategies that should improve students' chances of emerging from their doctoral programs with journal publications.

I noted earlier that the timeline shown in Figure 3-2 is a fairly liberal estimate. This is because the amount of time required to collect data—especially field studies—can vary significantly and often takes a year or more to complete. In field settings, academics have little to no control over the timing and pace of data collection. A significant amount of time and investment is required simply to get access to a field sample. More often than not, plans are changed, deadlines get pushed back or the data collection gets cancelled entirely. Assuming the data collection goes according to plan, the process of formatting and cleaning the data also takes time. Although academics have greater control in laboratory settings involving student participants, a significant amount of time is still required to design the study, secure the study site, recruit participants, and conduct the actual study itself. Thus, the one-year timeline for idea generation to data collection is fairly liberal and assumes that everything goes according to plan (which in many instances is simply not the case). Nevertheless, let me use this rosy outlook as the basis for my illustration going forward.

Figure 3-2. Timeline For Progression Through Publication Of Journal Articles

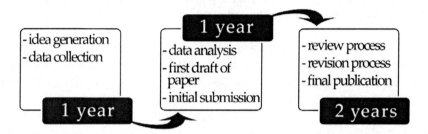

The two-year timeline for making an initial submission to a top-tier journal to getting final acceptance for publication may, by some accounts, also be liberal. First, the timeline assumes that authors take three months to conduct the necessary revisions to a paper before resubmitting it for another round of reviews. In some regards, this may be realistic. However, there are numerous instances in which new data must be collected in order for a revision to be successful. Second, an implicit assumption being made here is that the paper will be accepted at the first top-tier journal to which it is sent. It is an unfortunate truth that good papers are sometimes rejected. There are a variety of reasons why this occurs that are beyond the scope of this chapter. The fact of the matter is that it occurs[34] and when it does, the timeline becomes significantly longer if a paper goes through the review process at two or three top-tier journals before being accepted for publication.

2. Strategies For Doctoral Students

The discussion above does not paint the rosiest of pictures for doctoral students beginning their programs. Fortunately, there are a couple of strategies that students can adopt to make time an ally during the doctoral program. The key is to start working on research early. I will highlight two strategies that come from my observations of doctoral students and colleagues over the years, as well as from personal experience.

i. Strategy 1: From Seed To Blossoming Flower

This strategy is fairly simple to implement. Yet, it is quite often overlooked. In most standard doctoral programs, students spend the first two years doing coursework. This is typically delivered as a set of readings seminars that cover specific topics. Students are also directed to complete courses on research methods during this two-year period. More often than not, readings seminars require students to write a term paper that relates to the topic at hand. This is a perfect opportunity for students to begin to engage in fruitful research. Students are able to spend months on end during the semester researching and writing on a topic. This provides significant time for critical thought and refinement of ideas. Further, it is a useful forum for receiving feedback that helps the student improve the ideas. The end result is usually a paper with some good, though unrefined, ideas. A majority of doctoral students have little trouble getting to this stage, due, in no small part, to the fact that this is the basic requirement for most readings seminars. However, I continue to be amazed at the number of doctoral students who, upon fulfilling the requirements for their readings seminar, abandon their term papers and move on to another topic in another seminar. This, unfortunately, occurs far too often and, I believe, is a missed opportunity.

Assuming that a student has chosen a topic based on his or her interest in it, and assuming the topic has been properly vetted with the seminar instructor and other colleagues, it seems like an inefficient use of a semester to spend time and effort developing an idea only to abandon it. Doctoral students would serve themselves well by further developing the ideas and getting more critical feedback in an effort to get a journal publication out of this effort. Fortunately, there are a number of good forums for receiving feedback on one's ideas. One obvious source is the instructor of the readings seminar. Typically, these professors tend to be experts on the topic of the readings seminar, so they are likely to have a good sense of how promising and publishable an idea might be. Other faculty members within the student's department can also be a useful source of feedback. Finally, reviews from an academic conference are an excellent source of feedback that extends beyond one's own institution.

Incorporating feedback from these various sources often helps to improve the paper and move it closer to being ready for journal submission. By adopting an iterative process of writing, seeking feedback and rewriting, the student is nurturing the idea and helping it to grow into a finished product. In addition to building critical research skills, this strategy gives the student important insights into how to transform an idea into a completed research paper. It also allows the student to bring a paper or project to closure. I have personally followed this strategy and found it to be fruitful. One paper I began as a term paper for a readings seminar was published in the *Journal of Applied Psychology,*[35] a premier organizational behavior and industrial psychology journal. Another of my papers whose genesis can be traced to a term paper for a readings seminar was published in *Organization Science,*[36] a premier management journal. The point is that if a doctoral student is going spend a semester's worth of time on a paper (assuming the topic is good), it is worth getting something more than just a term paper out of it. This is especially true when one considers the limited time available before the job market comes beckoning. Figure 3-3 shows a summary of the recommended steps for turning a semester term paper into a journal submission. Although there is no guarantee of journal acceptance following this procedure, this sequence of steps enhances a doctoral student's ability to develop a pipeline of journal-ready submissions.

Figure 3-3. A Step-by-step Process For Turning A Term Paper Into A Journal Submission

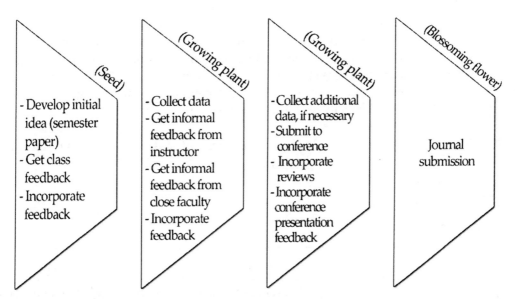

ii. Strategy 2: Building A House One Brick At A Time

The Chinese philosopher Lao-tzu proclaimed that even the longest journey begins with a single step. A second strategy that students might consider adopting is to develop an idea and refine it over the course of a series of doctoral seminars. This strategy resembles the first strategy outlined earlier in that it encourages doctoral students to pursue ideas developed in the context of seminars. However, one difference is that this strategy encourages students to use successive seminars as forums for further developing the idea and, potentially, spawning additional papers on the same topic. Through this approach, the student is able to spend a longer period of time delving into a topic from a variety of perspectives. Each seminar serves as a major step to advancing or expanding the idea in a way that is informed by the topic area. Of course, the nature of the perspectives adopted to inform the idea will be determined by the nature of the seminars the student encounters during his or her course work. An added advantage of this approach is that it enables the student to also consider a breadth of approaches to testing the idea as he or she progresses through a variety of research methods and statistics courses.

As an example of how this strategy might be adopted, consider a student who is interested in examining adaptive processes in software development. A seminar on team work processes and dynamics would serve as a useful stepping stone for understanding the phenomenon and identifying potential predictors for a model. Over the course of the semester, the student could focus on outlining the core theoretical base and key outcomes of interest. At the end of the semester, the student would have a completed draft of the front-end of the paper. The student could further refine the idea or expand it in subsequent seminars. For example, a seminar on decision-making might help the student incorporate an individual perspective or potentially even a multilevel perspective on the phenomenon. Similarly, a seminar on information systems strategy would enable the student to incorporate contextual influences at the organizational level or expand the idea to the organizational level of analysis. Through this process, the initial idea is continually enriched by different perspectives. Similarly, from a research methods perspective, the student can use a methods course to incorporate ideas on experimental design to design and conduct a study, and learn how to analyze data using a structural equation modeling technique learned in another course. Figure 3-4 provides an illustration of how this strategy can be used to develop an idea that could eventually be transformed into journal submissions.

Figure 3-4. A Strategy For Developing A Research Idea Across Doctoral Seminars And Courses

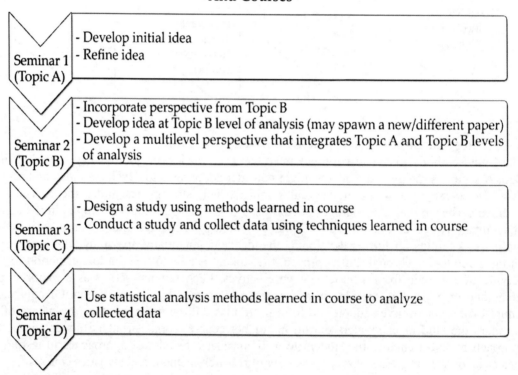

iii. Strategy 3: Learning From Those Who Know

A third strategy that students might consider is fairly straightforward. Simply work with faculty members who are conducting research. In fact, this is perhaps the most commonly used strategy for students to develop a pipeline of papers early in their doctoral programs. This strategy is particularly useful for students who may not have a particular topic of interest and are open to exploring various topics. There are several benefits to this approach. First, it offers the student an opportunity to learn the skills associated with crafting papers. Faculty members have various ways of approaching student collaborations. Some professors prefer to begin the process from scratch—in other words, they will brainstorm the idea, conceptualize the model, design the study, collect the data and write the paper, with the student being involved in all phases. Other professors may bring students into projects that are in advanced stages. For instance, the data may already have been collected, and the student will play a role in developing a model, obtaining results from model testing and crafting the paper. In other instances, the model may already have been conceptualized and the data collected, and the student's primary task may be to develop the paper. Whatever the case, the student has a great opportunity to learn, through apprenticeship, some important skills that may never be discussed in a classroom. Second, this approach allows the student to draw from the professor's knowledge base. When a student works on a professor's research project, chances are the professor will be highly engaged and provide a wealth of domain knowledge. This significantly increases the chances that a publishable paper will emerge from the student's efforts. Finally, this approach gives students the opportunity to write and publish more papers. A note of caution is needed here. It is tempting, especially during the early stages of the doctoral program, to want to work with many faculty members so as to have more papers. This is a risky strategy as the student risks being spread too thin and being unable to contribute meaningfully to the various projects.

I have observed many successful cases of students working with faculty members and having publications in top-tier journals by the time they are on the market. I have personally found this strategy to be fruitful as well. I began working on research projects with faculty members in the first year of my doctoral studies. These collaborations yielded top-tier journal publications in *Organizational Behavior and Human Decision Processes*[37] and *Information Systems Research*[38] by the time I was on the job market.

Summary

As the strategies outlined above suggest, there are a variety of ways in which doctoral students can develop a healthy pipeline of papers that will become journal submissions. The key is to have a deliberate plan and to execute the plan early. Doing so ensures that time becomes an ally in crafting journal submissions and publishing them.

3. The Challenge For Junior Faculty Members

At research universities, junior faculty members, like doctoral students, are under tremendous pressure to publish high-quality research in a short time span. The pressure to publish in top-tier journals is fairly standard. This pressure is enhanced by the fact that the number of responsibilities they are given—a majority of which have little or nothing to do with research—increases exponentially over time. Figure 3-5 shows a typical six-year tenure clock. In many academic institutions, a junior faculty member's tenure packet is submitted at the end of the fifth year or beginning of the sixth year. This six-year tenure clock is punctuated by a mid-tenure review that normally occurs during the third year of the tenure clock. Figure 3-2, shown earlier, shows the typical timeline for publishing a paper, particularly in a top-tier journal.

Figure 3-5. Timeline For Progression Through A Typical Tenure Clock

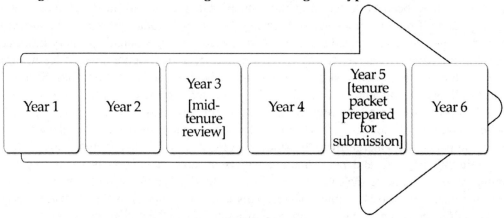

When it comes to journal publications, research institutions often differ in their standards for tenure. Therefore, here too, some simplifying assumptions need to be made. For the sake of argument, I will assume that the requirement is three unequivocal top-tier journal publications as well as a few publications in lower-tier journals to round out the portfolio. If you juxtapose Figures 3-2 and 3-5, you quickly realize that junior faculty members cannot focus on one paper at a time. Given the timeline shown in Figure 3-2, a paper submitted to a top-tier journal in year 1 may not get accepted until year 4 on the tenure clock—and that is assuming the paper is accepted at the first journal to which it is submitted. Additional constraints, which are not evident in Figures 3-2 and 3-5, make the task of developing enough papers for top-tier journals challenging. First, for most junior faculty members, the first year is the most difficult. During this year, the faculty member is teaching multiple courses (in some cases, for the first time) that require new preparation. Also, one or two committee assignments are not unusual. The faculty member is also taking time to get his or her bearings at the new institution. There will be social events that new faculty members need to attend. Second, there is the daunting task of cutting that huge dissertation document into one or more papers that are ready for journal submission. Collectively, these factors can easily render year 1 of the junior faculty member's tenure clock to be useless. This is, in fact, a reality for many newly minted PhDs. Unfortunately, many only realize the gravity of the situation by the time they start their second year.

Mission impossible? It certainly seems like it. The junior faculty member's mission, whether or not they choose to accept it, is to publish at least three top-tier journal articles (where each article takes about four years to work its way through the review process) within a five-year time span. Can it be done? Certainly. There are numerous examples of faculty members who have successfully accomplished this and more. The key is adequate planning and action. A deliberate plan needs to be in place from day 1. There is very little margin for aimless wandering and figuring out what to do next. It is critical that junior faculty members hit the ground running with their research program. Generally, junior faculty members who adopt some of the strategies discussed in various chapters in this book, including chapter 2 and all of section 3 (chapters 12-13), begin their first year already having a healthy pipeline of papers. This eases the pressure somewhat and puts them on a good trajectory to continue to develop additional papers for journal submission. In the remainder of this chapter, I will outline a few simple strategies that should help junior faculty members to produce a healthy record of journal publications. These strategies are based on observations of other faculty members who have successfully managed the publication process leading up to tenure.

4. Strategies For Junior Faculty Members

i. Strategy 1: The Loner

One strategy for developing a pipeline of papers is to take control of the process and manage it by yourself. Through the "loner" strategy, the junior faculty member works as a solo author on a majority of papers. The strategy has some advantages. First, this strategy provides the most control of a junior faculty member's management of his or her pipeline. Through this strategy, the junior faculty member controls the pace at which papers develop and are submitted to journals. Second, it avoids many of the hassles associated with collaboration by eliminating the need to coordinate schedules or adapt one's work style to accommodate those of a collaborator.

The "loner" strategy also has a few limitations. First, in order to be successful with this strategy, the junior faculty member needs to be strong in all aspects of research. Weaknesses in certain aspects cannot be supplemented by someone else's strengths, which might be the case in collaborative research. Second, the capacity for developing and processing multiple papers is much lower compared to what might be achieved in a collaborative structure. As Figure 3-6 shows, the ability to manage multiple papers requires more time and effort as the number of papers increases. At some point, the quality of input gets eroded as the researcher's effort gets spread too thin. Thus, there is a limit to how many solo papers a researcher can move forward at a reasonable pace. Under this model, papers do not progress unless the junior faculty member is actively working on them. For obvious reasons, adoption of this strategy tends to be the road less traveled. However, there are a few academics who have executed the strategy masterfully.

ii. Strategy 2: The Managed Program

In contrast to the strategy discussed above, the "managed program" strategy encourages the junior faculty member to build a network of core collaborators within a few well-defined topic areas. As one might expect, recommendations on just how many topic areas one should pursue differ depending on to whom you talk. My recommendation is either two or three topic areas. Naturally, one of the topic areas will be the subject of the junior faculty member's dissertation. A secondary topic may emerge as a result of work the junior faculty member has begun with faculty members during his or her time in the doctoral program. Alternatively, the pursuit of a secondary topic may emerge from one's own interests beyond the dissertation. Whichever way the junior faculty member arrives at the secondary or tertiary topic areas, it is generally a good idea to have topics that go beyond the dissertation. It shows a maturity in moving beyond one's doctoral program training. Opinions also vary on just how related the junior faculty member's topic areas should be. In my personal opinion, it matters not how related the topic areas are as long as the junior faculty member is able to keep up with developments in the literature on those topics. Unrelated topic areas provide the opportunity to branch off into research domains that can be a healthy break from the dissertation topic. Unrelated topics can also spark new ideas that can inform breakthroughs in the dissertation topic area. Related topic areas have the benefit of allowing the junior faculty member to capitalize on synergies based on existing domain expertise that has been developed during one's doctoral training. The time and effort required to ramp up on a new topic area are comparatively lower when the topic is related to the junior faculty member's area of expertise.

Figure 3-6. An Illustration Of The Relationship Between Number Of Papers Managed Simultaneously And The Amount Of Time And Effort Required

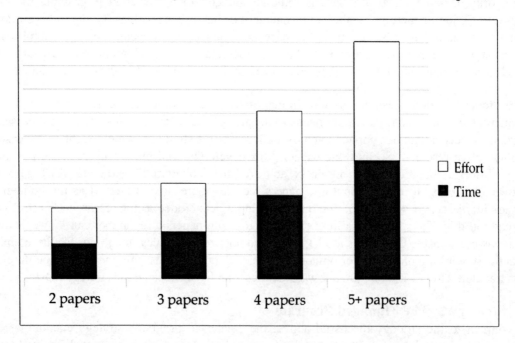

In terms of building one's network of collaborators, the "managed program" strategy requires the junior faculty member to be a good manager of people. It is often desirable to have collaborators at different stages of their career. The junior faculty member's peers are likely to share the same sense of urgency and drive to publish top-tier journal articles. Consequently, it will likely require less effort to manage turnaround times on drafts of papers and revisions on journal submissions. Senior faculty collaborators are often no less motivated to publish in top-tier journals. However, given the increased number of commitments and responsibilities they have to manage, it generally takes more time for them to turn papers around. A great benefit of working with senior faculty members is the tremendous insights they possess. Their insights often make the difference between whether a paper is publishable or not. They often also have more experience with navigating the review process and can help junior faculty members avoid common pitfalls. Thus, a healthy balance of peer and senior collaborators can enhance one's chances of gaining top-tier publications in a timely manner.

An obvious advantage of the "managed program" strategy over the "loner" strategy is that it greatly enhances the amount of bandwidth a junior faculty member has for processing papers that are at various stages of the journal submission process. Figure 3-7 illustrates how one can process multiple papers through partnering with collaborators. As the figure shows, a junior faculty member is able to juggle more papers as more minds are put to work in the collaboration task. The process becomes more manageable when a junior faculty member diversifies his or her role on various papers. For instance, taking a leading role on two or three different papers and a secondary and tertiary role on two or three others can be less strenuous than taking a lead role on five different papers. I have witnessed many faculty members achieving great success with this strategy.

iii. Strategy 3: The Opportunist

A final strategy that I have observed is what I like to call the "opportunist" strategy. This particular strategy bears some resemblance to the "managed program" outlined above, with one important difference—i.e., no clearly defined program. Whereas the "managed program" strategy advocates the development of a research program within two or three defined topic areas, the "opportunist" strategy has no such requirement. As the name of this strategy suggests, the junior faculty member pursues research collaborations on topics as they arise. This can be driven by a desire to work with a particular collaborator—the so called "we should work on something together" approach—or an interest in pursuing "hot" or emerging topics.

The "opportunist" strategy has many of the same advantages offered by the "managed program" strategy. It helps the junior faculty member build a network of collaborators through which he or she can expand the bandwidth devoted to developing and processing papers for journal submission. By diversifying the roles taken on various papers—i.e., lead role on some papers and a support role on others—the junior faculty member is able to have more papers in play in the journal submission and publication process. However, there are two key drawbacks to adopting this strategy. First, and perhaps most significantly, it carries the risk of producing a researcher who is not known for anything—i.e., not a topical expert. Even if the junior faculty member is successful at publishing a number of papers in top-tier journals across a variety of topics, he or she may be viewed as lacking an identity or area of expertise. Most research institutions prefer to have faculty members with recognized expertise on particular

Figure 3-7. An Illustration Of Managing Multiple Papers With Multiple Collaborators

Paper C: - Me: Writing hypothesis development section	Paper C: - Me: Hypothesis development section completed - Me: Writing method section - Collaborator 3: Streamlining theoretical background section	Paper C: - Me: Reading theoretical background section - Collaborator 3: Reading hypothesis development section	Paper C: - Me: First draft completed - Collaborator 3: Reading draft
Paper B: - Under first review at *MIS Quarterly*	Paper B: - Revise and resubmit at *MIS Quarterly* - Me: Read and reflect on reviews - Collaborator 2: Read and reflect on reviews	Paper B: - Me: Revising paper - Collaborator 2: Revising paper	Paper B: - Me: Revising paper - Collaborator 2: Revising paper
Paper A: - Me: Conducting data analysis - Collaborator 1: Revising introduction and hypotheses development section	Paper A: - Me: Analysis completed - Me: Writing discussion section	Paper A: - Me: Draft completed - Collaborator 1: Reviewing draft of paper	Paper A: - Submitted to *MIS Quarterly*

⟶

| January - March | April - June | July - August | September - November |

topics and this strategy is antithetical to that preference. Second, adopting such a strategy requires the junior faculty member to become familiar with a multitude of domains. Achieving a level of depth that produces a top-tier journal quality paper requires a significant amount of time and effort. Developing such depth across numerous topics can be significantly cumbersome. These two key drawbacks are consequential enough for junior faculty members who are working to establish themselves in academia, thus I personally would not recommend it. However, my own misgivings aside, this strategy has proven to be effective. Numerous faculty members have successfully published top-tier journal articles using this strategy.

Summary

As you might have gathered from the breadth of strategies just discussed, there is an element of equifinality to the achievement of a healthy pipeline of papers that are geared toward top-tier journal publication. Each strategy has yielded success for different academics in the field. It is pointless to attempt to predict which strategy fits best for different junior faculty members. The exercise of good judgment is paramount. My recommendation is for each junior faculty member to evaluate his or her own strengths and weaknesses in determining which strategy is best suited for him or her. Through such self-evaluation, an individual who is not good at managing collaborations may realize that the "managed program" strategy may not be the best fit. Similarly, an individual who enjoys working with others may find the "loner" strategy rather tedious and boring.

Two Complementary Steps

A final point worth considering is that while the strategies outlined in this chapter provide a roadmap for increasing journal submissions, other complementary steps are necessary to enhance the chance that these submissions will translate into publications. Two complementary steps are particularly relevant for enhancing the success of the strategies enumerated earlier. The first step involves working with good people. It goes without saying that many of the strategies outlined in this chapter (at least those that involve collaborating with others) are more likely to yield success when the collaborators involved are also skilled researchers. It does little good to expend effort on creating a pipeline of papers where you need to do the heavy lifting because your co-authors do not bring any useful skills to the table. In such circumstances, you would be better off working alone. Collaborations are more fruitful when complementary skills are brought to bear. This is true for the "managed program" strategy, where the junior faculty member pursues a carefully thought-through program of research. In pursuing such a strategy, one can increase the odds of success by being deliberate in the choice of collaborators and the sets of skills that will be brought to bear on various papers that are part of the program of research. Likewise, those pursuing the "opportunist" strategy enhance their odds of successfully publishing if they work with other skilled researchers who bring complementary skills to the collaboration. The second step involves making writing a part of your daily routine. A majority of institutions schedule your classes, schedule your department, college and committee meetings, and require you to schedule office hours to meet with students. Few, if any, require you to schedule time for research. Therefore, it is incumbent upon you to make writing papers a part of your daily routine rather than something you do when you can squeeze in the time for it. When writing papers is part of your daily routine, steady progress is more visible and your writing also improves. Clearly, this activity is relevant for the "loner" strategy, where the progress of a paper relies almost exclusively on one's ability to dedicate time to working on it. This activity is also relevant for those pursuing the "managed program" and the "opportunist" strategy as one needs to regulate the time devoted to working on multiple papers to ensure they progress toward journal submission and, hopefully, publication.

Concluding Thoughts

My main objective in this chapter was to outline a few strategies to help doctoral students and junior faculty members create a healthy pipeline of papers geared toward journal submission and publication. The strategies are intended to be a complement to existing advice about the mechanics of writing the journal article or managing the tenure process. I sought to outline some concrete steps that would enable junior members of the academy to turn their pipedreams into pipelines, as a colleague of mine once said. As I noted earlier, and reinforce here, following these strategies is no guarantee for success in publishing top-tier journal articles. Rather, the strategies are aimed at increasing the odds in your favor. The basketball player who does not take any shots at the basket guarantees that he or she will not score any points in a game. The basketball player who takes enough good shots at the basket is not guaranteed to score any points either but, at least, the odds of scoring are increased. In much the same way, doing nothing will guarantee that the junior faculty member or doctoral student gets no publications. Having a plan for developing and submitting papers to top-tier journals offers no guarantees but certainly increases the odds of success.

Hopefully, the strategies outlined in this chapter will prove useful in enabling you to establish your pipeline. If not, perhaps you will discover your own strategy that yields greater success. The main thing is to have a deliberate plan and begin putting that plan into action early enough in the process.

Key Takeaways

1. As research universities continue to enhance their standing as institutions of excellence in research, the standards for achieving tenure at these institutions continue to increase and consequently, junior faculty members are under constant pressure to produce publications in top journals
2. For doctoral students
    i. The challenge
        a. The average doctoral student takes five years to complete the program, while many papers also take about 5 years to complete (a year to conceptualize an idea, vet the

idea with colleagues, conduct a pilot study and then, orchestrate the data collection to test the idea; once data collection has been completed, it can take up to a year to format, clean and analyze the data, and then write the paper that will be the initial submission; and the review process itself can take two or more years before a paper is accepted)

b. Given this timeline, doctoral students need to hit the ground running if they are to have any chance at success

c. Note that 5 years for the publication process is optimistic—often, data collection challenges and a lengthy review process can expand this timeline considerably

d. Given the timeline challenges, it's important for doctoral students to start working on research early

ii. Strategy 1: From seed to blossoming flower

a. Doctoral students take seminars in which they read new literature and learn research methods—these are perfect opportunities to practice engaging in fruitful research

b. Focus on developing the ideas generated in courses, practicing research methods skills and getting critical feedback in an effort to get a journal publication out of the effort expended on coursework

c. There are a number of different sources for feedback including instructors of readings seminars, other faculty members within the student's department and reviews from submission to an academic conference

iii. Strategy 2: Building a house one brick at a time

a. Develop an idea and refine it over the course of a series of doctoral seminars

b. Use successive seminars as forums for further developing an idea and potentially, spawning additional papers on the same topic

c. Advantages of this approach include:

- Spending a longer period of time delving into a topic from a variety of perspectives

- Each seminar serves as a major step to advancing or expanding the idea in a way that is informed by the topic area

- This approach enables the student to consider various approaches to empirical validation while progressing through research methods and statistics courses

iv. Strategy 3: Learning from those who know

a. Work with faculty members who are conducting research

b. Students may start working with a faculty member on a project from initial conceptualization or on a mature project where data have already been collected and a model formulated

c. Be cautious about working with too many faculty members and spreading yourself too thin

3. For junior faculty members

i. The challenge

a. Tenure packets are often due at the end of the fifth year, while an optimistic timeline for the publication process is five years

    b. Junior faculty members can thus ill-afford to focus on one paper at a time because many schools require multiple papers in top-tier journals to grant tenure

    c. Compounding this challenge is the reality that the first year of appointment is often extremely busy with preparing new courses, serving on committees and social events at one's new institution

ii. Strategy 1: The loner

    a. One strategy for developing a pipeline of papers is to take control of the process and manage it by yourself

    b. Advantages: Gives you the most control over management of your pipeline and avoids the hassles associated with managing collaborations

    c. Disadvantages: Need to be strong in all aspects of research and lowers capacity to produce papers

iii. Strategy 2: The managed program

    a. This strategy encourages the junior faculty member to build a network of core collaborators within a few well-defined topic areas

    b. One of the topic areas will be the subject of the junior faculty member's dissertation

    c. A secondary topic may emerge as a result of work the junior faculty member has begun with faculty members during his or her time in the doctoral program (alternatively, the pursuit of a secondary topic may emerge from one's own interests beyond the dissertation)

    d. This strategy requires the junior faculty member to be a good manager of people

    e. It is often desirable to have collaborators at different stages of their career—junior faculty members are similarity motivated, while senior faculty members have valued experience and expertise

    f. Advantages include enhancing the amount of bandwidth for processing papers that are at various stages of the journal submission and review process

iv. Strategy 3: The opportunist

    a. This strategy resembles the managed program strategy but has no clearly defined program—the junior faculty member pursues research collaborations on topics as they arise

    b. Advantages are similar to the managed program strategy

    c. Disadvantages include the risk of not being known for anything

v. Complementary steps

    a. Work with good people—collaborations are more fruitful when complementary skills are brought to bear

    b. Make writing papers a part of your daily routine rather than something you do when you can squeeze in the time for it—when writing papers is part of your daily routine, steady progress is more visible and your writing also improves

CHAPTER 4

WRITING A PAPER

This chapter focuses on writing empirical articles for journals in the social and behavioral sciences. One qualifier is in order. The particular emphasis and lessons learned are from my experiences and, therefore, I will particularly focus on writing papers targeted toward information systems journals, such as *MIS Quarterly*, organizational behavior journals, such as *Organizational Behavior and Human Decision Processes*, human resources journals, such as *Personnel Psychology*, and marketing journals, such as *Journal of Marketing*. There are variations across journals and even within journals across time. So, besides the advice provided in this chapter and other sources to which I point, it is important to read the editorial statements of sitting editors and to look at recent published papers to understand the current idiosyncrasies of the journal that you are targeting.

There are many excellent articles on how to write a paper. Here are some useful sources that will help you in thinking about making a theoretical contribution and writing a paper for journals in the social and behavioral sciences: Bem (2003),[39] Bergh (2003),[40] Feldman (2004),[41] Rynes (2002),[42] Schminke (2004),[43] Starbuck (1999),[44] Weber (2003)[45] and Whetten (1989).[46] My goal is *not* to repeat what has been discussed effectively in these articles but rather to highlight a few additional things that may have been somewhat subtle or not mentioned in these other articles. Compared to these articles, my focus is more on the "do's and don't's" and "tips and tricks" in the process of writing a paper.

Before I begin, it would be beneficial for you to reflect on the following questions:
1. In your opinion, what is the most important reason papers get rejected?
2. In your opinion, why do you think papers suffer from the reason you gave (above)?
3. What are *your* biggest challenges as it relates to writing a paper? Be thorough and detailed.
4. Where do you face the most difficulties when you write? Note that this question is asking about the writing process itself.
5. What strategies have you tried to remedy the problems (identified in the previous two questions)?

Many people will say papers get rejected due to a lack of solid theoretical contribution. This is consistent with a major problem identified by editors of many leading journals in the social and behavioral sciences. In terms of the reason for this (i.e., answer to the second of the five questions above), it may be that the topic was uninteresting or the model was inadequate or the empirical study was poor. While these might be true, much can be done in writing a paper to ensure that these sorts of problems are minimized. My goal in this chapter is to discuss five strategies to aid activities related to the writing process—it is not my goal to discuss how to conduct research or how to position papers within any specific topic. I will illustrate the

strategies, with some suggestions from my own experiences, using examples from some of my early papers. The five strategies are:
1. Framing and telling an interesting story
2. Fishing
3. Writing and thinking
4. Outline of a paper
5. Hat trick

1. Framing And Telling An Interesting Story

The first lesson in writing an interesting article is to frame the paper in the most interesting way possible. I have heard it said that an idea is like a diamond—complex and multi-faceted. It is through framing that we shine light on to the idea, bringing out the brilliance and subtle nuances that might otherwise not be evident.

If reviewers are turned off by a paper in the first few pages—i.e., they don't believe an interesting story is in the paper—they are more likely to look for problems in the rest of the paper. In contrast, if they like the basic idea of the paper, they are more likely to look for ways to improve the paper. There is a very fine line between these two outcomes. It is important for authors to ensure that the reviewers are in the right frame of mind (insomuch as an author can influence this) for it can make the difference between the verdict of *reject* or *not-reject*. Notice that I am referring to it as *not-reject*. I do this for a reason—I really think of a *revise-and-resubmit* decision as a stay of execution.

Framing the paper is all about telling an interesting story. It is the framing that decides what story is actually being told. An interesting story hinges on saying something that has not been said before. For instance, one of my pet peeves, as it relates to papers on technology adoption—which is one of the most widely researched and mature topics in information systems—is how close the messages of submitted papers are to what has been said before. Not surprisingly, such papers seldom fare well in the review process. Reviewers and editors conclude that the paper offers little in the way of substantial theoretical contribution. They are not wrong.

Let me illustrate this with an example. Most research on the technology acceptance model (TAM) has found *perceived usefulness*, rather than *perceived ease of use,* to be the most important predictor of *intention to use a technology*.[47,48,49] I once reviewed a paper that found that perceived ease of use was more important [I was a reviewer of this paper]. This finding was buried somewhere in the results section. In fact, the authors later apologized and noted that it was quite likely that the finding was an error in the study design. At that time, I was a bit surprised the authors said that. Worse yet, I believed them. I then concluded that there was nothing new the paper had to offer and recommended rejection. This was a consistent recommendation across all reviewers. The editor rejected the paper. The moral? Perhaps, just perhaps, the paper could have been salvaged if the authors had framed the paper around questioning whether perceived usefulness would always be the most important determinant of intention and then, expounded upon the situations and circumstances when perceived ease of use may be more important. Such a framing would definitely have allowed them to tell a more interesting story than the ho-hum story of TAM. Interestingly, much later, there was a paper in *MIS Quarterly* in 2004 by Hans van der Heijden[50] that had similar contrary findings that were attributed to the type of information system, thus making the paper a good theoretical contribution.

Ultimately, it is far more likely that a paper framed around something interesting—e.g., perceived ease of use can be more important—rather than a re-make—e.g., TAM works in the context of web sites also—will lead to an interesting story that reviewers will find appealing and journal editors will want to publish. Over the years, I have gone from believing that the framing and the story is one of the many important things to get right to believing that the framing and the story constitute the single most important thing that can make or break an article. I wouldn't say that framing is a sufficient condition for publication—but, it certainly is the most important necessary condition.

I believe I got the framing right in a few instances. My first premier journal publication—i.e., a paper in *MIS Quarterly* in 1999[51]—tells an interesting story (in my biased view, anyway). I wrote the first draft of that paper for a PhD seminar class in the first quarter of my PhD program in 1993 taught by the late great Gerry DeSanctis. The first draft of the paper was about using ideas from text-based virtual reality games to develop a telecommuting tool that could provide greater social richness. Gerry seemed to like the paper and encouraged me to work on it outside the scope of the class. As I made my way through the PhD program, I became more and more enamored with text-based virtual reality multi-user games that I had used to set up the whole paper. As I discussed the paper with several people, some, especially Gerry and Fred [Davis], emphasized repeatedly that I should find something interesting to tell businesses— because the game per se was not interesting. I wrote a paper with a focus on the game as a metaphor to help people better appreciate telecommuting and text-based telecommuting tools, and provided implications for the design of telecommuting tools. It was rejected at the *Journal of Management Information Systems*. I then collected data to compare how trainees who underwent traditional training vs. game-based training reacted to a real telecommuting system. Interestingly, the game—with all its metaphorical properties for physical space—helped users better appreciate telecommuting and made them more favorable toward the system. Perhaps an aside [to this story] was that I used TAM as the underlying model to examine mean differences and moderation of key relationships. TAM was secondary in the framing of the paper. The paper used TAM but it was *not about* TAM. The paper was different from the typical TAM paper/submission in that I emphasized the problem and the solution, albeit using TAM as the underlying model used to compare the two types of training.

This is not to say that an extensively researched topic area automatically means any paper in that area is *DOA* (dead on arrival). It simply means that the stakes are higher. The bar is higher. It means that the story has to be more than interesting—it may even have to be exciting. There are at least three papers I co-authored related to TAM where the story had a way of carrying the day. Mike Morris and I wrote a paper on gender differences and TAM that appeared in *MIS Quarterly* in 2000.[52] This paper focused on a fundamental hole in TAM—the overlooked role of social influences. There had been work that had attempted to study social influences, although not necessarily as part of TAM. Fred Davis' original TAM paper in *Management Science* in 1989[53] included a test of the theory of reasoned action that incorporated social influences. Others have studied it. The results were inconclusive, with social influences being significant sometimes and non-significant at other times. Sometimes, PhD students are advised, told or even required to stay away from such a *mess*. I think such *mess* can present a great opportunity to make a contribution. For example, our paper on gender differences and TAM was really focused on integrating social influences into TAM, with gender playing a pivotal moderating role. In a related paper in *Management Science* in 2000,[54] where we proposed TAM2, Fred Davis and I incorporated social influences into TAM via different underlying mechanisms—namely, compliance, identification and internalization—tied to different causal pathways, with voluntariness playing a critical moderating role of key relationships. Finally, my paper on the determinants of ease of use in *Information Systems Research* in 2000[55] made a theoretical contribution to the TAM literature by focusing on the underlying cognitive and psychological processes that lead to the formation and change of ease of use perceptions. When one takes a 30,000-foot view, each of these could indeed be said to be a TAM paper. However, each of these papers offered much more than just a test of TAM in another context or more than an ad-hoc variable being added to TAM. Each presented an interesting story that related to a scientific gap.

2. Fishing

As PhD students, we are often taught that our papers need to be theory-driven and that we need to avoid *data fishing*. Data fishing is a practice in which a dataset is analyzed in an exploratory fashion without *a priori* theoretical expectations of possible patterns or causal relationships. When we read a typical empirical paper, there is almost always the following flow: introduction, literature review, theory development, method, results and discussion. One might think that the authors completed the literature review, developed a model, then designed a study, executed it, analyzed the data and wrote up the paper as a report of the testing of the originally proposed model that is reported in the paper. Many textbooks even teach such a sequence of activities represents a good research process. Thus, one could [usually erroneously] think that the authors wrote the paper in keeping with the chronological sequence in which the various phases of the research actually occurred.

Unfortunately, the research process doesn't work that way. It is invariably an iteration among the ideas (including the research question and framing), the theory development and the data/results, not to mention the ideas of the editors and reviewers. The sooner you recognize this need for iteration and are able to iterate [without emotional distress] across the various parts of a paper, the more likely you will find a way to frame the work in an interesting way. The emergence of interesting results is more likely to help you find a story to tell.

There is a fine line between fishing and iteration. Fishing would mean being entirely data driven. Discovery hinges on iteration. In the paradigm of positivist research, we rely on a priori theory quite a lot. This means that some *a priori* theory development is necessary. However, the ideas have to then be refined by letting the "data speak." Not letting the data speak will lead us to the dreaded *ivory tower theorizing*, which in the context of a researcher refers to the fact that the person has lost touch with reality.

Bem (2003, p. 187)[56] speaks eloquently to this issue:

> "When you are through exploring, you may conclude that the data are not strong enough to justify your new insights formally, but at least you are now ready to design the "right" study. If you still plan to report the current data, you may wish to mention the new insights tentatively, stating honestly that they remain to be tested adequately. Alternatively, the data may be strong enough to justify recentering your article around the new findings and subordinating or even ignoring your original hypotheses.

> This is not advice to suppress negative results. If your study was genuinely designed to test hypotheses that derive from a formal theory or are of wide general interest for some other reason, then they should remain the focus of your article. The integrity of the scientific enterprise requires the reporting of disconfirming results.

> But this requirement assumes that somebody out there cares about the hypotheses. Many respectable studies are explicitly exploratory or are launched from speculations of the "I-wonder-if…" variety. If your study is one of these, then nobody cares if you were wrong. Contrary to the conventional wisdom, science does not care how clever or clairvoyant you were at guessing your results ahead of time. Scientific integrity does not require you to lead your readers through all your wrongheaded hunches only to show—voila!—they were wrongheaded. A journal article should not be a personal history of your stillborn thoughts."

3. Writing And Thinking

There are two points I wish to highlight here. One is related to writing itself and the other is about writing and thinking. Both of Bem's articles (1995, 2003)[57,58] are excellent guides on what goes into a paper and how important writing is. Bem (2003, p. 205)[59] quite eloquently noted how important good writing is: "I believe the difference between the articles accepted and the top 15-20% of those rejected is frequently the difference between good and less good writing. Moral: Don't expect journal reviewers to discern your brilliance through the smog of polluted writing. Revise your manuscript. Polish it. Proofread it. Submit it."

Like some of the ideas sprinkled throughout this book, the credit for this idea goes to Fred Davis, who had, for many years, said to me that writing and thinking are tightly woven together. In the early days of my academic writing experiences, when my writing was quite poor (of course, reviewers of my papers frequently remind me that it still is!), I always found writing to be almost nauseating as I struggled with it and the output was, at best, an object of ridicule. However, I firmly believed that I had excellent ideas that simply were poorly expressed. Now, I see more and more that thinking about the ideas and expressing them are interwoven. The lack of clarity in thought is sure to be evidenced in the lack of clarity in the writing. The real *aha experience* comes when you are writing and you realize that there is a lack of depth in your idea, thus causing you to re-visit the underlying idea. Developing this skill takes time. The only thing I have found useful in this process is to write. The suggestions in Boice's (1990)[60] book about generative writing and spontaneous writing are enormously helpful. Nothing can substitute for the actual practice of writing and thinking and allowing the two to co-evolve. Both are extremely difficult skills. Practice early and often!

4. Outline Of A Paper

Researchers use many different techniques to create outlines of their papers and to write those papers. Some create a slide show to tell a story. Others just use a standard outline. Some prefer writing a clear abstract. One of Daryl Bem's suggestions that is quite effective is to think about a paper as an hourglass where the broadest part is at both ends of the paper—i.e., introduction and discussion. In his paper on writing an empirical journal article, Bem discusses the ingredients of various sections of an empirical paper. That paper, along with the many others listed earlier, are excellent sources of information on how to write papers.

Before discussing the outline and the ingredients of a paper, let me make some general comments about writing, drawing primarily from Bem's article. An introduction should not be narrowly conceived—it should be about the broader context. The writing itself must be clear and simple and accessible to PSYC 101 students. Bem asks that authors omit needless words, needless concepts, topics, anecdotes, asides and footnotes. For my part, I have found it useful to relegate points off the main theme into footnotes, particularly points that would ensure that a particular cite is incorporated or one that demonstrates knowledge of a particular literature base. He calls for a coherent story and thematic organization of the literature. This is an excellent point—a chronological organization, for example, does little to help the reader gain a holistic understanding of the literature. Literature reviews must focus on what we know. I agree that we must have informative headings. However, I disagree on his point about meta-comments—I do think roadmaps are of value. In my view, ensuring that the reader is not lost is crucial. I am not in favor of the elimination of meta-comments, not entirely anyway. He calls for a consistency in terminology—there is no need to change the terminology with a view toward breaking the boredom or monotony. A final point that strikes me is to never attack authors, only to attack ideas. To that, I might add that rather than attacking authors or ideas, we should always try to emphasize that we are *building upon and going beyond prior research* even if, in reality, we are indeed taking down one theoretical approach in favor of a new, different and contrasting one.

Let me start with a tool that I use to craft the outline of a paper—shown in Table 4-1. This table is a companion piece to Bem's (2003)[61] article, with this table focusing a bit more on the type of journals I mentioned at the outset of this chapter. The outlining approach that I present is consistent with the hourglass structure that Bem suggests for an empirical article, such that it starts broad, becomes more focused as it discusses details (of theory, method and results) and broadens out again in the discussion. I have also found the outlining tool to be effective in understanding papers written by others. Further, it can help rewrite papers that have been written (perhaps poorly) and that are in need of a complete overhaul. The outlining tool helps me focus on the most interesting story, to do so in the early stages of writing a paper, and to minimize or eliminate unnecessary appendages or tangential points that can creep into a paper and hurt it in the review process.

Table 4-1. Outline Of A Paper

Article title: _____

Version #: _____

Abstract:
Journals typically have a length limit on abstracts and it is typically between 100 and 200 words. In writing an abstract, remember that you are not trying to write an abstract of each section of the paper—such a structure is neither useful nor something that can be achieved. Abstracts should be one paragraph and discuss: the main research question and/or phenomenon being investigated, what was done, and what was found.

Introduction:
The introduction must tell the reader what the paper is about. You can accomplish this with a few effective paragraphs that focus on the business problem, the scientific problem, the paper's objectives and the expected contributions.

Business problem (or applied problem) and significance:
- The reader should be convinced that there is a significant problem or opportunity, which if unresolved could be catastrophic. This can be handled by focusing on the relevant problem plaguing (or opportunities facing) organizations that your research can help.
- Use numbers to make your case—e.g., 50% of all projects fail—and cite credible sources—e.g., Gartner.

Table 4-1 *Continued*. Outline Of A Paper

- Be succinct. The business problem should be presented in a paragraph of about ¾ page.

Theoretical problem and significance:

- Present a 30,000-foot view of the literature. Do not talk about subtleties in the research area, unless it is critical to understand the current paper's contributions. The interested reader will press on to the background section and your theory development where you can hit them with the details.
- Use the high-level view of the literature to highlight the gap that will be addressed in your research. For example: "While prior research has extensively studied individual-level technology adoption, little or no attention has been paid to the role of social factors and their effects on technology adoption."
- The reader should be convinced that there is a significant gap in the scientific literature that your work has the potential to plug.
- Be succinct. The scientific problem should be presented in a paragraph of about ¾ of a page.

Objectives:

- A clear statement or set of statements about the objectives of the paper. It is important that these objectives can be clearly tied to the business problem and scientific gap articulated earlier.
- One approach on conveying the objective is to provide a broad research objective—for example: this paper attempts to incorporate social factors in technology adoption research by drawing on research and theories related to gender stereotyping.
- An alternative is to present a set of objectives—for example: This paper has the following three objectives: (1) review important prior research on gender differences in organizational behavior and psychology; (2) develop a model of technology adoption that incorporates gender as a moderator of key relationships; and (3) empirically test the model in a longitudinal study in a field setting.

Expected contributions:

- Conclude the introduction with the contributions or insights that can be garnered as a result of such an investigation. Emphasize how your paper helps advance our understanding of the theory and phenomenon. You can discuss what nomological network you are extending or modifying. Also, it is important to discuss the theoretical contributions your paper will make—i.e., what theories will be advanced.

A comment about the intertwining and distinction across: (a) gap; (b) objectives; and (c) contributions. A gap exists in the literature. The objective is a way of filling the gap (there are many ways to fill a gap—so you could have the same gap tackled in different papers using different approaches, thus having different objectives across papers). Contributions are related to the theory or literature in which you identified the gaps. In sum, note that these three important elements of the introduction are related yet distinct.

Table 4-1 *Continued*. Outline Of A Paper

Literature review/Background:

This is information that a reader needs to know in order to understand the rest of the paper. It is typically meant for a reader who may not be intimately familiar with the area of research. You can expect a reviewer who is familiar with the topic to skip over this section in the first pass through the paper. This section should be crisp and should not be used as an opportunity to provide a report on all prior work. The focus should be on the relevant background. Some key elements that should be included in this section are:

- A discussion or overview of the specific theoretical framework or model on which the paper builds.
- Key findings from papers that you build upon or extend.
- Definitions of constructs that you draw from prior research.

Theory/hypothesis development:

For each hypothesis, list the relationship and the one or two reasons you expect the relationship to hold. Theory development is difficult and comes only with a lot of practice. As Whetten noted, theory development is about why relationships exist. Use examples to help make your case. I refer you to the many articles on theory-building and making a theoretical contribution.

Method:

The method section is perhaps most formulaic of all sections in a paper. Follow the format of the journal to which you plan to submit your paper. A good method section provides the necessary information to replicate the work. If the reader cannot replicate your study based on this section, it is a major problem. The following are essential:

Participants: Population, sampling frame, demographics and other relevant details.

Measures: Cites for adapted scales; new scales and steps taken to develop the scales.

Procedure: How was the study conducted, and what was measured and when? Again, think replication.

Results:

This section is also somewhat formulaic and published articles in the journal you are targeting should be studied carefully and used as templates. Journals vary in terms of where some of the information is reported—e.g., reliability and validity information is reported in the method section in some journals, while others report such information in the results section. The analysis procedure is another such detail—method or results. Ultimately, the reader must have the following information from the method and results:

- Reliability diagnostics
- Convergent and discriminant validity information
- Descriptive statistics
- Correlations
- Information regarding other threats—e.g., multicollinearity, outliers

Table 4-1 *Continued*. Outline Of A Paper

- Model tests and support for various hypotheses; also, identify surprising or unexpected findings (not just hypotheses that were not supported)

Discussion:
This section needs to incorporate five components. The length and content of each of these five components are described next:

Summary ("declaration of victory" statement): The first paragraph of the discussion section needs to be a sort of victory statement that notes that an important gap in the scientific literature was filled, that the model and most (or all) hypotheses were supported, and that presents the amount of variance explained in the key dependent variables (some journals care about this, some don't—do what's right for the journal you are targeting).

Theoretical contributions: This part of the discussion section should be about four paragraphs that focus on the major contributions of the paper. One paragraph should speak directly to the theory base from which the paper draws and builds. Other paragraphs should relate to contributions that emerge from interesting findings in the paper (this will vary across papers).

Theoretical implications: These three or four paragraphs are about the "so what" and "what's next" for researchers. The implications are about future research directions that emerge as a result of the findings in this paper (don't dwell here on the limitations of the current work and associated future research directions, which comes later).

Limitations: The limitations section should be a focused paragraph or two that recognizes limitations (some that may be alleviated) and identifies associated future research directions.

Practical implications: These three or four paragraphs should be about what the findings mean for organizations, managers and practitioners in the topic area related to the paper (e.g., system designers). The specific implications will obviously vary depending on the specific topic and findings. It is, however, important not to be superficial but rather to be insightful. For example, don't just call for practitioners to incentivize the behavior for which you find support—but rather say how this can be done and how organizational practice should change.

Together, the contributions and implications should close the loop on the business and scientific problems discussed in the introduction section.

Conclusions:
The conclusions section should be a succinct paragraph that highlights the golden nuggets. The conclusions section should not be another abstract. It is not about limitations or caveats. It should be about the major contribution of the paper and a key implication or two.

This outlining tool can also be used iteratively to flesh out a paper. I think and write in a very modular fashion, perhaps due to my structured, logical and analytical thought processes that developed during my days in engineering school and continued through my time as a computer scientist. In the first version of the outline, the goal is simply to get the framing, story and main ideas down. Using the outlining approach allows me to try many different storylines and pick the most compelling one. This method is less effortful, especially in the long-run, than getting a few months into the writing process only to discover that you have not really found the most interesting story. Once the basic outline is in place, you could then take any single section and flesh it out further—e.g., you could flesh out the introduction—and push it forward until it is completed and compelling. Alternatively, you could flesh out the various sections in a little more detail and iteratively expand it. The approach one takes to outlining and fleshing out various parts of the paper may vary based on how you like to think and work through the writing process. Nowadays, I like to have a high-level and a slightly more fleshed out outline first before embarking on writing the paper. Next, I tackle the introduction and write it entirely to make sure that the first few pages that a reviewer will be reading is interesting and thought-provoking. Table 4-1 presents my suggestions for the content that goes into various sections of the paper (skip any sections that do not apply to your paper)—keep in mind that this outline works best for an empirical paper using quantitative data in a positivist paradigm.

Once you have crafted the basic storyline and/or a working draft, you should not hesitate to critically review it even if that might mean having to completely rewrite the paper. Bem's (1995, p. 176)[62] article has spoken to this point in two very effective paragraphs:

"Finally, rewriting is difficult because it usually means restructuring. Sometimes it is necessary to discard whole sections of a manuscript, add new ones, and then totally reorganize the manuscript just to iron out a bump in the logic of the argument. Don't get so attached to your first draft that you are unwilling to tear it apart and rebuild it. (This is why the strategy of crafting each sentence of a first draft wastes time. A beautiful turn of phrase that took me 20 minutes to shape gets trashed when I have to restructure the manuscript. Worse, I get so attached to the phrase that I resist restructuring until I can find a new home for it.) A badly constructed building cannot be salvaged by brightening up the wallpaper. A badly constructed manuscript cannot be salvaged by changing words, inverting sentences, and shuffling paragraphs.

Which brings me to the word processor. Its very virtuosity at making these cosmetic changes will tempt you to tinker endlessly, encouraging you in the illusion that you are restructuring right there in front of the monitor. Do not be fooled. You are not. A word processor—even one with a fancy outline mode—is not an adequate restructuring tool for most writers. Moreover, it can produce flawless, physically beautiful drafts of wretched writing, encouraging you in the illusion that they are finished manuscripts ready to be submitted. Do not be fooled. They are not. If you are blessed with an excellent memory (or a very large monitor) and are confident that you can get away with a purely electronic process of restructuring, do it. But don't be ashamed to print out a complete draft of your manuscript; spread it out on the table or floor; take pencil, scissors, and scotch tape in hand; and then, all by your low-tech self, have at it."

5. Hat Trick

Once you use the outlining tool to flesh out the sections of your paper, the next step is to improve your paper so that it is the best it can be. The *hat trick* is named as such after I received advice from many people early in my PhD program about being able to switch between the "author hat" and the "reader hat." The hat trick can be vital to improving your paper.

Performing the hat trick is one of the hardest skills to develop, yet one of the most useful. As an author, you are so close to your material that your mind can fill in gaps when you read your work. A simple example is how a new reader picks up typos in your paper after you have edited it tens of times. It is simply because our minds easily fills in the missing "to," the missing "for," the missing "and," etc. These gaps are not the only gaps that our minds fill for us. Our minds can also fill in gaps in the logic and ideas—"fillings" that are, of course, inaccessible to our readers.

Combating the problem of selective blindness to missing elements that get filled by your mind is a major hurdle in transforming a mediocre paper into a good paper. It is the obstacle that must be crossed in order to stop writing for yourself and to start writing for your readers (the first set of whom are editors and reviewers). It might appear that an easy way to solve this problem is to ask someone else, such as a colleague (senior or junior), to read the paper and give comments. Of course, peer feedback is valuable and critical to the improvement of every paper. However, peer feedback cannot be a substitute for the hat trick. Why can a peer review not substitute for the hat trick? In a confusing paper, a peer may not be able to understand the main ideas, thus largely negating the purpose of a peer review. Also, rather than a peer review helping a bad paper become a better one, by effectively using the hat trick first, a peer review, which can come later, can be focused on transforming a good paper to a great paper.

Here are some suggestions for how to best perform the hat trick. Once you have completed a section of a paper or even an entire paper, put it away for two to four weeks. This time away from the paper will help you clear your mind. You will forget the intricate details of what you wrote. By distancing yourself from your paper, you are removing the "author hat." When you pick up the paper after some time has elapsed, you will almost certainly be donning the reviewer hat. Now, read the paper. You will almost certainly discover problems and issues that you had not noticed before. You will identify problems in flow and logic that your mind previously had filled in and glossed over. You will see typos that you had not seen before. The hat trick was a skill that I was completely lacking early in my career.

Nowadays, I consider myself to be reasonably competent at performing the hat trick. Of course, when you have this skill down pat, you can perform the hat trick without having to put the document away for an extended period of time. One might argue that putting the paper away for an extended period of time delays the process of completing and submitting the paper. This is indeed true and unavoidable. However, the journal acceptance rates and review cycle times being what they are, the time spent in creating a better product is well worth the time invested.

Concluding Thoughts

This chapter presented some tips on how to write an empirical journal article. There are several important complementary sources on how to write a paper to make a strong theoretical contribution and how to write an empirical journal article. This chapter focuses on a few specific tips and tricks. In particular, I discussed the importance of framing and developing an interesting storyline. I also talked about the iteration between theory and data. The most important part of this chapter focuses on how to develop an outline and use it as a guide in crafting a paper. Finally, I concluded with how important it is for you to be able to critically examine your paper and refine it further to make it the best it can be.

Key Takeaways

1. Good sources on writing, include: Bem (2003), Bergh (2003), Feldman (2004), Rynes (2002), Schminke (2004), Starbuck (1999), Weber (2003) and Whetten (1989)
2. Lack of a solid theoretical contribution is a common reason for rejection of a paper—an issue that can often be tied to the quality of the exposition
3. Framing and telling an interesting story
    i. If reviewers are turned off by a paper in the first few pages or so—i.e., they don't believe an interesting story is in the paper—they are more likely to look for problems with the rest of the paper
    ii. Quite in contrast, if they like the basic idea, they are more likely to look for ways to improve the paper
    iii. Frame the paper in the most interesting way possible
    iv. An interesting story hinges on saying something that has not been said before
    v. The framing and the story constitute the single most important thing that can make or break an article
    vi. An extensively researched topic doesn't mean any paper in that area is *DOA* (dead on arrival), it simply means that the stakes are higher
4. Fishing
    i. When we read a typical empirical paper, there is almost always the following flow: introduction, literature review, theory development, method, results and discussion—the research activities are usually not done in that sequence
    ii. The research process is an iteration among the ideas (including the research question and framing), the theory development and the data/results, not to mention the ideas of the editors and reviewers
    iii. There is a fine line between fishing and iteration—fishing would mean being entirely data driven, whereas discovery hinges on iteration
    iv. Let the "data speak" to avoid "ivory tower theorizing"

5. Writing and thinking
   i. Writing and thinking are tightly interwoven—the lack of clarity in thought is sure to be evidenced in the writing
   ii. As Bem put it: "Don't expect journal reviewers to discern your brilliance through the smog of polluted writing. Revise your manuscript. Polish it. Proofread it. Submit it."
   iii. Nothing will substitute for the actual practice of writing and thinking and allowing the two to co-evolve—both are extremely difficult skills... practice early and often!
6. Outline of a paper
   i. There are many tools for writing—you should find one that works for you: some create a slide show to tell a story, others use a standard outline, while some prefer to write a clear abstract
   ii. In using the outline approach, think about an hourglass where the broadest part is at both ends of the paper—i.e., introduction and discussion
   iii. An introduction should not be narrowly conceived—it should be about the broader context
   iv. Strive for a coherent story and thematic organization of the literature (a chronological organization, for example, does nothing)
   v. Roadmaps are of value—tell the reader where you are going
   vi. Never attack people or ideas in your writing—rather, build on ideas
   vii. The outlining tool provided in Table 4-1 can be used to iteratively flesh out a paper
   viii. Once you have crafted the basic storyline or draft of the paper, critically review it, even if that means completely rewriting the paper
7. Hat trick
   i. Practice the skill of switching between the "author hat" and the "reviewer hat"
   ii. As an author, your mind fills in the missing details in grammar and logic
   iii. Putting on the "reviewer hat" may require putting the paper aside for two to four weeks so that you can clear it from your mind and identify the missing details
   iv. Peer review can't substitute for the hat trick

CHAPTER 5

ADDRESSING REVIEWERS' AND EDITORS' COMMENTS

Great news! You've received reviews for your manuscript back from *MIS Quarterly* and it isn't a reject! The bad news—you have received upwards of ten pages of single-spaced comments from the editors and three reviewers. If your experiences are anything like mine, there is some kernel in the paper that the review panel (editors and reviewers) like. However, they want a stronger motivation, they want more robust theory, they have several questions related to the method, they want you to almost completely re-analyze your data, and they want some more and different implications. This may sound extreme but it is useful to start with how to tackle such a major revision and if you receive a more favorable revise-and-resubmit, it will be easier to handle. There have only been two occasions at premier journals where the editors and reviewers have really liked my paper in the initial submission where a *conditional accept* decision was made in the first round—a paper on gender differences and the theory of planned behavior that appeared in *Organizational Behavior and Human Decision Processes* in 2000[63] and a paper on usability that appeared in *Information Systems Research* in 2002.[64] Even in these rare cases, there were still many pages of comments that needed to be addressed.

Responding to comments and making the paper palatable to the review panel can be quite a challenge. To go back to some of the ingredients of a paper that I mentioned in chapter 4, I believe that adhering to a defined and interesting outline is important for yet another reason. Editors and reviewers of top journals, especially in some fields, are extremely critical—this point is made forcefully in an article in a premier journal in information systems (Dennis et al. 2006, p. 6):[65] "...reason that we as a discipline produce fewer elite research articles per capita is that many reviewers now expect papers to be 'flawless' to be worthy of publication in MISQ or ISR—a take-no-prisoners style of reviewing rather than the developmental style of reviewing sought by both MISQ and ISR." Saunders (2005, p. iii)[66] made a related point: "I think as a discipline we are too hard on ourselves. Too few articles are successfully navigating their way through the reviewing process into published form. Too many good ideas are not being developed and disseminated." Given the large number of editors (especially associate editors) and reviewers, I would be surprised if the culture and variance across people changes much in the years to come. Regardless, getting a *stay of execution* in the first round of review is important. From there, an author can move a paper forward, toward *life with a possibility of parole* in the subsequent round. Then, in the third round, it can be *paroled*. Then, parole turns into *probation*. Finally, it may be *home free*—i.e., in print! So, it is a step-by-step process with many rounds of reviews and revisions. I have had papers go ten rounds and have had some done in three rounds, two or three papers were accepted in the second round, and as noted, two accepted in the very first round. I have also had my fair share of rejections in the first, second, third and even, fourth rounds.

All these experiences, both good and bad, have taught me several lessons. I have organized my lessons learned into some actionable advice. I also provide some tools that will help in the process of revising a paper.

There are several useful articles that that discuss revising a paper: Agarwal (2006),[67] Bergh (2006),[68] Daft (1985),[69] Lee (1995),[70] Rynes (2006a, 2006b)[71,72] and Seibert (2006).[73] I believe these sources will complement and supplement what I discuss here.

I discuss six things that I hope will help you with successfully revising a paper:
1. Get over the negative emotion
2. Read, re-read, re-re-read, re-re-re-read, etc.
3. Make a punch list
4. Handle difficult comments
5. Write the new paper
6. Write the response document

1. Get Over The Negative Emotion

Especially early in your career, it is quite likely that you will take comments from reviewers and editors quite personally. This is the worst thing you can do. You have to get over the negative emotion. Set aside the reviews for a few days after the initial read or keep reading the reviews over and over again until you are convinced the reviewers either did not get it or were stupid or both. Do whatever works for you to get that negative emotion out of your system! It is only at that point that you are really ready to read the comments/concerns of the reviewers from the all-important perspective of addressing them in a revision. If upon reading a comment ten days after you read the reviews a first time, you still get upset, you are NOT over the negative emotion. It takes time. I have found that applying a 72-hour rule helps in this regard. I don't do anything substantive, including emailing the editor to seek any clarifications, within the first 72 hours of receiving a decision. Depending on how emotional you are in general, it may take you more or less time!

2. Read, Re-read, Re-re-read, Re-re-re-read, Etc.

Now, for the real reading of the reviews. You should read your review packet over and over again until you internalize the entire document. This is not trivial. This too takes time. What you do NOT want to do is to sit with the review packet open and start editing the paper. You need to first know every issue raised and every suggestion made—I reiterate: really internalize it. Like getting over the negative emotion, this takes time. As you read the reviews over and over again, you might also begin to appreciate and agree that some of the concerns discussed in the review packet are valid. As you become more and more logical (less emotional) and understand the content of the reviews, you may even believe that the reviewers have some ideas that can make your paper better! I like to read a review packet upwards of ten times before I begin the revision process so I can recall all the major issues. Relating to the previous point about the negative emotion, I like to read it until I have fully understood and internalized the issues, without any negative emotion.

3. Make A Punch List

Once you have read the review packet thoroughly, make a punch list. I make the first-cut list from memory. Then, I take a pass through the review packet once again and fill in the gaps. Rather than organize the punch list in the sequence in which they occur, I structure them according to the major sections in the paper. Reviewers tend to make comments at different levels of abstraction—e.g., "your theory sucks;" "I disagree with your use of social exchange theory as a theoretical lens;" and/or "I am not convinced about your rationale for H3." I like to keep the punch list at a somewhat high level of abstraction. This is important to ensure that you don't lose sight of the forest for the trees. Of course, you also shouldn't lose sight of the important trees! The detailed comments in the review packet are the trees. Yes, those details will eventually need to be addressed but a discussion of that comes later. Sitting down with the previous version of the paper and editing the paper, even if it is in response to issues in the review packet, has the potential to turn the paper into a *pretzel*. A paper that is merely edited to respond to the many comments will have many major problems—problematic flow, choppy writing, inconsistent arguments and random thoughts. A punch list is the first step in preventing such a problematic *pretzel-ized* paper.

Table 5-1 is an example of a punch list that my co-author, Hillol Bala, and I created from several pages of comments that we received on a paper. This paper was eventually accepted at *Information Systems Research.*[74]

Table 5-1. Punch List

Introduction
- Re-frame to address comments.

Background
- Expand background.

Theory Development
- We will build upon and extend three distinct theoretical perspectives—i.e., relational view of competitive advantages (e.g., Dyer and Singh 1998),[75] institutional perspectives (e.g., DiMaggio and Powell 1983)[76] and organizational inertia (e.g., Gilbert 2005)[77]—to develop 3 propositions on what drives organizational champions to adopt open process standards. We will offer three distinct mechanisms that can explain the adoption of process standards: (1) relational; (2) influence; and (3) inertia.

Table 5-1 *Continued*. Punch List

Methodology
- We will conduct a cross-case analysis to examine support for our propositions. We will follow the case study methodology suggested by Yin (2002)[78] and information systems (IS) scholars (e.g., Benbasat et al. 1987; Dubé and Paré 2003; Lee 1989).[79,80,81] Our approach will be consistent with prior exemplars of IS case studies (e.g., Sambamurthy and Zmud 1999).[82]
- We will classify our sample organizations (N=56) into three groups—namely, *early adopters*, *followers* and *skeptics/non-adopters*—and develop three cases. We will also compare these cases to understand the unique characteristics of organizations in each group.

Results
- We will discuss the three cases and elaborate on what drives the early adopters and followers to adopt process standards. Likewise, we will examine what drives the skeptics/non-adopters to not adopt process standards.
- We will discuss the support for our propositions.

Discussion
- We will revise the theoretical contributions in keeping with the focus of the revised paper.

4. Comments You Cannot Handle Or Don't Want To Handle

Let me begin by saying it's generally not a good idea to ignore the comments of editors and reviewers unless you absolutely cannot handle them.

As you make a punch list or go on to create a new outline or even write the paper, one of the facts that you have to face up to is that you may not be able to address all of the comments that have been raised. As an editor, I strived to avoid saying: "…and address all the remaining concerns of the reviewers" (I may say it if there are no inconsistencies across reviewers and the issues are straightforward). It is important, as an author, to explain why you weren't able to address some of the concerns. In many cases, there will be contradictory comments [typically across reviewers] or comments you simply cannot address. It is important to highlight such contradictions politely in your response document and clearly explain which option(s) you took and why.

In the end, explaining why you didn't or couldn't address some comments could be just as important as addressing those you did. Most reasonable editors and reviewers know that not every comment can be addressed, but they should feel an earnest effort was made to address all of the major concerns.

5. Write The New Paper

The hardest thing about rewriting a paper is avoiding the temptation of starting with the old paper and just editing it (adding, deleting or tweaking text) to create the new version. I regard every revision as a new paper. I start with an outline like I do the first version of any paper. The only difference in various sections is to make the outline sensitive to your punch list. In some cases, as I start with an outline for a revised paper, I may zoom in and expand some of the sections (and sub-sections) so that the outline is sensitive to the concerns raised by the review panel. Let me reiterate: I am strongly opposed to simply editing the previous version of the paper in order to arrive at the revised version. This does NOT mean that I advocate reinventing the wheel on sections that you have already written. It is fine to lift, clean and place an old section into the new paper. But, such grafting should be performed incrementally as the new paper gets written. All the earlier advice about how to write a paper (chapter 4) applies as you work your way through the revision of the paper.

After you write the new paper, you can examine it against your punch list. As you are working through the paper, you can periodically examine the paper against the review packet as well. But, I caution, you should not be enslaved by that document. It will not only *pretzel-ize* the paper, but also overwhelm you as you revise your paper.

In the end, as already noted, a reasonable panel of editors and reviewers knows that not every issue can be completely addressed but a solid paper that incorporates the spirit of the comments is much more likely to be successful than a *pretzel-ized* paper that tries to hit the letter of every comment and quite likely fails to do so.

The outline for the revised paper based on the punch list in Table 5-1 is shown in Table 5-2.

Table 5-2. Outline For The Revised Paper

Introduction

- The current framing will be changed to incorporate the notion of governance, configuration and safeguarding interorganizational relationships. *Interorganizational process standardization (IPS)*—the adoption, implementation and use of open process standards in interorganizational relationships—will be presented as a new/alternative approach to interorganizational configurations (Malhotra et al. 2005)[83] that will initially create a relationship-specific asset (we call it *relational specificity*) but later provides other competitive advantages, such as *dynamic relationship extension capability,* that may not be possible in other approaches to interorganizational governance.
- We will suggest that the adoption of *open process standards* is different from the adoption of *open technology standards* (e.g., TCP/IP, HTML, XML) and *process technologies* (e.g., ERP, CRM, SCM/IOS) in several important ways. First, the adoption of open technology standards does not necessarily require changes in organizational processes. Second, while

Table 5-2 *Continued*. Outline For The Revised Paper

process technologies may require radical or incremental changes in organizational processes, it is possible that firms customize these technologies to align with their existing routines, procedures and work practices. However, in the case of open process standards, firms have to alter their interorganizational processes (i.e., public processes) to conform to the specifications of the standards. Therefore, the changes are revolutionary as it originates externally (unless the firm itself is involved in the development of standards). Revolutionary changes in organizational processes are complex, risky and have significantly higher failure rates. So, we will argue that the adoption of process standards is a noticeably different decision situation for managers and, therefore, warrants scientific investigation.

Background
- We will provide definitions of open process standards and open technology standards and provide a discussion of the distinctions between the two.
- We will discuss how and why process standardization is important in interorganizational relationship contexts.
- We will provide a brief discussion of prior research on interorganizational governance and the role of standards in interorganizational relationships, with a particular focus on process standards research.

Theory Development
- We will build upon and extend three distinct theoretical perspectives—i.e., relational view of competitive advantages (e.g., Dyer and Singh 1998),[84] institutional perspectives (e.g., DiMaggio and Powell 1983)[85] and organizational inertia (e.g., Gilbert 2005)[86]—to develop 3 propositions on what drives organizational champions to adopt open process standards. We will offer three distinct mechanisms that can explain the adoption of process standards: (1) relational; (2) influence; and (3) inertia.
- The relational mechanism refers to managerial cognitions of the importance of relational governance, such as transaction specific investment, asset specificity and shared understanding between the trading partners.
- The influence mechanism refers to managerial cognitions of external pressures, such as coercive, normative and mimetic pressures, as well as aspects of network effects, such as positive network externalities or mass adoption of open process standards.
- The inertia mechanism refers to managerial cognitions of resource and routine rigidity and the ability to coordinate and integrate public and private business processes.
- The propositions are:

P1: Organizations will adopt open process standards despite perceived threats of losing competitive advantage and perceived uncertainty of standards diffusion if organizational champions perceive that interorganizational process standardization will ensure relationship specificity and provide long-term dynamic relationship extension capability.

Table 5-2 *Continued*. Outline For The Revised Paper

P2: Organizations will adopt open process standards despite perceived threats of losing competitive advantage and perceived uncertainty of standards diffusion if organizational champions perceive that there is a significant coercive, mimetic or normative pressure for such an adoption and there are positive network externalities.

P3: Organizations will adopt open process standards despite perceived threats of losing competitive advantage and perceived uncertainty of standards diffusion if the organizational champions perceive that there is a less degree of resource and routine rigidity (i.e., organizational inertia) that can potentially seize the benefits of open process standards.

Methodology

- We will conduct a cross-case analysis to examine support for our propositions. We will follow the case study methodology suggested by Yin (2002)[87] and information systems (IS) scholars (e.g., Benbasat et al. 1987; Dubé and Paré 2003; Lee 1989).[88,89,90] Our approach will be consistent with prior exemplars of IS case studies (e.g., Sambamurthy and Zmud 1999).[91]
- We will classify our sample organizations (N=56) into three groups—*early adopters*, *followers* and *skeptics/non-adopters*—and develop three cases. We will also compare these cases to understand the unique characteristics of organizations in each group.
- Depending on whether we are allowed to reveal organizational details (we have requested permission from the legal departments of the various participating organizations), we will provide details of these organizations in a tabular format (e.g., industry, nature of B2B relationships, technology standards, employees involved in B2B activities), which will be organized as one table for each case/group.

Results

- We will discuss the three cases and elaborate on what drives the early adopters and followers to adopt process standards. Likewise, we will examine what drives the skeptics/non-adopters to not adopt process standards.
- We will discuss the support for our propositions.
- Based on our new data analysis, we have the following findings:

The early adopters were primarily large organizations who were part of the standards development efforts. These organizations were typically dominating in the interorganizational relationships. For these organizations, the key mechanisms were the influence and inertia mechanisms. We found that early adopters were influenced by the normative pressure to standardize processes as they were involved in the standard development initiatives and they had the ability to overcome organizational inertia. For the followers, we found that the three mechanisms had an interactive effect. Particularly, we found that, in the presence of higher coercive power, organizational champions placed less importance on inertia and relational mechanisms. However, in the presence of strong relational specificity, organizational champions placed more importance on influence mechanisms, especially mimetic influence.

Table 5-2 *Continued*. Outline For The Revised Paper

Despite the obvious institutional pressures and understanding of the importance of relational specificity, the skeptics were reluctant to adopt open process standards because of high degree of organizational inertia, especially routine rigidity. We observed that the champions in these organizations had different strategic beliefs regarding the adoption of process standards. Particularly, the perceived uncertainty of standards diffusion was high. These organizations considered the adoption a revolutionary change and were reluctant to reconfigure their existing capabilities (Lavie 2006).[92]

Discussion
- Our key theoretical contributions are:

Prior research on the adoption of or migration to open technology standards has primarily focused on three set of factors: network effects or externalities, standardization costs and path dependency (see for example, Weitzel et al. forthcoming; Zhu et al. forthcoming).[93,94] While this extant research has captured important antecedents and aspects of influence mechanisms, our research extends this research by adding two additional mechanisms that are pertinent to interorganizational process standards: relational and inertia. Thus, we contribute to the study of complex interorganizational standards adoption.

Prior research on the adoption and implementation of interorganizational systems (IOS), such as EDI, has primarily focused on institutional pressures and instrumental benefits of such adoption. Therefore, we extend this research by adding the relational and inertia perspectives.

Finally, prior research on interorganizational governance has primarily focused on relational aspects, such as transaction-specific investments and joint decision-making. We extend this research by adding the influence and organizational inertia perspectives.

- Future research: We believe that our research could serve as the starting point for future research on interorganizational process standardization, which is an underinvestigated area. Therefore, we will provide detailed future research directions.

References
Benbasat, I., D. K. Goldstein, M. Mead. 1987. The case research strategy in studies of information systems. *MIS Quarterly* **11**(3) 369–386.

DiMaggio, P., W. W. Powell. 1983. The iron cage revisited: Institutional isomorphism and collective rationality in organizational fields. *American Sociological Review* **48**(2) 147–160.

Dubé, L., G. Paré. 2003. Rigor in information systems positivist case research: Current practices, trends, and recommendations. *MIS Quarterly* **27**(4) 597–636.

Table 5-2 *Continued*. Outline For The Revised Paper

Dyer, J. H., H. Singh. 1998. The relational view: Cooperative strategy and sources of interorganizational competitive advantages. *Academy of Management Review* **23**(4) 660–679.

Gilbert, C. G. 2005. Unbundling the structure of inertia: Resource versus routine rigidity. *Academy of Management Journal* **48**(5) 741–763.

Lavie, D. 2006. Capability reconfiguration: An analysis of incumbent responses to technological change. *Academy of Management Review* **31**(1) 153–174.

Sambamurthy, V., R. W. Zmud. 1999. Arrangements for information technology governance: A theory of multiple contingencies. *MIS Quarterly* **23**(2) 261–290.

Weitzel, T., D. Beimborn, W. König. forthcoming. Unified economic model of standard diffusion: The impact of standardization cost, network effects, and network topology. *MIS Quarterly*.

Yin, R. K. 2002. *Case Study Research, Design and Methods*, 3rd ed. Sage Publications, Newbury Park.

Zhu, K, K. L. Kraemer, V. Gurbaxani, S. Xu. forthcoming. Migration to open-standard interorganizational systems: Network effects, switching costs, and path dependency. *MIS Quarterly*.

6. Write The Response Document

The last thing I do when I am revising a paper is to write the response document. Some might argue that it is a good idea for this to be the first thing done. My reasoning for doing it last is that it is difficult to know all the intricacies of what has been revised until the revisions are actually complete. Of course, writing the response document first can guide your thinking about what you can do to address the various issues and then, you can come back and edit and refine the response document after all the revisions are completed. While there are many options between writing the response document first vs. last—i.e., filling in varying levels of details as you address various comments. I do not favor the options in-between (where you go back-and-forth between the paper and response document to varying extents) as it makes you iterate too much between the paper and the response document, thus making the paper more likely to resemble an ill-fated *pretzel,* which is doomed to be a disaster when it comes to logical flow.

Reviewers vary in how and when they read the response document. Some read it first. Some read it last. Some read it and the paper together. Some never read it. Your response document needs to accommodate all types of reviewer reading styles—yes, even those who will never read it, at least not in much detail.

Don't editorialize the comments of anyone on the review panel—reviewers and editors (including editor-in-chief). They said it. They chose the words they used. They liked the words they used. They don't need you to tell them what they think. State the comments in the words of the editors and reviewers. This means keeping their comments verbatim in the response document... yes, even if there is bad grammar or typos. Including the comments in full will make it easier for the editors and reviewers to assess the responses. Let me note here that you should not delete any positive things that the editors and reviewers may have said about the work. Just because a comment does not need a response, it does not mean it should be dropped. It is good to remind the editors and reviewers of the positive comments they made about the paper. There are at least two good reasons for doing this. First, to remind them of the positive reactions they had to the paper so they recall what they liked about your paper and why they liked it. Second, reviewing is a thankless and unpaid task (at most journals)—reviewers will feel good about the appreciation conveyed (more on this later)—I know I do.

There are two good formats for a response document. One where the comments are typed in full, interspersed with the responses—you might use a different font or typeface for the comment (italics) vs. the response (regular typeface). The second is a table format with comments in the left column and your response to each comment in the right column. Excerpts illustrating both formats are shown in Table 5-3.

Table 5-3. Response Document Formats
(a) Comments And Responses Interspersed

Responses to Reviewer 2 Comments

I was really delighted to see a paper on this topic, and I am really optimistic about the prospects for this paper. You have great data, and I know you'll be able to tell a compelling story.

We thank reviewer 2 for the favorable comments and support. We have made every effort to address the various comments and suggestions of the reviewer.

That said, I was very disappointed with your analysis of the data, and by extension with the conclusions you drew. Although you appear to have touched all the methodological bases and are using all the right words, what you've actually done is a sort of quantitative analysis with words, and the result is a multivariate-type variance model that adds little to the literature and doesn't do justice to your data. Your analysis doesn't fare well when evaluated either as case-oriented qualitative research or as process-oriented grounded theory.

Your point is well-taken. We certainly understand that our attempt at grounded theory was disappointing. As noted earlier, following the suggestion of the Senior Editor and reviewers, we have completely re-framed the paper and now use a cross-case analysis rather than a grounded theory approach.

Table 5-3 *Continued*. Response Document Formats
(b) Table Format

Responses to Referee 1 Comments	
Comment	**Response**
The subject matter of this paper on B2Bi is relevant to ISR readers. The author/s provide some insightful comments about intra-organizational adoption and use of ICT. I definitely think this could be turned into an interesting contribution, but my main concern is that it claims to use a qualitative methodology, yet the paper is organized, structured and framed as one which is commonly used to report the findings of survey research.	We thank for you for the encouraging comment. As noted in our response to the Senior Editor, we have re-framed the paper based on the comments of the Senior Editor and the referees. Specifically, we have dropped the grounded theory approach and use a cross-case approach. We hope the new approach addresses this concern.
My main concern in reading the paper was that I gained no feel for who these IT champions were, and how they perceived their roles within the B2Bi process. The language used in the paper talked about 'factors' that influence IT champions, but the method used is a softer, qualitative approach, where interviewees respond to a range of questions posed by an interviewer.	We provided more details on organization and the champions from each organization (p. 21). We adopted a cross-case analysis methodology and followed guidelines and exemplars of prior research using a cross-case methodology (e.g., Benbasat et al. 1987; Dubé and Paré 2003; Lapointe and Rivard 2005; Lee 1989; Sambamurthy and Zmud 1999; Sherif et al. 2006).[95,96,97,98,99,100]

Every response document should begin with a preamble. This preamble should open with your [profuse] thanks to the editors and reviewers for their insightful comments and time. The preamble should then summarize the main changes made to the paper. One of the primary objectives of summarizing the major changes is that it gives the editors and reviewers a bird's eye view of the major changes and [hopefully] a feeling that the main concerns have been addressed. Once again, most reasonable editors and reviewers know that not every concern can be addressed, but they should feel an earnest effort was made to address all of the major concerns. An example of a preamble is shown in Table 5-4.

Let me make a very important comment about the tone of your response document. Be polite. It is unlikely that you will win a "shouting match" with the editors and reviewers. If you disagree, do so politely. I heard this comment made by someone: "The reviewers are always right even when they are wrong." How true! Besides, it is easier to catch flies with honey, rather than vinegar. Being polite is also the more professional approach. An example of what I perceive to be a sufficiently polite response was shown earlier in Table 5-3(a).

Table 5-4. A Preamble To A Response Document

We are grateful to the Senior Editor (SE) and reviewers for the many helpful suggestions to improve the paper. We are also thankful to the workshop participants, especially the SE, who provided us further guidance in revising the paper. We appreciate the opportunity to revise the paper for further consideration for publication in the *Information Systems Research's* (*ISR*) special issue on the *Digitally Enabled Extended Enterprise in a Global Economy.*

In this document, we present the comments from two rounds of review: (1) SE comments based on the workshop in Ann Arbor; and (2) SE and reviewer comments from the initial round of review. The comments are in the left column and our responses to each comment are provided in the right column. We also provide an appendix to this document explaining RosettaNet partner interface processes (PIPs). We have made major changes in the following areas:

1. *Focus of the paper:* The paper has been scoped down and based on the suggestions of the SE and the reviewers. We now focus on the *assimilation* (i.e., the extent of deployment) of interorganizational business process standards (IBPS). We have eliminated any discussion of outcomes of IBPS implementation.

2. *Grounded theory to theory-driven approach:* Instead of a grounded theory approach to identify a broad set of "factors" that lead to IBPS adoption, we now have a theory-driven approach. Drawing on three different theoretical perspectives (i.e., relational view of the firm, institutional theory and organizational inertia theory), we present three mechanisms underlying various levels of IBPS assimilation. We present hypotheses on how these mechanisms will influence the assimilation of IBPS at dominant and non-dominant firms.

3. *Cross-case analysis:* We re-analyzed the data following a multiple case study approach (see Sambamurthy and Zmud 1999 for an exemplar).[101] We selected representative cases of organizations that reached different assimilation stages (i.e., awareness but no adoption, adoption but no deployment, limited deployment and general deployment) in the 2-year duration of our study. We tested our hypotheses by examining interview transcripts and other documents. We present and discuss the results from qualitative and quantitative analyses (see Sherif et al. 2006 for an exemplar).[102]

4. *More details on organizations:* We provided more details on the data collection procedures (e.g., interview protocol), participants and organizations to give the readers a better feel for the context of this research.

In sum, the paper is re-framed and re-organized based on the suggestions of the SE and reviewers. We hope that these major revisions meet the review team's expectations. At this stage, in some places, we have erred on the side of including more information and do feel we can shorten the paper to meet the length restrictions—we welcome the review team's input on the same as well. Once again, we are thankful for the comments and suggestions, and the opportunity to revise our work for further consideration for this special issue at *ISR*.

Another stylistic point relates to whether or not to include page numbers in the response document to point to the location of specific text in the paper to help the reviewers see where changes have been effected. Including page numbers makes it easier to find relevant text in the paper. However, it makes it a bit harder to hide the not-so-well-addressed issues. It may be a good thing to do in the entire response document if you believe you have fully addressed most of the issues. A related stylistic comment is whether to repeat key text from the paper in the response document. Doing so will allow you to point to the text that will help the editors and reviewers see that you have completely addressed a particular issue. Of course, I am not advocating a cut-and-paste of all text inserted into the paper—just text pertaining to important points and text pertaining to issues you know you have nailed. It makes it convenient for the editors and reviewers to see the combination of the paper and the response document, and it likely makes them more favorably disposed towards your paper. Be cautious about doing this if it is an issue that is not well-addressed and/or if the revision is not quite on-target because the changes were just too difficult to make. In such cases, obfuscating and playing a bit of hide-and-seek may help you survive the round. One negative consequence of such an approach is that your paper may survive the round but ultimately, get rejected. I am not advocating a weak revision and an obfuscated response document as it merely prolongs the agony—but who knows, you may get lucky. The bottom line is to revise the paper to the best of your ability and make the paper and response document as accessible to editors and reviewers as possible.

Concluding Thoughts

The better the journal, the more challenging the task of responding to editors' and reviewers' comments will be. Many times, this enormous challenge will have to be handled more than once before a paper can be published. Not only is responding to the comments important, but also writing a persuasive response document that is clear and polite is vital. This chapter discussed several tips and tricks to achieve these goals.

Key Takeaways

1. Getting a paper published takes several rounds of convincing editors and reviewers
2. Get over the emotion
    i. Set aside the reviews for a few days after the initial read
    ii. Do whatever works for you to get the negative emotion that you experience (when you receive most review packets) out of your system—it is only at that point that you are really ready to read the comments/concerns of the reviews
3. Read, re-read, re-re-read, re-re-re-read, etc.
    i. Read your review packet over and over again until you internalize the entire document—this is not trivial and it takes time
    ii. Know every issue raised and every suggestion made—really internalize it
    iii. DO NOT sit with the review packet open and start editing the paper—this will result in a *pretzel-ized* paper

4. Make a punch list
    i. Make a high-level list of the reviewers' major comments
    ii. Try to do this from memory to ensure you have really internalized the review packet
    iii. Then, fill in the holes with the aid of the review packet
    iv. Structure the punch list according to the major sections of the paper (i.e., framing, theory development, method, results and discussion)
5. Comments you cannot handle or don't want to handle
    i. It's generally not a good idea to ignore the comments of editors and reviewers unless you absolutely cannot handle them
    ii. In many cases, there will be contradictory comments or comments you simply cannot address—it is important to highlight such contradictions politely in your response document and explain clearly which option you took
    iii. Most reasonable editors and reviewers know that not everything can be addressed but they should feel an earnest effort was made to address all of the major concerns
6. Write the new paper
    i. Rewriting is difficult—not only does your mind fill in gaps (as it always does when you write), but also it is hard to pick up these logical holes
    ii. Set the paper aside for a while before revisiting it
    iii. Avoid simply editing the previous version of the paper in order to arrive at the revised version
    iv. It is fine to lift, clean and place an old section into the new paper—but, such grafting should be performed incrementally as the new paper gets written
    v. As you are working through the paper, you can periodically examine the paper against the review packet as well
    vi. After you write the new paper, examine it against your punch list
7. Write the response document
    i. There are many approaches to writing the response document—some write it first, as this helps identify what needs to be done to revise the paper, but it may be difficult to know what has been revised until the revision is complete; others write it last, but this approach may suffer from not having a plan in advance of the revision
    ii. Avoid an in-between model where you iterate between the response document and the paper
    iii. Don't editorialize the comments of the editors and reviewers
    iv. Always include the comments in full, making sure to include positive comments—including positive comments helps remind the review panel what they liked about your paper and why they liked your paper
    v. Acknowledge and thank the reviewers for the work they have done
    vi. There are two approaches to structuring a response document: one where the comments are typed in full, interspersed with the responses and another is a table format with comments in the left column and your response to each comment in the right column
    vii. Every response document should begin with a preamble that should open with your

    thanks to the editors and reviewers for their insightful comments and time, and then summarize the main changes made to the paper

viii. Be polite in your response document

  ix. Consider including page numbers that reference your changes [only] if you are able to address all issues well

   x. Other sources that discuss revising a paper include: Agarwal (2006), Bergh (2006), Daft (1985), Lee (1995), Rynes (2006a, 2006b) and Seibert (2006)

CHAPTER 6

HOW TEACHING CAN HELP RESEARCH

In this chapter, I discuss how teaching can help your research in different ways. It is not my intent to discuss teaching tips and tricks or strategies for teaching excellence. There are already several excellent sources for the same. Besides chapters 14 through 16 of this book, here are a few examples: Bain's (2004) *What the Best College Teachers Do,*[103] MaKeachie's (1999) *Teaching Tips,*[104] Rotenberg's (2005) *The Art and Craft of College Teaching: A Guide for New Professors and Graduate Students,*[105] Provitera-McGlynn's (2001) *Successful Beginnings for College Teaching,*[106] and Filene's (2006) *The Joy of Teaching: A Practical Guide for New College Instructors.*[107]

I have frequently heard criticisms about the downside of teaching—how it hinders the pursuit of research, how it robs time away from doing research, how it may be good to be in a just-in-time-mode in terms of preparing for class (e.g., dedicate two to three days a week toward teaching—preparing, delivering, etc.), how new preparations are evil, etc. While there is likely some truth to these statements, I argue that there is also some falsehood.

I discuss four important ways by which you can get teaching to help your research:
1. Prepare early, not often
2. Listen to your teaching
3. Integrate research into teaching
4. Be fully aware of three myths related to teaching

1. Prepare Early, Not Often

As Yogi Berra would say, "let's start at the beginning." As far as teaching goes, the beginning is the preparation of a course, especially a new one. Even if it is a course that you have already taught—say once before—preparation is still required for the new semester. While preparation for a new course involves substantially more time and effort than gearing up to teach a course you have taught before, the latter also takes time and should not be underestimated. A new preparation involves phenomenal effort, especially to do it right. Identifying books, querying others in your school and other schools for syllabi, creating or modifying slides for each class meeting, picking readings, creating assignments, coordinating with your teaching assistant on grading policies or worse, grading new deliverables by yourself, and, of course, trying to stay ahead of the many things that could go wrong—e.g., software that does not work, classroom changes, weather-related cancellations, too much material, too little material. Rehashing an old course requires reviewing the old materials, incorporating changes in the topic/field since the last time you taught the course (just ask anyone who taught telecommunications courses starting in 1995), and redesigning assignments and exams, especially if they are for undergraduates as the materials have possibly made it on to some web site somewhere, and being sensitive, on an ongoing basis (sometimes as the semester unfolds), to new developments in the field.

While some day-to-day preparation is essential, be it quickly brushing up on the materials or reviewing slides, for the heavy lifting, I am an advocate of preparing the entire course at the beginning of the semester—even if it means taking 3 weeks out of the summer to do nothing but getting prepared to teach in the fall semester or even if it means taking 2 weeks in December and a week in January to do nothing but getting prepared to teach in the spring semester. What is the value in doing this? Two reasons. First, rather than just staying a week ahead of the students, uncertain over where the course is headed and unable to respond to students' questions probing into the future or related to concepts to be discussed in the future, you will have a clear idea of where you are headed and have a good level of mastery over the materials. Second, rather than being consumed by teaching throughout the semester, you will have more time to focus on research during the semester even during a heavy teaching semester.

What does it mean to prepare the entire course before the semester begins? By this, I mean, identifying readings, doing the readings, preparing the slides, preparing the assignments, the answer keys and the exams. Do as much of it as you can before the semester begins, leaving room for adjustments. This will do you a world of good during the semester. You will not be as stressed as you would be if you were following a just-in-time model for preparation. Teaching will not consume your every thought. You won't obsess about it constantly. The result? You will free up significant amount of your time, despite having to teach, to focus on research. You will not have to think of it as a teaching semester wherein little research gets done. Sure, you will still need to review the slides, skim the readings the night before each class session meets and find the current magazine articles or newspaper clips to augment your lecture. At least, you will not be spending the entire weekend or the early part of the week getting the materials organized for the upcoming week or two. You will also not be spending the entire weekend or the early part of the week creating assignments, making up answer keys or writing exams. Instead, you can focus on research.

Prepare early. This ensures that you do not have to prepare often. You do not have to spend your effort and more importantly, valuable thinking time in the shower, among other places, worrying about your course(s)!

2. Listen To Your Teaching

Teaching offers some of the most valuable lessons to help you in the pursuit of your research. I discuss this in greater detail (later in this chapter) when I discuss the myth "teaching is a waste of time." But, let me share the basic idea here. Teaching is one of the best ways to learn how to communicate new subject matter to an audience unfamiliar with the subject. A student audience can often be skeptical, not unlike reviewers! Dissemination of information is at the heart of both teaching and writing papers. In both cases, the actual frontline materials—i.e., presentation or paper—is merely the tip of the iceberg. An iceberg that runs very deep. All the careful preparation and work that is executed a priori *must* be made evident in the presentation. Most of all, the main thing that is shared between teaching and research is communication to your audience. Your ability to hear what they hear, motivate the topic, answer questions that occur to the audience (preemptively), persuade them that what you are saying is important and worth knowing, and your ability to leave them satisfied are key building blocks to effective communication. If you are not getting through to your students, reflect on your teaching style and you will be reflecting on something deeper—i.e., your ability to communicate what you know very well to a possibly skeptical, unfamiliar audience. If you correct the errors in your teaching, you will have taken a vital step towards strengthening your communication in your writing and/or presenting.

Two key mistakes that new teachers tend to make are: (1) pitching material at too difficult a level for the audience to comprehend; and (2) filling in gaps in the logical flow of the class session with details from one's own knowledge base that the audience obviously cannot access. Not surprisingly, these are also two errors quite common in writing. Fortunately, these errors can be fixed by paying close attention to teaching.

Just listen to yourself as you teach. Look at the faces of your students. Are you getting blank stares? If yes, it's not always and automatically the students' fault—it could be that you are not reaching them. Chances are your writing could have the same problem.

3. Integrating Research Into Teaching

Bringing your research into your classroom can provide tremendous benefits if it is done correctly. A couple of the direct benefits from a classroom perspective are that it establishes you as a normal person to your students when you discuss your research and the challenges you faced in collecting data. It also indicates to your students that you do other things besides teach. It can help you explain why sometimes it takes you a couple of days to respond to their emails (in fact, it may set up the perfect excuse!). While students might occasionally complain that their professor is just interested in research but not in teaching, for the most part, they usually do like to have professors who are contributing to the body of knowledge in some field, preferably closely related to what she or he is teaching, because this means their professor is an expert on some topic. I have frequently tried to explain my job to them: "I am in the business of creating and disseminating knowledge." When they give me a puzzled look, I clarify it with: "I research and teach. When I am doing research, I am trying to create new knowledge. When I am teaching, I am trying to disseminate [new] knowledge." They seem to get it. I emphasize that I like both parts of the job and note that I believe doing one without the other is problematic. I tell them that if I were to only do research, then, I might never be able to connect it to the real world to influence practice—presenting my work to organizations and teaching the principles that emerge are the two ways that I disseminate the knowledge that I have created. I also tell my students that if I were to only teach, then, I would just be a talking head who is teaching someone else's ideas and teaching out of a book. At the end of this discussion, I have usually successfully explained my job to them and sometimes, even made them curious about my research.

While all the above points speak to the benefits of integrating research into teaching at some level, the most important benefit is the opportunity it provides to pilot new ideas, theoretical justifications, examples and implications. Do the students buy it? Does it pass the test of making sense to a college student? Does it sound persuasive? If you cannot successfully explain it to a college student, you have no chance of successfully getting your point across to your mother, which, of course, is the ultimate litmus test! Failure to explain and persuade the captive audience of college students stuck in your class invariably means that it is unlikely that you can persuade skeptical reviewers of the importance of your ideas, theoretical justifications, examples and implications.

Of course, another benefit that we can derive from integrating our research and teaching is using our students as subjects—typically for card sort procedures to develop/refine scales, to fill out survey instruments for pilot studies and/or to participate in studies.[108]

One example of how I integrated research into teaching is related to the topic of usability. It worked out well both from research and teaching perspectives. The series of papers that I published on this topic includes: *Information Systems Research* (2002),[109] *Communications of the ACM* (2003),[110] *Management Science* (2006)[111] and *MIS Quarterly* (2006).[112] I began work on usability in 1997, soon after I joined the faculty of the University of Maryland. I was working on defining the constructs and writing items for the various categories and subcategories that comprised usability. I wanted to gauge how well students understood the definitions and the items. I was also working on using the constant sum method, rather than a 7-point scale, for the responses as this allowed to get weighted ratings. There were many things I was trying to do with the construct and its operationalization. Each semester from the time I began teaching e-commerce application design and development, I included a couple of class sessions on usability and had an assignment on usability that required the students to use the items that I had developed to rate web sites and provide explanations for why they assigned the weights they did for various categories and subcategories of usability. They also needed to justify why they assigned the ratings they assigned for the various sites they evaluated. Using the information from each student's assignment, I was able to see if the items were measuring what I sought to measure—the reasons provided by the students in justifying their weights and ratings provided the necessary information to gauge their interpretation. In addition to helping the development of a robust instrument that could be used for live data collection, the process served the important purpose of giving me a familiar topic to teach. As I continued with field data collection, I shared the results in later semesters of teaching, which had the added benefit of helping students see that I was a contributing expert in the field of usability.

4. Myths

There are a few myths I have heard about teaching on which I would like to comment. Obviously, as I call them myths, you already know what I think of them, but these are nuggets of advice that you may receive. I am sharing here an alternate and more positive view of these mythical nuggets.

i.   Myth #1: Teaching Is A Waste Of Time

The more research-oriented the departmental environment, the more you may hear about how junior faculty members need to put up with teaching because it is part of the job. You may hear that it is necessary to be adequate at teaching but excellence in teaching will never help an assistant professor get tenure (it just wouldn't hurt). You may hear that spending too much time on teaching is definitely going to interfere with research. Nothing can be further from the truth. Teaching is not a waste of time. I am not going to lecture you on the virtues and importance of teaching for its own sake as that subject could be written up as a book in its own right. Instead, I am going to focus on why teaching should be important even for research-focused faculty members who could not care less about teaching.

I have had the good fortune of being in the classrooms of some excellent teachers. I have also had the good fortune of knowing many great teachers. While I have shamelessly stolen their practices over the years, I have often wondered what makes a good teacher good. Chapters 14-16 provide a lot of information on how to be (or become) an effective teacher. While there are many books that present various techniques, tips and tricks, I found what appealed to me most, as a student, were three important abilities for a teacher to possess:
a.   To know me—not as a person, but my background, my experiences, the projected future direction for my career
b.   To make me care about the importance of a topic
c.   To help me understand

When you think about a lecture that you are preparing, you give consideration to many factors so that you can prepare a good lecture that ensures the message reaches your students. Here are some of the things you should do after you have gained mastery of the material to be taught that relates to each of the three points mentioned above:

a. Knowing Your Students

You should try to consider your target student audience. Teaching an introductory information systems course to freshmen across all majors on campus will certainly be different from teaching the topic to more mature business majors that in turn will be different from teaching the topic to juniors who are information systems majors. Your reasons for why students should care about the lecture material should be different, your examples should be different, your stories should be different, your slides should be different, your exercises should be different and your homework assignments should be different (although there may be some similarities).

b. Providing Information About Why The Student Should Care About The Topic

Once you know your audience, you should provide the motivation in a way the target student group can best understand it, with a focus that will make the target student group care. You can try to accomplish this in different ways. For example, you may be teaching an MBA course on systems analysis and design. You can tell the students how much money is wasted by organizations if they do not heed the principles involved in the feasibility analysis topic. Feasibility analysis is a critical step in system analysis and if it is executed poorly, the system could fail to produce the desired outcome and result in millions of dollars being wasted. You can give them examples of failures—ranging from supernova-sized failures to those that happened in a local mom-and-pop business. You can tell them why they would be better off knowing, understanding and applying feasibility analysis. Also, in economic downtimes, such as it is now, one additional detail to emphasize how expertise in this topic will be helpful to them in securing a job!

c. Helping Students Understand

In any topic area, there are many things you can discuss. You have spent months reading and experiencing the concepts and practices. However, you should focus on the aspects that are *most* interesting and valuable to your target group of students. You should try to speak their language. You should try to relate to their experiences and backgrounds. You should try to tell a tale that will help them grasp the knowledge you are sharing. You should try to help them leave with a feeling that they have learned something new and that they have learned something they can use or apply.

Few would disagree that if you do a good job week-in and week-out on each of these three fronts, you would be a good teacher, maybe even a great teacher. If you could go back to the days when you were a student, these three aspects may have distinguished your mediocre teachers from the good ones and the good ones from the great ones. Practicing these three things is also going to make your research papers better. No, this is not a typo. I did say practicing these elements in your teaching is going to make your research papers better.

How? Why?

The various things that I discussed above require certain abilities if they are to be done well. These abilities when put to use are, in fact, the same abilities that make a paper better. These same abilities also help a researcher to write a better paper. When a researcher writes a paper, he or she must ensure that these three elements are fully considered.

a. Knowing Your Audience

The paper must appeal to the audience. Who are the readers of the journal in which you are trying to publish? What do they care about? A paper needs a focused introduction that emphasizes why businesses (or practitioners) should care and why researchers should care about the message in your paper. What is the relevant scientific gap and what does the current paper do to plug that gap? Your positioning of the relevant gaps—both practical and theoretical—should be sensitive to the target journal's audience. Clearly, what would be interesting to a psychology journal audience will not be the same as what would be interesting to an information systems journal audience. To use an example from my experience—let me discuss a paper I wrote on telecommuting that was published in *Personnel Psychology*. Although using a motivational model from information systems and studying telecommuting with system use as the dependent variable, the paper was written to address problems that would be of interest to the *Personnel Psychology* audience—i.e., how we can enhance telecommuting via the right system design, which is different from what might appeal to the IS audience, such as what design attributes would maximize telecommuting system use? An important difference: the focus for the *Personnel Psychology*[113] paper was really about telecommuting, which is an important way to support employees and their work.

b. Providing Information About Why The Reader Should Care About The Topic

Once you have identified the target journal and audience, the motivation for the topic needs to be appropriate. A particular topic may be of interest to many researchers and practitioners in many fields. However, providing the right motivation is critical. Let me return to the example about my article in *Personnel Psychology*. While maximizing system use and finding the ideal design characteristics were important, would personnel psychologists really have cared about it? What they care(d) about were the bottlenecks facing telecommuting, the advantages of telecommuting, and a solution that can help organizations maximize the advantages and eliminate the bottlenecks of telecommuting. While millions of dollars may be spent in failed telecommuting initiatives, would personnel psychologists care about that? They care(d) about making organizations more flexible in meeting the needs of employees and about allowing working mothers the flexibility to achieve work-life balance.

c. Helping Readers Understand

You should ensure that you cite the relevant prior literature from the fields related to the target journal and readership. I have had experiences where a reviewer has literally counted the references and indicated that only say 8 out of 71 references were from information systems journals. This extends beyond just relevant literature to the theoretical arguments—i.e., the *why* (theoretical justification, examples, etc.) associated with the relationships. The *why* should appeal to the readership. In my works on gender and age differences targeted to organizational behavior and psychology journals, the literature review focused on relevant research in those fields even though the study was conducted in a technology context. One key hypothesis in a paper that appeared in *Organizational Behavior and Human Decision Processes* (2000)[114] was that social influence will have a stronger effect on intention (to perform a behavior—in this context, use a new technology) among women when compared to the effect social influence would have among men. The arguments included why women may be more responsive to social influences in general and the discussion was not just focused on reasons why women might be more responsive to social influences in the technology context.

Now, let me relate this back to teaching. Your every class session provides an opportunity to practice these abilities. Your every class session provides a chance for you to get instantaneous feedback from your students, from the questions they ask and from the enthusiasm they show. Just as you try to heed reviewers' comments, you should heed students' feedback, both verbal and non-verbal. Your students, if asked, will surely share with you what worked and what did not work. Classroom sessions are the lowest risk practice sessions you can ever have. Classroom material is often the easiest material you can possibly try to communicate to an audience. The material is never the same from class to class. That's the beauty of it. Each class is a new opportunity. The skills you build transcend teaching. But, only if you pay attention to them. Note what you are doing, note the reactions and use feedback [from student reactions] in a diagnostic way. Try it again—in the next class session on a different topic. Soon, you'll see the topic through the eye of a student. Soon, you can see your next paper through the eye of a reader or reviewer—not after you receive the reviews but when you are writing the paper.

ii. Myth #2: A Three-course Load Is Always Better Than A Four-course Load

Many research-oriented schools have a three-course load as part of the standard package for an assistant professor. Some schools, however, do not. They have a four-course load. Assistant professors often spend a lot of time and effort negotiating their way out of the four-course load and getting (or trying to get) relief on the teaching front. Sometimes, it may even work. My point is simple. It is a lot more important to bring that teaching into a condensed mode rather than worrying about the total contact time. One easy example of when a four-course load is better than a three-course load is if you are teaching four sections of the same course in the fall semester and doing it all say on Tuesdays/Thursdays of the fall semester. That beats teaching twice a week in fall (two sections) and twice a week in spring (one section) to fulfill a three-course load commitment, regardless of whether they are three sections of the same or different courses.

I recall one semester where I was teaching two sections of a programming course on Tuesday and Thursday mornings, and teaching two sections of an e-commerce application development course in the afternoons of those same days. That four-course load typically left me completely exhausted at the end of Tuesdays and Thursdays. I needed a drink at the end of those days—actually, a few large drinks. However, I was ready to crank out research on Mondays, Wednesdays and Fridays because the course materials for both courses were already set up as I had taught the classes previously. My routine for Tuesdays and Thursdays began at 7 a.m.—reviewing the materials for both classes. My teaching began at 9:30 a.m. and I had a break at 12:15 p.m. I picked up teaching again at 2 p.m. and I was done teaching at 4:45 p.m. The break in the afternoon was dedicated, over lunch, to the preparation of the afternoon lectures.

iii. Myth #3: Avoid New Course Preparations Like The Plague

If you read my discussion of myth #1, I need to do very little explaining here. New course preparations have the same advantages that I outlined in the context of why teaching will benefit research and why teaching is not a waste of time. New course preparations are something to optimize—note that I do not say minimize or avoid. New course preparations will teach you many of the things that teaching will help you learn. You will learn to motivate material, to speak to your audience, to focus on what is interesting, etc. New course preparations offer the added advantage that it is new material—like the findings from a new study that you are writing up into a paper. New courses, like new papers with new findings, rely on the framing and story-telling skills you have acquired in the past, and help you improve upon your skills using the new materials—they are not like courses you have taught before where you can rely on past student reactions and your own feelings (much like you can rely on reviewers' input on previous papers/revisions).

Concluding Thoughts

This chapter presented the message that teaching is not the evil and detrimental task it is made out to be in terms of its impact on research. I discussed how teaching can provide various opportunities to improve your research, particularly because both research and teaching share the underlying idea of having to communicate effectively to an audience. Communicating about both research and teaching have the same underlying principles of recognizing who the audience is and speaking to what their interests are. I also debunk three myths related to teaching—myths that say that teaching is a waste of time, a three-course load is always better than a four-course load and that new course preparations should be avoided.

Key Takeaways

1. Excellent sources for teaching tips and tricks include: Bain's (2004) *What the Best College Teachers Do*, MaKeachie's (1999) *Teaching Tips*, Rotenberg's (2005) *The Art and Craft of College Teaching: A Guide for New Professors And Graduate Students*, Provitera-McGlynn's (2001) *Successful Beginnings for College Teaching*, and Filene's (2006) *The Joy of Teaching: A Practical Guide for New College Instructors*
2. Prepare early, not often
   i. Course preparations, especially new ones, consume considerable time—protect your research time by preparing your courses entirely at the beginning of the semester
   ii. The value in preparing early is that you can stay ahead of students and see where the course is headed; also, rather than being consumed by teaching and a feeling of unpreparedness constantly throughout the semester, you will have more time to focus on research during the semester
   iii. Do as much of your preparation as you can before the semester begins, leaving room just for adjustments so you will not be as stressed as you would be if you were practicing a just-in-time preparation model—the result is that you will still have much

of your bandwidth even during a teaching intensive semester for research

3. Listen to your teaching
   i. Teaching is one of the best ways to learn how to communicate new subject matter to an audience unfamiliar with the subject—a student audience can often be skeptical, not unlike reviewers!
   ii. Dissemination of information is at the heart of both teaching and writing papers
   iii. If you are not getting through to your students, reflect on your teaching style and you will be reflecting on something deeper—i.e., your ability to communicate what you know very well to a possibly skeptical, unfamiliar audience
   iv. Two key mistakes that new teachers tend to make are: (1) pitching the material at too difficult a level for the audience to comprehend; and (2) filling in gaps in the logical flow of the class session with details from one's own knowledge base that the audience obviously cannot access
   v. The two mistakes noted above are relevant to research as they are frequently committed in writing papers as well
4. Integrating research into teaching
   i. Bringing your research into the classroom has two direct benefits:
       a. It establishes you as a human being to your students when you discuss your research and the challenges you face in collecting data
       b. It indicates to your students that you do other things besides teach—this can in turn help set expectations about your availability outside the classroom
   ii. Explain to students that research and teaching go hand-in-hand—if you were to only do research, then, you might never be able to connect it to the real world to influence practice; alternatively, if you were to only teach, then, you would merely be a talking head
   iii. An important benefit of integrating teaching and research is the opportunity it provides to pilot new ideas, theoretical justifications, examples, and implications, and to use students as subjects for research
5. Myths about teaching
   i. Myth #1: Teaching is a waste of time... in fact, teaching is not a waste of time—the best teachers get to know their audience, help motivate students to care about the topic and help them understand the topic, which are skills that are key to researchers as well
       a. Knowing your students: Consider your target student audience (teaching an introductory information systems course to freshmen across all majors on campus will certainly be different from teaching the topic to more mature business majors that in turn will be different from teaching the topic to juniors who are information systems majors)
       b. Providing information about why the student should care about the topic: Once you know your audience, you should provide the motivation in a way the target student group can best understand it, with a focus that will make the target student group care

    c. Helping students understand the topic: Focus on the aspects that would be *most* interesting and valuable to the target group of students

    d. Knowing your audience: The paper must appeal to the audience (who are the readers of the journal in which you are trying to publish? what do they care about? the relevant gaps—both practical and theoretical—should be sensitive to the target journal)

    e. Providing information about why the reader should care about the topic: The motivation for the topic needs to be appropriate to the chosen journal

    f. Helping readers understand: Ensure that you cite the relevant prior literature and leverage appropriate theoretical arguments

ii. Myth #2: A three-course load is always better than a four-course load

    a. It is a lot more important to bring your teaching into a condensed mode rather than worrying about the total contact time

    b. For example, a 4-course load is better than a 3-course load when you are teaching 4 sections of the same course in the fall semester and doing it all on Tuesdays and Thursdays of the fall semester—this beats teaching twice a week in the fall semester (two sections) and twice a week in the spring semester (one section) to fulfill a three-course commitment, regardless of whether they are three sections of the same course or different courses

iii. Myth #3: Avoid new course preparations like the plague

    a. New course preparations will teach you many of the things that teaching will help you learn

    b. New courses will help you learn to motivate material, to speak to your audience and to focus on what is interesting, etc.

    c. New course preparations offer the added advantage that it is new material—like findings from a new study that you are writing up into a paper

    d. New courses, like new papers with new findings, rely on the framing and story-telling skills you have acquired in the past and help you develop your skills further with the new materials

CHAPTER 7

BUILDING AND MANAGING COLLABORATIONS

Let's start with what the word *collaborate* means—Dictionary.com defines it as follows:
intr. v. col·lab·o·rat·ed, col·lab·o·rat·ing, col·lab·o·rates
To work together, especially in a joint intellectual effort.
To cooperate treasonably, as with an enemy occupation force in one's country.

There is something about these two definitions that makes me think that they were created to describe research collaboration. I am certain you can see it in the first definition but you might be wondering what it is about treason and enemies that relate to academic research. The joint intellectual effort is related to the focus on research projects and papers. The enemies, loosely speaking of course, are the journal editors and reviewers, and the land that we seek to occupy is the journal space. A successful collaboration results in occupation of the land that the journal editors' hold dear, in occupation of the land that reviewers guard as tough, sometimes fair, sometimes unfair and sometimes belligerent, gatekeepers. The usefulness of the enemy metaphor is that it helps us to carefully think about framing and story-telling in our papers. Of course, I do not mean to suggest that the journal editors and reviewers are enemies in the true sense of the word, especially as many have been kind to me by accepting many of my papers! I believe that thinking about editors and reviewers as enemies (or adversaries) can give us the focus we need to ensure that we do not take things for granted or make stupid, avoidable mistakes. As you read this chapter, keep chapters 2 and 3 in mind as well.

I organize my thinking on building and managing collaborations into three sets of five: five reasons to collaborate, five reasons not to collaborate and five rules for collaboration (these five rules are really my "lessons learned").

The five reasons to collaborate are:
1. Creates efficiency gains
2. Leverages complementarities
3. Whole can be greater than the sum of the parts
4. Creates an environment for lifelong learning
5. Provides a support group

The five reasons to not collaborate are:
1. Flying solo is important
2. Coordination costs are high
3. Leads to the blame game
4. Ruins relationships
5. Having to reconcile work styles

Five rules that drive or limit my collaboration (aka the lessons I learned from collaborating) are:

1. Ensure motivational alignment
2. Ensure rank alignment
3. Be mindful of your strengths and weaknesses
4. Always mix business and pleasure
5. Keep the number of collaborators manageable

Before I embark on the reasons to collaborate, I must note that I am neither advocating collaboration nor am I against it. There are some reasons to collaborate, there are some reasons not to collaborate and then there are contingencies (rules) that make collaborations work or that can turn a collaboration into a disaster. All of these should be taken into consideration in conjunction with each other. Let me illustrate: as a reason to collaborate, I note creating efficiency gains and leveraging complementarities. However, I also note that I caution junior researchers to keep the number of collaborators manageable and to not form collaboration teams of all possible dyads [at your place of employment]. In the end, care and thought should go into building and managing collaborations so that the benefits (reasons to collaborate) outweigh the costs (reasons not to collaborate) and the rules (listed here or those you may develop) are observed.

Five Reasons To Collaborate

Below, I discuss the five reasons to collaborate and provide a brief rationale associated with each reason.

1. Creates Efficiency Gains

This is one of the simplest and most logical reasons for collaboration. Two heads can be better than one. You can execute research projects quicker. You can write papers quicker. You can share subject pools. Collaboration is also very helpful in making things more efficient in another interesting and important way—much like there is evidence demonstrating that having a "workout buddy" is more likely to result in successful weight loss outcomes—having a collaborator is likely to create social pressure that can result in focus and faster completion of research activities—e.g., writing a paper. Efficiency gains may also result because both of you (or as many collaborators as there are) may plan more carefully in order to execute research activities in a timely manner.

2. Leverages Complementarities

One of the best reasons to collaborate is to work on research that you would not normally be able to work on by yourself from a topical and/or methodological perspective. For example, in my case, collaborations helped me use qualitative methods for data collection—something I would not have otherwise touched with a 100-foot pole.

3. Whole Can Be Greater Than The Sum Of The Parts

Even if you were not leveraging complementarities and working on unique projects, but instead were working on a project that either collaborator (or any of the collaborators) could have worked on alone, there are advantages to collaborating. Collaboration can result in a better product. Discussion of ideas, arguments about theoretical justifications and research designs, ideas from one person's background, training and interests that are unique, and a simulated review of sections of a paper that was written by one of the collaborating partners are a few of the advantages that could result from collaborating. Overall, collaboration can be key to a better paper emerging—something that even given twice the time, one person could not have produced. Putting things in perspective, brainstorming and generating strategies to solve issues will all benefit from collaboration. This benefit of collaboration becomes particularly important when you face daunting comments from editors and reviewers as interactions among collaborators can help greatly to develop a winning strategy to address comments and revise a paper.

4. Creates An Environment For Lifelong Learning

Perhaps no other profession creates an environment for lifelong learning to the same extent that academia does. There are many things that one can learn from collaborators. As mentioned earlier, there is always an opportunity to learn about new theoretical perspectives, topics and methodologies. No matter how similar the interests are between your collaborators and you, each person brings a set of unique ideas to the table, reads different things and is shaped by different experiences. Collaboration thus creates a great environment for lifelong learning. Each meeting is an eye-opening experience as each person shares ideas. It keeps the profession and research fresh through the drudgeries of designing studies, collecting data, analyzing data, writing papers, getting beaten up by reviewers and editors, revising papers, all of which culminate finally in getting papers published. It is this journey where you have countless dialogs and arguments with your collaborators that create the excitement and lifelong learning that, in this profession, so many of us value.

Another type of learning that can come from working with collaborators is skill-based—i.e., you may find yourself lacking in some skill(s), such as data analysis, theory-building and/or writing, that may be a key strength of one or more of your collaborators. Working with them thus affords you a fantastic learning opportunity. Hopefully, you possess some skill(s) that can help your collaborator(s) as well. Such mutually beneficial learning will keep collaborations alive and well for a long time.

Counterintuitive as it may seem, collaborating with PhD students can also help (even for faculty members) as students frequently go in different and unique directions with their research that can then lead the faculty member to reading and learning some new and interesting things.

5. Provides A Support Group

Collaborators can be a great support group. Collaborators can help with issues even on projects and papers where they are not "official" collaborators. They can sympathize and empathize with you to get you over those tough times after you have received a rejection. More importantly, they can give you the tough love that is necessary before your paper goes out for review by providing a harsh yet constructive critique of the paper simulating a review process so that problems that you could not see (maybe because you were too close to the paper) are spotted and fixed before the paper is submitted to a journal. Of course, peers, who are not your collaborators, can do the same just as easily, but collaborators already have a bond with you, have greater familiarity with your work and there is, hopefully, an agreement based on reciprocity. Thus, collaborators can not only be a source of emotional support during tough times, but also be helpful critics of your works.

Five Reasons Not To Collaborate

Chances are you are now completely convinced that you must collaborate because it offers some fantastic benefits. Yes, it can. However, there are some notes of caution that should be heeded. My sole purpose in raising these issues is to ensure that, if and when you collaborate, you can think through these issues, discuss relevant ones with your collaborators at the outset and think of ways upfront to ensure problems don't crop up later. Also, some of the reasons I outline here can, if not heeded, become an Achilles' heel to your promotion and tenure case—so think through them and plan accordingly.

1. Flying Solo Is Important

Some institutions greatly value sole-authored publications. They are viewed as demonstrations of your unique contributions. They are also viewed as a sign that you can do it all by yourself. This tends to be particularly important if your advisor is a highly respected scholar. There may even be some merit to this rationale. It is quite likely that the papers from one's dissertation can be carried over the finish line by the advisor, even if he or she is only a 2nd author. With an advisor co-author, advice received during all phases of the research process—i.e., literature review, model development, study design, data collection, writing, editing, revision strategy, rewrites and revision process—can turn out a great product fit for the best journals. Flying solo—i.e., doing all these activities by yourself—will show that you were not just a passive observer, and that you have learned the art and science needed to produce top-quality journal articles. In the end, some number of lead-authored publications may be enough, but sole-authored publications will be valuable or even necessary at some schools. A mix of sole-authored, lead-authored and other publications (which are neither sole-authored nor with you as a lead author) will be a good record, thus suggesting that the pursuit of sole-authored papers is important. This reason not to collaborate is, therefore, not that alarming after all. If time and ability were no constraint, is there then a downside to having only sole-authored papers? Yes, it is possible. Someone might actually observe: "S/he doesn't work well with others and is not a team player." Ultimately, perhaps the moral here is that you should have some solo work as well as some collaborative work.

2. Coordination Costs Are High

Coordinating the schedules of busy people is rather difficult. Not only do you have to coordinate schedules with your collaborators, but also you have to coordinate so that the time spent working together is meaningful enough to make substantial progress and have meaningful conversations to help move your work toward publication. You may frequently find yourself in a situation where your teaching days are not the teaching days of your collaborator, your semester off is the busy semester for your collaborator, or your period (time of day) of peak performance does not overlap with your collaborator's. When all is said and done, there will be significant coordination costs in a collaboration. For a collaboration to be successful, coordination should be discussed upfront so that neither resentment nor lack of progress becomes the only outcome. In this context, working with more than one collaborator on a particular project can turn into a nightmare—the adage, "two's company, three's a crowd" comes to mind.

3. Leads To The Blame Game

The first step to ruining a working relationship is the blame game. Like any sports team that we read about, when things are going well for the team, problems can be masked. In contrast, when things do not go well, problems surface. For example, if a series of favorable decisions (e.g., acceptances, invitations to revise-and-resubmit) are rolling in, all will be well with the collaboration; if, however, a few papers are rejected and the issues delineated by the reviewers point to certain aspects or sections of the paper, it could result in the blame game—i.e., finger pointing. Successful collaborations should leave no room for the blame game—the most likely scenario for that to happen is joint ownership of the project/paper and not a divide-and-conquer strategy. If there is a blame game being played, read on…

4. Ruins Relationships

Collaboration can ruin relationships. Many things, big and small, can work their way to being killers of otherwise smooth professional interactions or even friendships. The blame game can result in a ruined relationship. Other issues that could create problems include but are not limited to: authorship order, failure to meet deadlines, quality of work and work style differences. Such issues can turn a good, solid professional relationship or friendship into a bickering and hostile interaction. The only way to really overcome this is to talk about the various issues—like the ones listed above or others as they occur. In the best case scenario, when issues surface, communication can help strengthen the relationship and/or help you mature as a researcher. For instance, instead of the blame game, it could be an opportunity for one or more of the collaborators to learn and remedy a potential deficiency that exists in their knowledge or skill base. The issues will never go away. Problems will occur. But like any other interpersonal relationship, good communication is at the heart of successful collaborations.

5. Having To Reconcile Work Styles

People have different work styles. One of the best parts of academia is that we can do whatever we please (within limits, of course). We all have our own idiosyncratic way of doing things. We do things the way we see fit. Working with collaborators calls for some compromises, changes and tolerance. Your collaborator may prefer to meet in the morning whereas you may hate morning meetings. They may prefer to write the abstract first whereas you may prefer to write it last. There are an infinite variety of differences between people and their various work styles. Collaboration often calls for adjustments. Successful collaborators use differences as learning opportunities to appreciate and benefit from each other's different viewpoints and approaches. However, uncompromising collaborators can create frustrating experiences. I have referred to meetings with difficult collaborators as "root canals." Do not sign up or stay in a collaboration that is going to make you feel that you'd rather be at the oral surgeon's!

Five Rules Of Collaboration

Earlier, I said I neither advocate nor oppose collaboration. The reality, of course, is that given the pressures of publication and the high standards of journals, collaboration is necessary for success. Picking the right collaborators can be the difference between success and failure. In sharing the rules for collaboration, I note some things that have worked well for me thus far. These have driven my choice of collaborators over the years and, to some extent, the process of collaboration. Some of these rules I formulated through years of successful and unsuccessful collaborations. Some of these rules I formulated simply by watching or hearing about others' successful and unsuccessful collaborations.

1. Ensure Motivational Alignment

It is best to collaborate with those who have similar motivations. Motivations come from multiple sources. One source of motivation is, of course, intrinsic. Another source of motivation is tied to which school one is at and what types of journals are valued at that school. When the personal and school-based motivations are aligned, collaborations can work well. If there is a misalignment of motivations across collaborators, there will be frustration, lack of effort and lack of interest from one collaborator or another (including you!). Ensure motivational alignment no matter how well you know the potential collaborator(s) and no matter how much you want to work with him or her (them).

2. Ensure Rank Alignment

Rank alignment also plays a significant role in whether or not a collaboration can be successful. While assistant professors can constantly hear the ticking sound of the tenure clock, once tenured, the ticking stops. Once at the rank of professor, there may be no sounds heard at all! At the rank of associate professor or professor, there is an opportunity to pursue higher risk projects. There are positives and potential negatives to collaborating with seasoned researchers. On the positive side, senior researchers have knowledge and experience, some of which is gained through editorial experiences. On the negative side of the ledger is that the same sense of urgency that you experience will not be experienced by a tenured [full] professor! Schedules may slide. There will probably be more urgent and pressing matters, e.g., committees, editorial work, reviewing work and administrative duties, that eat away at their schedules that in turn can cause research to sometimes be moved to the back burner. I am not advocating completely avoiding collaborations with senior faculty members—just go in with your eyes open about their schedule. You can balance this with other collaborations with peers or by doing sole-authored work or by knowing you have to do much of the time-sensitive work yourself. You can also go into collaborations with senior faculty members knowing that you will likely need to spend more time on various facets of the project.

One clear solution is to work with peers at your or other institutions. If the motivations and ranks are aligned in a collaboration, things couldn't be better for the collaborative process. These can be very successful collaborations that produce high-quality papers. Related to this, collaborating with PhD students can also result in solid work as students tend to work hard and are interested in papers so as to be more attractive on the job market. This, however, must be tempered by the fact that much time must be invested in their training. Sometimes, one junior faculty member may not possess the rounded skill set to carry a project over the finish line with a PhD student. One way to address this is for junior faculty members to collaborate with a PhD student in tow; alternatively, a junior and a senior faculty member can collaborate with a PhD student in tow.

3. Be Mindful Of Your Strengths And Weaknesses

Not all PhD graduates emerge equally equipped out of the gate. While there are some similarities—e.g., strength in research design and data analysis, weakness in theory-building—specific areas of strength and weakness, and the extent of each strength or weakness varies—e.g., a strength could be data analysis using LISREL and a weakness could be theory-building. Be honest with yourself and identify your strengths and weaknesses. I am strongly in favor of early collaborations being about complementary strengths. One of my early weaknesses was writing (most of the reviewers of my papers still think so!) so I sought out collaborations where

I could learn to write more effectively. I was fortunate to work with Fred Davis, a phenomenal writer (but was perhaps running out of patience with my complete lack of writing skills), and one of my early collaborators, Mike Morris, also a fantastic writer (Fred Davis once likened Mike's writing to that of Robert Louis Stevenson!). These two collaborations helped me learn quite a bit about writing, making me push myself to learn more about writing and ultimately, I think, actually helping me become a better writer.

My other early collaborators—Sue Brown and Cheri Speier—have their own unique strengths. One of Sue's is a versatility in methodologies. I learned quite a bit about qualitative methods, which has led more recently to my working on other research projects that use qualitative data. Cheri has an ability to process a lot of material (literature) very quickly and get a lay of the land in a completely new domain. I benefited from learning the tips and tricks that she employed.

I like to think that my ability to work effectively with organizations to collect data that are otherwise difficult to collect is one of my strengths. Hopefully, getting better quality data for our collaborative research projects was of value to my collaborators. It is my belief that collaborators will stick around, if the strengths and weaknesses of the collaborators are complementary as this is likely to result in producing works that any one person cannot otherwise produce. If the gains are purely efficiency gains, when the ticking of the tenure clock stops, the pressure is eased substantially and the collaboration has less impetus to sustain.

4. Always Mix Business And Pleasure

I have had the best of luck with my collaborations when I have been able to mix business and pleasure. All of my early collaborations were with people who already were, or very soon became some of my best friends in the field—Sue Brown, Fred Davis, Mike Morris and Cheri Speier. The old adage goes, "find something you enjoy doing and you will never have to work a day in your life." Working with my friends ensured that when we worked, we were still having a lot of fun and not just because we enjoyed the research that we were doing but because we enjoyed each other's company (at least I enjoyed theirs—you'll have to check with them for the other way around!). Many of my later collaborations were also with good friends as it has become an important rule that I enforce before I begin any collaboration.

Working with friends has its share of advantages, such as open and easy communication about various issues. However, I must hasten to add that collaborations with friends also create a potential way to lose the friendship. As I mentioned earlier, communication is key. I firmly believe that the friendship is far more important than anything else—e.g., authorship order. While it is important to not sweat the small stuff—e.g., authorship order—it is still necessary to be fair so that one person does not feel any resentment, for if one does, it is a sure fire way to kill the collaboration and worse, the friendship. Communicate early and often to keep things above board, and you will always enjoy your work during the collaborative phases of the project! Overall, mixing business and pleasure, and working with friends makes communication easier and work more pleasurable.

5. Keep The Number Of Collaborators Manageable

This is really a natural byproduct of some of the other rules. Keep the number manageable because satisfying other rules, gaining all benefits and avoiding pitfalls (reasons not to collaborate) become more unlikely with a large number of collaborators. Do not create all possible dyads and triads in your new workplace just because it helps you explore new topics or just because it presents an opportunity to build ties with everyone at work. Be selective and don't stretch yourself too thin. If you have a large number of collaborators, you risk upsetting someone if and when you drop the ball! While it may seem attractive to hedge your bets and work on many things, you may just as well hedge your bets by trying to do high-quality work on a few projects/papers! Quality over quantity always.

Concluding Thoughts

The five reasons to collaborate, five reasons not to collaborate and five rules of collaboration present my perspective. They cannot possibly represent an exhaustive list. Of course, others may disagree with some of the points made here—perhaps more than in any other chapter of this book. Find what works for you. While I neither advocate collaboration nor oppose it, it is likely that in academia, collaboration is necessary in order to build a successful—i.e., tenureable—portfolio. So, build collaborations carefully and take them seriously.

Key Takeaways

1. There are good reasons to collaborate, good reasons NOT to collaborate and some general guidelines that should drive or limit collaboration
2. Also, when you think about collaborations, keep chapters 2 and 3 in mind
3. Five reasons to collaborate
   i. Creates efficiency gains
      a. Two heads are better than one
      b. You can execute research projects quicker
      c. You can write papers more rapidly
      d. You can share subject pools
      e. Having a collaborator is likely to create social pressure that can result in focus and faster completion of research activities
   ii. Leverages complementarities
      a. Collaborating means you can work on research on which you would not be able to work by yourself
      b. You can use methodologies that you would not have been able to use, if you are working alone

  iii. The whole can be greater than the sum of the parts
   a. Collaboration can result in a better product
   b. Discussion of ideas, arguments about theoretical justifications and research designs, ideas from one person's background, training and interests that are unique, and a simulated review of sections of a paper that was written by one of the collaboration partners are a few of the advantages that could result from collaborating
   c. Putting things in perspective, brainstorming and generating strategies to solve issues will all benefit from collaboration
   d. Interactions among collaborators can help greatly to develop a winning strategy to address comments and revise a paper
  iv. Creates an environment for lifelong learning
   a. There is always an opportunity to learn new theoretical perspectives, topics and methodologies
   b. You may find yourself lacking in some skill(s)—e.g., data analysis, theory-building, writing—that may be a key strength of one or more of your collaborators
   c. Collaborating with PhD students can lead to the pursuit of interesting projects as students frequently go in different and unique directions that can then lead the faculty member to reading and learning some new and interesting things
  v. Provides a support group
   a. Collaborators can help with issues even on projects and papers where they are not "official" collaborators
   b. They can sympathize and empathize to get you over those tough times after you have received a rejection
   c. They can give you the tough love that is necessary before your paper goes out for review by providing a harsh yet constructive critique of your paper
 4. Five reasons not to collaborate: Discuss these issues with your collaborators at the outset and think of ways to address the problem areas upfront so you have a mutual understanding with your collaborators
  i. Flying solo is important
   a. Sole-authored publications are viewed as a demonstration of your unique contribution and your ability to perform all phases of the research by yourself
   b. Sole-authored publications are particularly important if your advisor is a highly respected scholar—publishing papers by yourself will show that not only were you not just a passive observer, but also you have learned the art and science needed to produce top-quality journal articles
   c. Some number of lead-authored publications is valuable but sole-authored publications may be necessary at some schools—a mix of sole-authored, lead-authored and other publications (which are neither sole-authored nor with you as lead author) will be a good record
  ii. Coordination costs are high

      a. Coordinating the schedules of busy people is rather difficult

      b. Not only do you have to coordinate schedules with your collaborators, but also you have to coordinate so that the time spent working together is meaningful enough to make substantial progress

      c. For collaboration to be successful, coordination should be discussed upfront so that neither resentment nor lack of progress becomes the only outcome

  iii. Leads to blame game

      a. When things do not go well (e.g., rejections), the blame-game could be played out

      b. Successful collaborations should leave no room for the blame game—the best way to avoid the blame game is joint ownership of the project/paper and not a divide-and-conquer strategy

  iv. Ruins relationships

      a. Issues that could ruin relationships include but are not limited to authorship order, failure to meet deadlines, quality of work and work style differences

      b. Such issues can turn a good, solid professional relationship and/or friendship into a bickering and hostile one

      c. Talk about the various issues before or as they occur. In the best case scenario, when issues surface, communication could help strengthen the relationship and/or help you mature as a researcher

   v. Have to reconcile work styles

      a. We like to do things the way we see fit—however, working with collaborators calls for some compromises, changes and tolerance

      b. Successful collaborations use differences as a learning opportunity to appreciate and benefit from different viewpoints and approaches

5. Five rules of collaboration (my "lessons learned")

   i. Ensure motivational alignment

      a. Motivations come from multiple sources—one source of motivation is, of course, intrinsic, and another source of motivation is tied to the school at which one is and the types of journals valued at that school

      b. If there is a misalignment of motivations across collaborators, there will be frustration, lack of effort and lack of interest from one person or another

      c. Ensure motivational alignment no matter how well you know the potential collaborator or how much you want to work with the potential collaborator

   ii. Ensure rank alignment

      a. Assistant professors can constantly hear the ticking sound of the tenure clock, while tenured professors do not

      b. At the rank of associate professor and professor, there may be an opportunity to pursue higher risk projects that may take longer

      c. Collaborating with a seasoned researcher has advantages that include working with someone with a great deal of knowledge and experience—however, they have less of an urgency than assistant professors do and thus schedules may slide

      d. Balance your work with senior faculty members by:
- Collaborating with peers
- Doing sole-authored work
- Doing much of the time-sensitive work yourself

      e. Consider collaborating with PhD students

iii. Be mindful of your strengths and weaknesses

      a. Be honest with yourself about your strengths and weaknesses—early collaborations should be about complementary strengths

      b. Collaborators will stick around if the strengths and weaknesses are complementary as this is likely to produce works that any one person cannot otherwise produce

      c. If a collaboration is purely about efficiency gains, when the ticking of the tenure clock stops, the pressure is eased substantially and the collaboration does not have to (will not) sustain

iv. Always mix business and pleasure

      a. Working with friends ensures that when you work, you can still have fun—not only because you enjoy the research, but also because you enjoy each other's company

      b. Working with friends has its share of advantages, such as open and easy communication about various issues

      c. Collaborations with friends also create a potential way to lose the friendship—communication is key to avoiding this

v. Keep the number of collaborators manageable

      a. Satisfying other rules, gaining all benefits and avoiding pitfalls (reasons not to collaborate) becomes more unlikely with a large number of collaborators

      b. Do not create all possible dyads and triads in your new workplace just because it helps you explore new topics or just because it presents an opportunity to build ties with all your colleagues—be selective and don't stretch yourself too thin

      c. If you do have a large number of collaborators, you risk upsetting someone if and when you drop the ball!

CHAPTER 8

MANAGING THE PhD PROGRAM: YEARS 1 AND 2

The first two years of the PhD program are, in many ways, the most enjoyable years of the PhD program. They expose a student to academic research, the process of which can be very much like finding a new love. The excitement of reading about various research topics leads to the good problem of having many possible research ideas running through the heads of new PhD students. It creates and requires new ways of thinking and perceiving, both of which can also be immensely exciting. However, the first two years also have the highest attrition/dropout rates. One of the main reasons students leave a PhD program is that they fail to manage the first two years effectively and consequently, find the program becomes overwhelming, with no apparent light at the end of the tunnel.

Managing the PhD program effectively is not a trivial task. Almost everyone will acknowledge that a PhD program can be overwhelming, especially in the early stages. The immense amount of information, the adjustment to the new lifestyle, the statistics, the need to pursue research and the need to serve as a graduate assistant for up to 20 hours a week may all prove to be too much for some students, thus driving them to quit. Those who brave the early storm may yet be running from deadline to deadline in just-in-time mode, with little or no pause to reflect on what they have learned, what their key knowledge/skill gaps are and what they need to do to fill the gaps. Although the comprehensive exams are a point when students can reflect on what they have learned, that too is an experience that students often fear and just want to survive.

Some of the challenges that are caused early in students' academic careers are a directly a function of the design of the PhD programs in most North American schools. Students run helter-skelter cramming in some number of classes each week, doing their duties as a 20-hour graduate assistant, reading papers (for courses and beyond) and working on research projects all into a standard work week. The programs are not necessarily designed to give students a chance to pause and reflect but rather to see how well students survive the rigorous intellectual and even time management challenges of a PhD program. Survival is frequently tied to being organized, able to meet requirements, and the acquisition of acceptable levels of skills in statistics, research methods and various topical areas. Yet, frequently, I have found that the students with some of the best ideas fall victim to the pressure and time constraints, and do not make it successfully through these early hurdles due to the lack of time management, organization and planning skills. I will discuss my advice around four major points:

1. Time management and organization
2. Planning document
   i. Faculty mentor
   ii. Learning goals
   iii. Research projects

3. Summer research
4. Being well-rounded
   i. Methods and statistics
   ii. Theory-building and writing

1. Time Management And Organization

No matter how organized someone is when he or she begins a PhD program, the number of things to be done and the enormity of the various tasks take their toll even on the most organized student. Of course, many who choose to enter a PhD program do so for the intellectual and work-related freedom (that, of course, comes after one completes a PhD and gets a job) and thus, time management and organization may not be their strong suit. Without effective time management and organization skills, the PhD program tends to be most overwhelming and creates a feeling of constantly being behind.

One way to deal with this is to have lists, lists and more lists. After fumbling through my first quarter of the PhD program in a bit of a daze and getting two Bs out of three classes, I started making layers of lists to manage my time. For the first time in my life, I had to-do lists at varying levels of abstraction. I had lists of things to do over the quarter, broken into lists organized by month, broken further into lists by weeks and finally, daily lists. Almost always, I was behind [on all lists!] but I felt more in control and knew exactly what needed to be done. These lists slowly morphed into a document that I created for myself at the start of each quarter. The next section discusses the document.

2. Planning Document

A tool that I found useful in making a dent in the organizational and progress assessments of most students (and in my own career) is the planning document tool that I include below. It evolves over the course of my PhD career. Most recently, it has been revised to suit today's environment and is shown in Table 8-1. The document is fairly self-explanatory but I draw attention to three important elements:

i. Faculty Mentor
The role of a faculty mentor, aside from the PhD program director, is essential. A faculty mentor or mentors is not a dissertation advisor because a dissertation advisor role is largely not applicable until one reaches the dissertation stage and that typically happens in the third year. Instead, what a faculty mentor does is to provide the student with guidance on research projects, courses and various aspects of the program. Faculty members, who are formal mentors, are also more likely to take responsibility for student learning. Having different mentors will potentially expose the student to different perspectives, experiences, topic areas and styles. . In sum, having one or more faculty mentors gives a student a chance for varied

exposure without creating expectations on the part of either the faculty member or the student that this would be an advising [dissertation] relationship.

ii. Learning Goals

Learning goals are important to help students get the opportunity to learn and experience all facets of a PhD program/curriculum necessary to be successful. Learning goals help students look beyond specific classes by shifting the focus to strengths and weaknesses. Hopefully, thinking about learning goals will create some reflection and importantly, perhaps a research assistant assignment that will help students accomplish these goals. There are many things to learn in order to be a well-rounded PhD student at the end of two years. Some skills are easier to learn than others. For instance, learning the basic ideas behind analyzing data can be relatively simple. However, understanding all the assumptions, options of statistical tests, and dealing with messy data takes practice, practice and more practice. It is easy to lose sight of learning goals—i.e., goals that relate to acquiring skills. One important thing that must be considered with regard to learning goals is that students typically come into a PhD program with their own unique combination of preferences and strengths. Similarly, they also come with weaknesses. For example, seldom are new PhD students good at academic writing, but many come into the program with strong quantitative skills. Alternatively, some come with strong reading and writing abilities (albeit not academic writing) but weak quantitative skills. Of course, all of these are relative strengths and weaknesses within each PhD student. Failure to think about learning goals will only result in students avoiding weak areas and favoring those they perceive to be their strengths.

iii. Research Projects

Research projects are the most important aspect of learning in the first two years of the PhD program. Research projects fit best with the apprentice mode of training and learning. While the first two years are filled with classes in the major/core field (e.g., information systems), a supporting field (e.g., psychology) and statistics, research projects are where these newly acquired book-learning can come to life in practice. Collaborative research projects with faculty members are the best way to learn how to do research, especially to acquire the tacit knowledge related to conducting research and writing papers. In terms of learning the craft, one of the biggest challenges for students is finding time to work on research that is meaningful (i.e., not just papers that satisfy course requirements) where the student will be called to work on various aspects of the paper, from theory development to study design to data collection to data analysis to writing. Often, not all of these things will be accomplished by the student in a single project—however, paying attention to learning goals will allow students and PhD program directors to ensure that every student gets an opportunity to work on all phases of a research project, especially those phases on which the student could use the most training.

Do the topics of research projects [that students pursue to learn the skills] matter? One could make the case for both yes and no. Engaging in research projects in a topic area that they like or enjoy could take students down the path of a potential dissertation topic. However, given the focus on the need to acquire skills, regardless of the area, a project that is at some level of maturity is going to be better than a project where the student has to engage in activities that he or she may not have the skills to perform. For example, scoping out the gaps in an entirely new research topic is not likely to result in much if a student is assigned to the task in his or her first semester. Instead, assigning the student to review the literature, summarize and attempt to synthesize the literature in a research topic will be more fruitful. Similarly, asking the student to work with data that have already been gathered by a faculty mentor, with the student using their statistics classes as avenues to learn about the juxtaposition of the science and practice of data analysis will be of greater value to the student [and maybe even some value to the research project itself].

I would recommend PhD students discuss this document with a faculty mentor and/or PhD program director three times a year: at the start of fall, spring and summer. This will allow for reflection on the previous semester's activities and learning, followed by a look ahead and development of a concrete plan for the upcoming semester. The ideal time to discuss this document is before the GA assignments for the upcoming semester have been made so that assignments can match students' needs with faculty interests/projects.

Table 8-1. Doctoral Student Review And Planning Document

Student name:		
Report for:	select one / select one	
Plan for:	select one / select one	
Semester/year entered the PhD program	select one / select one	
Date comps passed (if applicable)	select one / select one	
Dissertation topic (if applicable)		
Dissertation advisor (if applicable) or Faculty mentor		
Dissertation committee (if applicable)		
Coursework		
select one / select one		[select one]

Table 8-1 *Continued*. Doctoral Student Review And Planning Document

		[select one]
		[select one]
		[select one]
select one / select one		[select one]
		[select one]
		[select one]
		[select one]
select one / select one		[select one]
		[select one]
		[select one]
		[select one]
select one / select one		[select one]
		[select one]
		[select one]
		[select one]

Other courses (provide semester/year, course number and grade)

Reflective statement on what you learned last semester (from coursework, research, projects, etc. Be descriptive – ½ to 1 page). *NOTE: The field area will re-size automatically as you type*

Research

Major areas of interest

Table 8-1 *Continued.* **Doctoral Student Review And Planning Document**

Statement of research interests (be descriptive about issues tied to the areas listed above – ½ to 1 page; incl. dissertation interests here). *NOTE: The field area will re-size automatically as you type*
Journal publications
Conference proceedings
Description of current research projects (be descriptive about issues tied to your major areas of interest – ½ to 1 page; incl. progress on dissertation here). *NOTE: The field area will re-size automatically as you type*
Working Papers
Progress report on any working papers listed on previous semester's report (be descriptive – ½ to 1 page). *NOTE: The field area will re-size automatically as you type*

Table 8-1 *Continued*. Doctoral Student Review And Planning Document

Research and learning goals for the upcoming semester (be descriptive – ½ to 1 page; incl. goals for dissertation here). *NOTE: The field area will re-size automatically as you type*

Teaching

Teaching goals for the upcoming semester		
Semester/Year	Courses taught	Student Evaluations
select one / select one		
select one / select one		
select one / select one		
select one / select one		
select one / select one		
select one / select one		
Reflective statement on your teaching experience last semester (be sure to include what you did well and what areas you'd like to improve; be descriptive – ½ to 1 page). *NOTE: The field area will re-size automatically as you type*		
Teaching goals for the upcoming semester (be sure to include how you, with or without external help, plan to remedy difficulties from the past semester; be descriptive – ½ to 1 page). *NOTE: The field area will re-size automatically as you type*		

3. Summer Research

Summers can be the most valuable time in a PhD student's first two years because they present opportunities to focus heavily on research. There are typically no classes in the summer. Hopefully, the student is supported through the summer on an assistantship or fellowship that is not too demanding in terms of time. In any case, the summer time with some duties is unlikely to be as onerous as the regular semester that is filled with similar duties *and* three or more courses. In some respects, the first summer is far more crucial than the second summer. The first summer provides an opportunity to bring to life and put into practice the ideas that a student learns in their first year. I strongly advocate that students collect data during the first summer, even if it is for a fairly simple project. The data collection experience will open the student's eyes to the difficulty associated with collecting data, and make them far more realistic and far less critical of papers they read! A related idea is for students to have two projects going in parallel over the summer—one which is independent and another that is collaborative with a faculty member.

The first summer research project in collaboration with a faculty member can result in a submission to a journal where the student is a co-author. Another approach is to conduct an empirical study that ties to a paper that the student wrote for a class earlier in the first year. The topic area of the first summer's research project can be governed by the same principles from the earlier discussion of research projects (chapter 3). It is far more important for a student to acquire the skills related to research by working on a project than it is for a student to have a specific topical focus in the first year.

The second summer research project is a little different. The key difference is that the 2nd year summer research project can be used to scope out a topic for a dissertation so students don't fall into a trap of aimlessly wandering in the 3rd year when the air (pressure) is let out of the balloon after they complete the comprehensive exam requirements. In most cases, the second summer comes with the enormous *perceived* pressure of preparing for the comprehensive exams. I say it is perceived pressure because students who have done the right things along the way should neither feel the pressure nor have much difficulty in passing comprehensive exams. Yet, I grant that the pressure is somewhat understandable as it is a "go/no-go" point in most programs.

A note to PhD program directors… It behooves PhD programs to take some responsibility for PhD student learning by giving them a chance to succeed in the 2nd summer. Some PhD programs have the comprehensive exams administered at the start of the summer so that the students do not spend the entire summer on just preparing for the exam. Instead, they complete the exam right at the start of the summer so that the rest of the summer can be dedicated to research. I believe this is a better approach than having comprehensive exams at the end of the 2nd summer.

4. Being Well-rounded

One broad piece of advice I give to first- and second-year PhD students is: "Aim to become well-rounded by the end of the second year." By "well-rounded" I mean possessing in good measure the variety of skills necessary to be successful in academia, particularly in research.

Being well-rounded is easier said than done. Frequently, I find that all PhD students together in a cohort would make one well-rounded PhD student. Students come into the program with different strengths, develop a liking for certain facets of research over others and develop or acquire more skills in some areas over others. This means first- and second-year PhD students would be well-served to frequently take themselves outside their comfort zone and push themselves to stretch their academic abilities by attempting things in which they are not comfortable as a way to address their weaknesses. For instance, someone whose isn't very good at writing should get involved in a paper where his or her role will be that of the primary writer.

Beyond the actual practice of working on research projects, which is vital to becoming well-rounded, there are two broad sets of skills that students must acquire. Although they fall under the header of "methods and statistics" and "theory-building and writing," a better categorization may really be "structured and easier learned skills" and "nearly impossible to teach skills."

i. Methods And Statistics

Methods and statistics represent the most structured skills that PhD students must learn. At least theoretically speaking, students usually grasp the basics of methods somewhat easily. But, it is enormously difficult for most students to actually put into practice. These skills are best learned, developed and committed to memory through actual practice. Practice turns laundry lists of validity threats and so on into actual issues to contend with and resolve. In the case of statistics, students may struggle with it for different reasons. Some students have a fairly limited background in statistics. Other students have a hard time relating their textbook knowledge of statistics to actual practice. In still other cases, students come quantitatively challenged and thus, face a hard time with statistics. Those with a more analytical mind and/or an engineering background seem to have an easier time with statistics. However, working on actual research projects with real data is almost always more useful to developing data analysis skills than textbook knowledge. Students should assess where they stand with respect to these skills so they can remedy this weakness, if necessary.

ii. Theory-building And Writing

From nearly a decade and a half of working with PhD students, I conclude that theory-building is the hardest skill for PhD students to learn. There are several good articles on what constitutes good theory and theoretical contribution: Bacharach (1989),[115] Dubin (1976),[116] Eisenhardt (1989),[117] Feldman (2004),[118] George and Jones (2000),[119] Langley (1999),[120] Poole and Van de ven (1989),[121] Sutton and Staw (1995),[122] Weick (1989, 1995)[123,124] and Whetten (1989).[125] Editorials by editors of various journals reiterate some of the key points made in these articles. Weber (2003)[126] discussed the nature of theory, the characteristics of good theory and identified the four steps to follow to make theoretical contributions to be: (1) articulate the constructs of a theory; (2) articulate the laws of interaction (relationships) among the constructs of a theory; (3) articulate the lawful state space of a theory; and (4) articulate the lawful event space of a theory.

Zmud (1998)[127] discussed what a "pure theory" paper is and how it is different from a "non pure theory" paper. He also discussed (p. xxxi) different ways theories in information systems, for instance, can be developed: "Information systems theory can be developed in three major ways. First, new theories can be developed. By a new theory, I am referring to ideas that have not previously appeared in either the information systems or reference discipline literatures. Second, existing theories (from either information systems or reference disciplines) can be applied 'as is' to information systems phenomena that had previously not been informed by these specific theories. Third, existing theories can be improved while being applied to information systems phenomena. Each of these pathways represents a means for making a value-added contribution to the information systems field, and the third pathway can produce value-added contributions to reference disciplines."

Weber (2003),[128] in his editorial comments, stated theory "is an *account* that is intended to explain or predict *phenomena* that we perceive in the world" (p. iv, emphasis in original). His articulation of the various ways in which theoretical contributions can be made are consistent with those described in Whetten's (1989)[129] influential ideas. Whetten noted and discussed four building blocks of theory development: *What* (constructs), *How* (relationships), *Why* (justification) and *Who, Where, When* (conditions). Whetten further stated that although *What* or *How* by themselves do not constitute a theoretical contribution, they can be critical ingredients that expand the set of constructs and relationships and under some circumstances can even be publishable in premier journals (see Weick 1995).[130] Refining some of these ideas, Weber argued that, in his view, there may be five ways to make a theoretical contribution even with the *What*: articulating new constructs to build new theory, introducing new constructs into existing theory, deleting constructs from an existing theory, adding and deleting constructs from an existing theory, and defining constructs more precisely within the scope of an existing theory. He further suggested similar possibilities for making theoretical contributions with the *How*—i.e., relationships.

Why is likely the "...most fruitful, but also most difficult avenue for theory development" (Whetten 1989, p. 493).[131] Weber's (2003)[132] commentary echoes this point by suggesting that theory should be able to account for phenomena. Also, he notes that constructs and relationships serve as bases for building richer explanations for phenomena of interest. Whetten noted that *Who, Where, When* also possess potential for a good theoretical contribution if the conditions being examined are qualitatively different from prior research and/or if the nature of the relationships and outcomes are substantially different from prior research that helps us understand the limits and boundaries of existing knowledge, thus furthering our understanding of the phenomenon at hand. This is consistent with Weber's suggestions that theoretical contributions can be made by delineating the lawful state space and event space of theories. Rich descriptions of how these contingencies can translate into strong contextual theoretical contributions is articulated well in Johns (2006)[133] and Alvesson and Karreman (2007).[134] While clearly noting that references, data, lists of constructs, diagrams and hypotheses are *not* theory, Sutton and Staw (1995)[135] suggest that "theory is the answer to queries of *why*" (p. 378, emphasis in original)—a view highly consistent with Whetten. Sutton and Staw's (1995)[136] description of theory and the *why* is still very important in our pursuit of making a theoretical contribution: "Theory is about the connections among phenomena, a story about why acts, events, structure, and thoughts occur. Theory emphasizes the nature of causal relationships, identifying what comes first as well as the timing of such events. Strong theory, in our view, delves into underlying processes so as to understand the systematic reasons for a particular occurrence or nonoccurrence. It often burrows deeply into microprocesses, laterally into neighboring concepts, or in upward direction, tying itself to broader social phenomena. It usually is laced with a set of convincing and logically interconnected arguments. It can have implications that we have not seen with our naked (or theoretically unassisted) eye. It may have implications that run counter to our common sense." As Weick (1995)[137] put it succinctly, "a good theory explains, predicts, and delights" (p. 378).

In addition to these comments, leading scholars have frequently noted that one of the important considerations for research is *relevance* of the problem. While scientific rigor is an important and necessary condition, perhaps most research in the behavioral and social sciences, seeks to study relevant problems (Benbasat and Zmud 1999; Lee 1999; Zmud 1996).[138,139,140] *Relevance* is a focus on phenomena that are interesting, applicable and current (Benbasat and Zmud 1999).[141] This suggestion implies the need to focus on problems that are relevant to today's organizations and society.

While not disagreeing with Sutton and Staw's (1995)[142] commentary, Weick (1995)[143] provided some additional important insights into theory development and making a theoretical contribution. Weick (1995)[144] suggests that, in addition to the pursuit of theory, it is important to recognize such *theorizing* as it represents the interim struggles of scientific discovery (see also Runkel and Runkel 1984)[145] and "consists of activities like abstracting, generalizing, relating, selecting, explaining, synthesizing, and idealizing" (p. 389). Such activities, Weick (1995)[146] argued, result in the very elements that Sutton and Staw (1995)[147] termed as not being theory. While Weick (1995)[148] agreed that the five elements articulated by Sutton and Staw (1995)[149] are indeed *not* theory, he went on to state that if a clear interim struggle is articulated and such a struggle leads to one or more of those five elements, those research processes are indeed important to know, understand and publish.

Underlying all of these articles is the theme that theory-building is both an art and a science. Various scholars share several tips and tricks about what they have done that has worked for them. Unlike data analysis where, through examples, one can understand the steps, the processes and follow the rules with different data sets, much of the process of good theory-building happens in the head of the scholar and the outcome (good theory) is a manifestation of a process that cannot be easily articulated.

Good theory-building comes only with a great deal of practice and, especially in the early stages, through practice and apprenticeship. Theory-building is an ability to build upon and go beyond current research in an effective way. It is the ability to know what has been done and to be able to develop logical arguments to justify new relationships. Most students, early in the PhD program and sometimes even later in the PhD program and beyond, believe that theory-building is essentially a collection of statements that either someone else has already made or for which someone else has already found empirical evidence. Breaking students out of the mold of relying completely on the extant literature to develop new theory requires a substantial shift in their thinking and the need for students to give themselves the creative license to have original ideas, arguments and examples. While students are inundated with enormous prior literature and structured ways of doing data analysis and research design, by giving themselves the creative license, students can balance the use of prior literature with the development of their own ideas.

Writing is a very important and difficult skill to acquire. What I have to share about writing and several resources that will help with writing and revising empirical journal articles have been presented in chapters 4 and 5.

Other Resources

Insofar as related resources for PhD students go, one good source is Decision Line: http://www.decisionsciences.org/DecisionLine/col-doctoral.htm. Several articles by Varun Grover, four of which have been integrated into chapter 11, are useful and a few others that have caught my eye are: Robey's (2001)[150] answers to PhD students' frequently asked questions (FAQs) and Schneiderjans' (2001)[151] bill of rights for PhD students (yes, you read this correctly: bill of rights!).

Concluding Thoughts

This chapter provides advice to help PhD students face challenges they will encounter in the first two years of the program. One of the biggest challenges is time management. I provided a review and planning document that I have found useful. One of the most important goals of the first two years should be to emerge from the program being as well-rounded as possible in terms of skills. My overall advice could be summed up as: work on research early and often. By using the planning document and focusing specifically on learning goals, rather than just outcomes (e.g., courses or papers), a student can move to the dissertation stage with the skills necessary to produce a high-quality dissertation and continue on the road to success.

Key Takeaways

1. The first two years of the PhD program create and require new ways of thinking and perceiving, which can be immensely exciting—however, the first two years also have the highest attrition/dropout rates
2. One of the main reasons students leave the program is that they fail to manage the first two years effectively and consequently, find the program to be overwhelming with no appear light at the end of the tunnel
3. Survival is frequently tied to being organized, able to meet requirements and performing to an acceptable level in coursework
4. Time management and organization
   i. Without effective time management and organization skills, the PhD program tends to be even more overwhelming, exhausting and creates a feeling of being behind

       constantly

    ii. To deal with this issue, create lists, lists and more lists

        a. Create lists of things to do over a quarter, broken into lists organized by month, broken further into lists by weeks and then, days

        b. These lists can be used to create a planning document at the start of each quarter

5. A planning document (shown in Table 8-1) can be a useful tool for organizational and progress assessments of most students, with the three important elements of this document being:

    i. The faculty mentor(s)

        a. A faculty mentor is not a dissertation advisor

        b. Having different mentors will potentially expose the student to different perspectives on research

    ii. Learning goals

        a. Learning goals are those goals that relate to skills that need to be acquired

        b. Learning goals are important to help students get the opportunity to learn and experience all facets of the PhD program necessary to be successful

        c. Learning goals help students look beyond specific courses and instead, focus on their individual strengths and weaknesses in terms of skills

        d. Failure to confront areas of weakness will result in students avoiding them and favoring those areas they perceive to be their strengths

    iii. Research projects

        a. Collaborative research projects with faculty members are the best way to learn how to do research, especially to acquire tacit knowledge related to conducting research and writing papers

        b. One of the biggest challenges for students is finding time to work on research that is meaningful (i.e., not just papers that satisfy course requirements) where the student will be called upon to work on various aspects of the paper, from theory development to study design to data collection to data analysis to writing

        c. Paying attention to learning goals will allow students and PhD program directors to ensure that every student gets an opportunity to work on various phases of a research project

        d. The topic of the research project matters less than a focus on acquiring key skills

        e. PhD students should discuss this document with a faculty mentor and/or PhD program director three times a year: at the start of fall, spring and summer

6. Summer Research

    i. Summers can be the most valuable time in the first two years because it presents an opportunity to focus heavily on working on research projects as there are typically no classes in the summer

    ii. The first summer is far more crucial than the second summer because it provides an opportunity to bring to life and put into practice the ideas that a student learns in the first year

iii. Students should be encouraged to collect data during the first summer, even if it is for a fairly simple project—such data collection will open the student's eyes to the difficulty associated with collecting data

iv. The second year summer research project can be used to scope out a topic for a dissertation so that students don't fall into a trap of aimlessly wandering in the third year without knowing what to do

v. For PhD program directors: Consider having the comprehensive exams administered at the start of the summer so that the students do not spend the entire summer just preparing for an exam, but rather complete the exam right at the start of the summer so that the rest of the summer can be dedicated to research

7. Being well-rounded

i. PhD students should aim to become well-rounded by the end of the second year—this means first- and second-year PhD students should strive to take themselves outside their comfort zone and do things to address their weaknesses

ii. Two broad sets of skills that students must acquire are: (a) methods and statistics; and (b) theory-building and writing

  a. Methods and statistics
  - Methods and statistics represent the most structured of all skills that a student learns—yet, students may struggle with it for different reasons
  - Know where you stand so you can remedy this weakness, if applicable
  - Working on research and real data almost always trumps textbook knowledge—these skills are best learned and committed to memory through actual practice because practice turns laundry lists of validity threats and so on into actual issues to contend with and resolve

  b. Theory-building and writing
  - Theory-building is the hardest skill to learn
  - There are several good articles on what constitutes strong theory: Bacharach (1989), Dubin (1976), Eisenhardt (1989), Feldman (2004), George and Jones (2000), Langley (1999), Poole and Van de ven (1989), Sutton and Staw (1995), Weick (1989, 1995), and Whetten (1989)
  - Whetten (1989) noted and discussed four building blocks of theory development: *What (constructs), How (relationships), Why (justification) and Who, Where, When (conditions)*
  - One of the important considerations for research is relevance of the problem, with relevance being the focus on phenomena that are interesting, applicable and current (Benbasat and Zmud 1999), thus suggesting the need to focus on problems that are relevant to today's organizations and society
  - Weick (1995) suggests that, in addition to the pursuit of theory, it is important to recognize *theorizing* as it represents the interim struggles of scientific discovery and "consists of activities like abstracting, generalizing, relating, selecting, explaining, synthesizing, and idealizing" (p. 389)

- Underlying many of the excellent articles on theory and theory development is a theme that theory-building is both an art and a science and is nearly impossible to articulate
- Good theory-building comes only with a great deal of practice and through apprenticeship and through granting oneself the creative license to create new theory
- Chapters 4 and 5 present an extensive discussion and point to resources that will help with building writing skills

8. Other good sources for PhD students and PhD program directors are:
   i. *Decision Line*: http://www.decisionsciences.org/DecisionLine/col-doctoral.htm
   ii. Varun Grover's essays on doctoral student success (see chapter 11)
   iii. Robey's (2001) answers to PhD students' frequently asked questions (FAQs)
   iv. Schneiderjans' (2001) bill of rights for PhD students

CHAPTER 9

MANAGING THE PHD PROGRAM: YEAR 3 AND BEYOND

One of the major differences in going from the second year into the third year of the PhD program is the end of the structured road and the start of a highly unstructured one. This chapter discusses the challenges of the lack of structure and some suggestions on how to deal with those challenges. I also offer some general thoughts about pursuing a dissertation, which is the primary activity of PhD students from the third year onwards. I organize my advice into five areas:

1. Third-year slump
   i.   Take a break
   ii. Impose structure
2. Dissertation
3. Collecting more data than meets the dissertation requirements
4. Learn to write
5. Dissertation as papers

1. Third-year Slump

Many different terms have been used to refer to one of the most dangerous situations associated with the third year of the PhD program. Be it the "third-year slump" or "third-year black hole" or "third-year blues," they all refer to one of the biggest problems that befall many PhD students. The first two years of most PhD programs create enormous time and deadline pressure on a constant basis—almost like overfilling a balloon with air. The third year, especially after the comprehensive exams, is like letting the air out of a balloon. A major challenge for students in the first two years is to react and respond to the constant external pressure to deliver. In contrast, in the 3rd year, the students have to be driven by an internal desire to perform. For many, the burnout from the first two years can turn the third year into a slump in terms of effort and accomplishments, as they try to recover from the constant pressure of the first two years or enjoy the sudden lack of pressure such that they (students) forget about the dissertation.

Another reason why the third-year black hole exists is the shift from the structured phase of the program to the unstructured phase. Even if students are working collaboratively with faculty members on research projects, the first two years tend to be fairly structured. The beginning of the third year is typically marked by the pursuit of a specific dissertation topic or question, even if the broad topic was already known before the student gets to the third year. In the third year, students spend a lot of time reading and have a hard time measuring progress. The third year thus presents one of riskiest times in the program—a time when lack of progress can turn a student who was previously on course to be successful into one who fails to graduate.

There are two possible preventive measures for the ills that can befall third-year PhD students:

i. Take a Break

I am a strong advocate of a substantial break after the comprehensive exam "pass" verdict is announced. Unfortunately, the verdict tends to come in the fall when the semester has already begun. I still favor perhaps one or even two 4-day breaks away from everything that allows a student to decompress and enjoy the fruits of his or her labor. Perhaps just as beneficial would be two such breaks between a few days of work.

ii. Impose Structure

If planning was important in the first two years, it is imperative in the third year and beyond. The first two years have tremendous structure built into them through course work, whereas the third year, from which point there is no course work, has less structure. There are many ways to impose structure. Goal-setting research can serve as a useful guide in this process: have specific, short-term goals. Quite like the lists advocated before, here too, I call for layers of lists. The idea of specific, short-term goals can be operationalized as:

a. Have a plan for the semester
b. Break the semester plan into a monthly plan
c. Break the monthly plan into a weekly plan
d. Break the weekly plan into a daily plan
e. Recognize that plans will need to adapt and evolve
f. Recognize that tasks take a lot longer to accomplish than one usually expects (or plans)

The planning document discussed earlier is one way to create a plan for each semester. However, the planning document is far more abstract and needs to be converted to actionable items that can help you accomplish the goals in the planning document. You should take the initiative to develop abstract (semester) and concrete (monthly, weekly and daily) plans to keep you on track and working to finish your program on time.

2. Dissertation

Students vary greatly in how much time it takes them to find a suitable dissertation topic. Even students who do everything they are supposed to do in the first two years may meander for a long time before finding their dissertation topic. There is unfortunately no magical solution to this problem. However, a few different people have provided excellent suggestions in this regard. Gordon Davis' book (2nd edition co-authored with Clyde Parker)[152] titled "Writing the Doctoral Dissertation" is a must-read for every PhD student. He discusses various matters related to completing a successful dissertation, such as choosing a topic, choosing an advisor, forming a committee, how to make steady progress and how to measure progress. One of the reasons for the black hole described earlier is the lack of a dissertation topic. Gordon (2003, p. 186),[153] has spoken eloquently on this issue: "Another difficulty for candidates to avoid may be putting off topic selection. For this there may be no fixed answer. The serious mistake, however, would be mentally segmenting the graduate study process into a series of disconnected phases such as course work, field exams and, only then, thought of a dissertation topic. One would better be counseled to keep rough notes on dissertation possibilities throughout the program, possibilities which may change throughout the early substantive and methodological course work. What a fix to be in, to be starting from zero after subject matter and methodological courses are completed, then trying to think up research possibilities and unfamiliar methods to discuss with yourself or other potential advisors! (Actually, some institutions, possibly your own, include discussion of research plans as part of written and oral qualifying exams.)"

Many useful ideas are also presented in *Decision Line* articles targeted toward helping PhD students not only find a dissertation topic but also pursue it effectively. Issues that get excellent treatment include, as noted earlier, choosing a topic, finding an advisor, forming a committee, monitoring your progress and taking corrective action as needed. The articles that caught my eye are: Gordon Davis' (2000)[154] overview of his book, Aronson's (2001)[155] article on working on the dissertation, and Grover and Malhotra's (2003)[156] article on advisor-student interactions.

In a *Decision Line* article, Robey (2001, p. 11)[157] noted: "Choose your advisor first and allow the advisor to develop a topic with you… You must also understand that the dissertation is not the only research you will ever do. If you have trouble deciding among different topics, pick the topic that is most timely or most feasible and choose it as your dissertation. You can do the remaining topics later if they still seem interesting… Choose a dissertation topic that is sufficiently interesting so that you will be motivated to work on it. Don't make it your life's work. Few people become so well known for their dissertations that their later careers are materially affected. Smart students (and advisors) view the dissertation as part of doctoral education, so a good dissertation is one from which the student learns and which is finished in reasonable time." The above point is frequently summarized as: "a good dissertation is a done dissertation." However, I don't necessarily agree with everything Robey says above. While it is indeed important for a dissertation to be completed and it forms an important part of doctoral education, I believe that a good dissertation is one that leads to publishable papers and other papers that can make the topic area the focus of your life's work, as I discussed in chapter 2. Grover's chapter 11 also discusses the issue of a done dissertation.

3. Collecting More Data Than Meets The Dissertation Requirements

As I talked about in chapter 2, it is important to think of research projects more broadly than narrow research studies where data are being collected. If one is conducting longitudinal field research, the importance of collecting more data than goes into just a dissertation becomes very critical. More broadly speaking, designing a study or studies with more data than what goes into the dissertation is thus critical to generating multiple many publishable papers from one research project. By collecting a lot of additional data in the 3rd and/or4th years of the PhD program, you can fuel several years of papers. Although not by design, I stumbled on ideas for other papers based on data I had collected but had no active plan to use in my dissertation papers. For instance, gender and age differences in technology adoption were direct off-shoots from data I had collected as part of my dissertation. Similarly, I had collected other data that I have still not used in papers but could certainly use in the future! See chapter 2 for more detail on this issue.

4. Learn To Write

I have already talked about writing an academic journal article in chapter 4. The dissertation represents a unique opportunity to do that. Many students rely far too much on the advisor to do the writing or providing editorial suggestions to the point where they are not willing to or able to take ownership of the writing process. For many, learning to write may be the last major hurdle to scholarship and all too often, a hurdle to becoming a scholar that they may never scale. There are several excellent resources on writing better—many of which are discussed in chapter 4.

5. Dissertation As Papers

The last point of discussion here is regarding how a dissertation should be organized. It is interesting to compare the more traditional behavioral and social sciences research dissertations with the more modern form of a dissertation that is organized as papers.

The traditional approach for a dissertation uses the following seven sections:
i.   Introduction
ii. Literature review
iii. Model development
iv. Method
v.   Results
vi. Discussion
vii. Conclusions

Such a traditional approach builds on an older model of crafting papers from a dissertation wherein a literature review could be published as a standalone review paper, when a model development (theory) paper could be published as a standalone paper and when the empirical test of the model could be the third standalone paper. Although it is possible to publish review papers (see chapter 18 where Dr. Burton-Jones talks about "who needs data?"), given the small number of papers that have been published under this umbrella and the nature of a review paper (compared to a "literature review" section of a traditional dissertation), a traditional literature review is unlikely to lead to a premier journal publication in this day and age. Further, with the pressure on journals to use their pages carefully and consequently, to enforce page limits explicitly (e.g., *Management Science*) or implicitly (e.g., most editors typically evaluate the length to contribution ratio), literature review papers have a limited likelihood of publication.

Similarly, a model development paper (sans data) is likely to evoke the reaction of "this paper is great but come back with an empirical test." Effectively, such a reaction calls for the merger of the model development with the empirical test. Further, the pressure to write shorter papers means clear, crisp literature review sections will need to be embedded in the paper. Many journals, e.g., *Academy of Management Journal*, don't have much of a literature review section—just the core points integrated into the introduction and theory development sections.

The current pressures for journal publications warrant a dissertation that can be converted to articles that can be quickly sent out for journal review. This can be best accomplished by a focus on a dissertation format with the following sections:
i.   Introduction
ii.   Paper #1
iii. Paper #2…
iv.   Paper #n
v.   Conclusions

There is nothing magical about three papers for a dissertation although I have frequently heard this model referred to as a "three-essay" or "three-paper" model. It can be two papers or four papers. Such a dissertation has an overarching introduction that scopes the broader problem and catalogs potential unanswered questions that might be tackled in each of the different papers. Each paper is a self-contained empirical journal article that is in the neighborhood of the length that might be expected at various journals—about 40 pages double-spaced. Similar to an overarching introduction, a conclusions section presents insights at a higher level of abstraction than any of the individual papers and ties the insights to the introduction. If more than one paper is based on the same data set, there is sure to be some redundancy across the papers.

An added advantage of the multiple paper model for a dissertation is that, at the completion of the dissertation, there are three papers ready to be submitted. There is no protracted pursuit of crafting individual papers from the traditional monolithic dissertation. Of course, I would recommend choosing the longest moratorium so that University Microfilms International (UMI) delays making your dissertation freely available, thus ensuring that ideas from the dissertation papers are not intentionally or unintentionally stolen, especially considering it is far easier to steal ideas out of a dissertation following the multi-paper (multi-essay) model when compared to a traditional dissertation.

Last but not least, writing the dissertation as a series of papers helps students learn what they need to know to be successful—i.e., crafting good journal articles. Learning to write a traditional dissertation in today's environment fails to focus on the valuable journal article writing skills that are crucial to the continued success of an academic, but instead focuses on writing a "book" that no one will publish or read.

Concluding Thoughts

The third year and beyond in the PhD program is quite unlike any other time in a PhD student's life. No undergraduate or masters or early PhD program experiences provide a feel for how unstructured the later part of a PhD program can be. Managing this time effectively and completing a good dissertation, while collecting data that will feed papers that go beyond the dissertation, is an important way to get a jumpstart on the road to success as you begin your career as a new assistant professor.

Key Takeaways

1. One of the major differences in going beyond the second year into the third year of the PhD program is the end of the structured road and the start of a highly unstructured path—this transition is riddled with challenges
2. Third-year slump
    i.   For many, the burnout from the first two years can turn the third year into a slump in terms of effort and accomplishments as they try to recover from the constant pressure of the first two years
    ii. Another reason why the third-year slump exists is the shift from the structured to the unstructured—because of having to choose a dissertation topic, in the third year, students spend a lot of time reading and have a hard time measuring progress
    iii. Keep rough notes on dissertation possibilities throughout the program to help in avoiding mindless searches for a dissertation topic
    iv. Two preventive measures that can help avoid the pitfalls associated with the third year are: take a break and impose structure
        a. Take a break: After the pass verdict on the comprehensive exams has been rendered, take one or even two 4-day breaks away from everything
        b. Impose structure: Have specific goals and have short-term goals
            - Have a plan for the semester
            - Break the semester plan down into a monthly plan
            - Break the monthly plan into a weekly plan
            - Break the weekly plan into a daily plan
            - Recognize that plans will need to adapt and evolve
            - Recognize that tasks take a lot longer to accomplish than you might usually expect (or plan)
    v.   The planning document discussed earlier, i.e., Table 8-1, is one way to create a plan for each semester
3. Dissertation
    i.   Students vary greatly in how much time it takes them to find a suitable topic
    ii. There are many useful ideas presented in *Decision Line* articles and in Gordon Davis' book titled "Writing the Doctoral Dissertation" that provide guidance for selecting a dissertation topic, choosing an advisor, forming a committee, how to make steady

       progress and how to measure progress
- iii. Choose a dissertation topic that is sufficiently interesting so that you will be motivated to work on it
- iv. A good dissertation can lead to other papers that can make the topic area the focus of much of your career, especially early career

4. Collecting more data than meets the dissertation requirements (see also chapter 2)
- i. It is important to think of research projects more broadly than narrow research studies where data are being collected
- ii. If one is conducting longitudinal field research, the importance of collecting more data than goes into just a dissertation becomes very critical
- iii. Learn to write: The dissertation represents a unique opportunity to learn to write without too much reliance on an advisor

5. Dissertation as papers
- i. The traditional dissertation is organized around an introduction, literature review, model development, method, results, discussion and conclusions—this approach builds on an older model of potential papers from dissertations when a literature review could be published as a standalone review paper, the model development (theory) could be published as a standalone paper and the empirical test of the model could be a third standalone paper
- ii. The current pressures for journal publications warrant a dissertation that can be converted to articles that can be sent out for journal review soon after graduation (without taking 1-2 years to carve out papers)
  - a. This can be best accomplished best by a focus on a dissertation format that is: Introduction, Paper #1, Paper #2… Paper #n, Conclusions
  - b. This model is typically referred to as a "three-essay" or "three-paper" model—however, there is nothing magical about the number three and dissertations based on this model can be composed of two papers or four papers
  - c. Each paper is a self-contained empirical journal article that is in the neighborhood of the length that might be expected at various journals—i.e., about 40 double-spaced pages
- iii. An added advantage of the multiple paper model for a dissertation is that at the completion of the dissertation, there are three papers ready to be submitted
- iv. Choose the longest moratorium so that University Microfilms International (UMI) delays making your dissertation freely available, thus ensuring that ideas from the dissertation papers are not intentionally or unintentionally stolen
- v. Writing the dissertation as a series of papers helps students learn what they need to know to be successful—i.e., writing good journal articles

CHAPTER 10

IF I ONLY KNEW THEN…
Tracy Ann Sykes

Assistant Professor
Walton College of Business
University of Arkansas
Fayetteville, AR
tracy@tracyannsykes.com

When Dr. Venkatesh asked me to contribute a chapter to this book, I was both honored (of course!) and completely flabbergasted. Being a relatively newly minted graduate of a PhD program, I still have trouble seeing myself in the role of an advisor to others. However, it eventually occurred to me that the things I could write confidently about were those things related to my own experiences in the PhD program—both the good and the not so good. The old saying that hindsight is 20/20 is a cliché because it is so true. Much of what I am going to write about could be discussed in the "Research" section of this book, but I am writing this chapter from a student's perspective and I truly hope it is of value to other students. I am going to discuss several things that I think I did well or got right in my PhD program and several things that, had I a time machine, I'd probably do differently.

Things I got right:
1. Worked on many projects, but only within a few streams
2. Advanced the portfolio: Never wasted an opportunity
3. Worked with organizations
4. Kept a big book of ideas
5. Didn't allow myself to get discouraged

Things I'd do differently:
1. Deal with the perfectionism-procrastination paradox
2. Get on top of time management/deadline issues
3. Risk breadth for depth
4. Balance work and life
5. Get over the impostor syndrome

Things I Got Right

When I graduated in 2009, I was told that I had a strong curriculum vita (CV), especially as it pertains to publications, a focused area of expertise and probably most important: a healthy research pipeline. Because these are all things that are discussed in other chapters of this book, I'll focus on discussing the five things that I believe I did right that helped me on this road.

Of course there might be other reasons, but these are the things that remain most prominent in my mind as things that I actively pursued and used to build a stronger CV.

1. Worked On Many Projects, But Only Within A Few Streams

When you first enter a PhD program, it is like stepping into a different world that operates under slightly different rules. Instead of focusing on clear, small goals as one does in high school or in an undergraduate or master's degree, one is inundated with new information at an alarming rate. I remember thinking that I could feel my brain trying to rewire itself to handle all the information and organize it so that it would make sense. Even more amazing is that I found most of it fascinating. The more I read, the more engaged I was in wanting to read more. Every article, every book gave me a new direction to explore. Thankfully, I got control of myself fairly early (due to my advisor and PhD student mentors) and put a moratorium on branching out into every direction at once.

I was very lucky. I found a topic area—namely, social networks—that captured my imagination and happened to be generating interest in the information systems field even when I was an undergraduate student, ever before my entry into the PhD program, when I was working with professors as a volunteer research assistant. I found an article by Nahapiet and Ghoshal (1998)[158] that really spoke to me. I've always been a people person and most interested in individual behaviors, i.e., the idea that the connections between individuals formed a type of capital that we use every day seemed to be somehow intuitively correct. I began to read articles in every topic with this lens in mind, wondering: how could this work be advanced by looking at the issue from a social networks viewpoint? This was despite my advisor, rather than because of him! He was adamant that this new "lens" was problematic, not very interesting and not at all related to information systems, which is my primary field. Most people would have given up! However, besides being a bookworm, I am very determined. I held my ground with my advisor and I like to think he's finally come around. Ultimately, I kept my focus on exploring social networks as a lens to explore information systems topics. I used almost every course that had a paper requirement to further this focus. Across a few courses, I took a paper and continued to develop it from one course to the next. I feel that this really helped me to gain a depth of knowledge and experience in a single, broad subject area, which gave my CV a maturity that working in several different areas might not have.

2. Advanced The Portfolio: Never Wasted An Opportunity

This point is related to the one above. I never let an opportunity pass me by when it came to building my portfolio of achievements. "Aim for the moon. If you miss, you may hit a star"[159] were words I took to heart. I approached every paper, even if only for a class, as if it were for the broader information systems audience of a top-tier journal. One paper[160] developed in a class during my first year ended up being re-worked and sent to the *International Conference on Information Systems* (ICIS), which is widely regarded as the premier information systems conference. Every opportunity to work with a senior student or professor was taken, so long as it had some component that matched my research interests. In my PhD program, one component of the dreaded comprehensive exams was to prepare a grant proposal based on a call for proposals from the National Science Foundation (NSF) in one week. My prior focus on social networks actually made this daunting task easier in that I found a way to incorporate social networks into the proposal, which saved me from having to do a lot of new work on writing up a theoretical background section. Further, many of the ideas I used from this mock proposal ended up in my dissertation, although in a somewhat different form. I asked to be involved in a small research grant opportunity so that I could have something related to grants on my CV; also, of course, because it involved at least one of my areas of interest. Finally, I was told about a science assistant position with the NSF. With a little prodding from my advisor, who thought it a fabulous idea, I applied and got the position! This helped me to build a CV that was different from the competition, with a more complete portfolio of achievements.

3. Worked With Organizations

Working with organizations has been vital to my research productivity. It has allowed me to collect data that is suitable for top journals from a very early stage in my PhD program as well as help me really round out my education. Collecting data from organizations, rather than from students, laboratory experiments or simulations provides a host of situations that must be navigated carefully. Every time I've collected data from organizations, several issues have arisen that throw my original plans for the experience out the window. Much like any battle, original plans never survive the first encounter with the "enemy." Learning to deal with these issues has given me greater insight into problems organizations face, ways organizations operate and given me ideas as to what future directions my research might take that would benefit them as well as my portfolio.

With my time machine, I learned that I worked well with organizations even before I entered the PhD program. I was co-teaching an MBA course (as the only instructor on the ground) in Finland, back in 2000 to a class of about 70 students. Many of the students worked at Nokia and other leading European firms. I befriended many of them and some of them were of great help as they rose through the ranks of the organization. To this date, I collect data with the help of some of the people I met before I ever enrolled in the program! Go back through your rolodex (or whatever electronic version of it that you have), you never know who could be a great potential data collection contact.

Working with organizations has also afforded me opportunities to network with managers and employees that can be mined as sources of information or future research opportunities. I think working with organizations really affords us great potential as a field to be of practical as well as theoretical relevance. By understanding the problems that organizations deal with on a daily basis, we can better tailor our research toward addressing their problems. Having our research considered useful by organizations furthers this symbiotic cycle.

4. Kept A Big Book Of Ideas

The idea for this came from my early schooling where I learned to take a lot of notes and to journal daily. I found early on that I usually have creative ideas on and off depending on lectures I attend, articles or books I read, newspaper articles, discussions with peers or friends and the list goes on. I blame it on an attention deficit problem I've always had. My thoughts are often hyperactive and it's hard to keep track of them sometimes. From my first seminar in the PhD program, I started keeping a small notebook with me wherever I went. In this notebook, I would jot down thoughts and ideas as they came to me related to classes, discussions, etc. Not all, in fact, most of these ideas were not suitable for further development, but some were! Best of all, because I had written them down, I didn't lose them when my attention wandered to something else. I think being widely read really helps us generate the most ideas. Also, just because an idea that you have at one point seems to be pointless or has a lot of problems doesn't mean that somewhere down the line, with added experience, skills and maturity, that it won't be the kernel of something really interesting.

5. Didn't Allow Myself To Get Discouraged

Perhaps the most important thing that allowed me to develop a strong CV and healthy research pipeline was not allowing myself to get discouraged, or at least not letting myself remain discouraged for long. PhD programs are excellent proving grounds for mental fortitude. You are constantly bombarded with information, tasked with assignments of one type or another to the point where you may even forget what day it is. At least, I often felt this way. When something didn't go the way I expected, an assignment was proving too difficult or an exam seemed to be impossible, I kept myself focused on what I really wanted—the PhD degree. I can easily understand why it's called a "terminal degree" because often I felt that the program was going to kill me! All joking aside, I was able to keep my mind and eye on the prize, as it were, and used it to motivate myself, especially when I was at my lowest. Having been very active in terms of writing papers in the program, I also received many rejections and these did (and still do) tend to get me down. At such times, I have to work on picking myself back up and keep going. This has yet to come easy for me.

Being stubborn can be an asset. I didn't let my advisor's initial dislike of my topic area stop me from pursuing it, and I didn't let setbacks in any form keep me from getting back up and trying twice as hard. Of course, the line between being an asset and being a problem is a fine one. Students should definitely listen to their advisors and if they find themselves in a similar situation, they need to be able to explain their reasons for wanting to go down the paths they want to pursue. If you can't craft a solid argument, then you probably shouldn't pursue it. If every time you bring the topic up and everyone says it's a bad idea, it probably is. Don't be discouraged; figure out a way to re-tool your original idea into something that is more acceptable to your audience (and advisor).

Things I'd Do Differently

Of course, no experience is perfect. I had many ups and downs in my program. Thankfully, I was able to get through the program despite them. As with the things that I think I did well, there are probably a whole host of things that I could have done better, or that had detrimental effects on my progress, but the five items I discuss here are the things that stand out in my memory as having caused me more problems than I like to think about.

1. Deal With The Perfectionism-Procrastination Paradox

I think the number one thing that increased my stress levels, caused me to miss deadlines and was just one of the biggest issues that I had and still have to deal with is the perfectionism-procrastination paradox, especially as it pertains to writing. I'm a perfectionist when it comes to writing. I spend hours and hours writing, editing and rewriting before allowing anyone to even see what I've written. Of course, you'd never believe it if you see the reviews I usually get for my papers. This is an old habit and a truly horrible habit when you are in a PhD program wherein you are expected to write quite a lot. Why? Because when you don't want anyone to look at your writing until it is "perfect," no one will be able to offer guidance, critique or anything else that could actually help achieve a better product. It leads to a situation where you know you *have* to write something, you know you won't be happy with whatever you end up writing and consequently, you put it off in favor of anything else you could be doing that makes you feel productive. Like reading more articles or even washing your car! This particular habit probably extended average writing times on any given paper, assignment, and even this chapter (for instance!), or whatever I was supposed to be writing by at least a week. My time machine should help me change this. I think I would have been more productive or at least had more free time. I have since learned that it is much better to just "bang out" a draft, knowing it won't be perfect or even great, but at least I will have something. Further, if you are working with co-authors, at least they will have something tangible that they can comment on or edit and keep the process moving forward. Here's a little tip from someone (me) who used to edit journal manuscripts for professors: editing is always easier than writing (composing).

In a related vein, the best way to improve your writing is to just write. The more you write, the better you'll be at it. The better you are at it, the quicker you're likely to get and the more you'll be able to draft quickly to get feedback from your advisor, co-author, etc. Several chapters in this book speak to the issue of writing and writing well—in particular, I think chapter 4 that provides an outlining tool to write a paper is one that I personally found very useful.

2. Get On Top Of Time Management/Deadline Issues

As I mentioned earlier, I often felt overwhelmed by the sheer amount of work and number of claims on my time in a given day, week or semester from classes, outside readings, teaching, work for my assistantship, time for family and on some days, even sleep. Sleep was usually the first thing that got severely curtailed, followed by time spent with family and friends, followed by any readings outside of a class context and then if time were really crunched, I'd start prioritizing class work into categories along the lines of "must put 100% effort in," "can try for a B" and even "do as little as possible to still get a passing grade" (perhaps now that I have my PhD, I can admit it publicly!). I am almost certain that most PhD programs actively try to overwhelm a student in the first year. Perhaps this is to show students that they can, in fact, survive almost impossible amounts of work. However, looking back, I now realize that much of my being overwhelmed was due to not having the best time management skills.

The three skills that I think would have helped me the most and what I'm still trying to master are: planning ahead, prioritizing and creating contingency plans, whenever possible. Planning ahead is so important and it's something with which I still struggle. The thing that helps me get more done these days is creating several to-do lists, each with a different time frame as focus. I have monthly to-dos, weekly to-dos and even daily to-dos. By breaking up my tasks into smaller bite-size pieces for the daily to-do list, I stop dwelling on ALL of the stuff that I have to get accomplished in a short amount of time. I just focus on getting the tasks done. This saves a lot of worry, time and wasted effort.

Next is prioritizing the to-dos. One pattern of behavior that I sometimes fell into (and have heard others doing the same) is trying to juggle several big projects at the same time. Inevitably, the outcome is doing less than optimally on each. If you can break it into one major task to accomplish per day and stick to it, you end up being a lot happier with the end product than when trying to spend just a few hours on each of three big tasks. Today, work on project A, get the high-priority item done! Tomorrow, work on the high-priority item for project B, etc. Of course, sometimes things happen or are scheduled in such a way as to make it necessary to work a few hours on multiple big tasks but if you keep up with your planning, this should be kept to a minimum.

Finally, contingency planning is also very important and probably, the hardest of the time management skills. I think it is supposed to come to us over time as we experience more work and varying situations. I'm still trying to get the hang of it. The one thing that seems to help me is trying to plan at least one hour a day for "catch-up" work. If my daily to-do list has three items but someone unexpectedly drops by my office for feedback or to give me an update on some project, I will not have used my allocated time to do my tasks. So, I try to have the catch-up time in order to finish up. Sometimes this works but often it doesn't seem to be enough—but as I said, I'm still learning.

3. Risk Breadth For Depth

Sticking to my limited areas of research interests allowed me to build a strong portfolio. However, that being said, I did eventually add two areas to my program of research, in addition to social networking: developing country contexts and health informatics (although still with a social network focus). I didn't add these until later in my program. I wish it were possible to use my time machine and try to get myself to do this earlier. Until I added these two areas to my areas of focus, I was in danger of being labeled a one-trick pony that was too focused on one area that, not so strangely, was related to my dissertation work.

Depth helped me to establish myself but breadth is important to show diversity and an ability to work in multiple distinct but related areas.

4. Balance Work And Life

I hate to say it, but one reason I think that I was successful in my PhD program was that I didn't have a lot of work-life balance. Mostly, my life was work and I didn't have a spouse or children so I wasn't taking time away from anything on account of my PhD program. Although, I do now have a neurotic cat that can't stand the sight of manuscripts—if I leave white paper out, he turns it into confetti. If I could do it over, I would definitely try to achieve more balance across work and non-work activities. I wish I had read Gordon Davis' chapter in this book (chapter 19) before I ever started my program or at least during my program! Of course, I would have achieved greater balance if I also had those all-important time management skills.

When I had interviews or campus visits, I was humbled to be asked: "How is your CV so strong?" How do you answer that type of question? If you say you were just that good, you are being arrogant. If you say it was because you didn't have a lot of outside interests and worked long hours 7 days a week, you sound like you have no life (and are a boring person!). I remember answering the question in a few ways, mostly that I did a lot of work, didn't have a lot of claims on my time that wasn't related to my program and, of course, was lucky. I was counseled at some point by a potential future colleague to not say anything related to luck as it made me sound less sure of my skills. I guess there is no 100% right answer.

If I could go back, I'd definitely make some changes—not huge, but some. I think I would set aside one evening a week to do something fun—like go to a movie, a bookstore or coffee shop—and just relax. I do have many interests outside of work but for a variety of reasons, these interests took a backseat to my PhD program and related work. I think I could have balanced work and life better if I had simply set aside some time each week to do something fun. This time would be inviolate and not to be used for work, ever. I did learn that if you don't have these breaks planned, you can start resenting whatever it is you are working on. This is especially problematic when it happens to be your dissertation!

5. Get Over The Impostor Syndrome

Feel like you are a fraud? That you ended up in your PhD program by accident and that soon someone is going to figure out they made a mistake by admitting you? These and similar feelings are quite common to many people, especially academics. It is called impostor syndrome, a psychological phenomenon where people have difficulty internalizing their accomplishments. Impostor syndrome is something that I still occasionally feel. I like to think that most people do in the early stages of a career. It caused me to doubt myself a lot during my PhD program. Even today, if I have to give a talk in front of other academics or experts, I go in thinking that I'm about to make a complete fool of myself because surely the people to whom I'm going to be presenting are all smarter than me!

The amount of time and energy I spent convincing myself that I didn't know what I was doing (writing a paper, preparing a presentation, summarizing articles, etc.) makes me sick. I could have finished most tasks quicker, been a lot happier and not struggled so much! If you have these feelings of being a fraud, sit yourself down and give yourself a firm talking to. It isn't true. Most everyone feels that way at some point or another and every endeavor that you carry out successfully, every accomplishment, every triumph that you earn needs to be viewed as the signs of competence, ability and worth that they actually are. The more you sit around telling yourself that you shouldn't be where you are and that you can't accomplish what needs to be accomplished, the more likely you are to convince yourself that you shouldn't and that you can't—this is the stuff of which self-fulfilling prophecies are made. There are enough real trials and tribulations on the road to attaining a PhD or tenure that you don't need to make up more.

Impostor syndrome also had the bad side effect of making me believe that I was not capable so when I faced real problems, I spent a lot of precious time thinking that the problems were signs that I didn't belong in the program, rather than seeking help to address them. One challenge I faced was with statistics. I was convinced that I was a math dummy and it was just another sign that I was attempting to do something that I wasn't equipped to handle. Thankfully, I had good friends and mentors who convinced me that I wasn't being "dumb" and that I should look into the reasons for my difficulties. In doing so, I found that I have a mild form of dyscalculia (like dyslexia, but with numbers) and had a huge hole in my mathematical training (I never took a trigonometry course). This left me with a deep feeling of not being able to handle any mathematical courses and statistics was close enough (to mathematics) as far as I was concerned. After getting tested and learning these things about myself, I was able to learn how to be more confident with statistics and other math-related topics. Today, I pride myself on my data analysis skills, especially as it relates to handling complex network data. I also learned that my style of working could be improved to compensate for my attention deficit disorder—even nowadays, I work for about 20 to 30 minutes and then take a break for about 10 minutes. These "breaks" are often my working on another project or work task, but switching to different tasks helps me better concentrate on them and has improved my productivity. If I had tackled the problem from the beginning, I would have wasted a lot less time!

Being aware of our own deficits is good, but manufacturing ones that aren't there is not.

Nowadays, when I accomplish something, a journal submission that comes back with a revise-and-resubmit verdict, a good idea or some project that has been finished, I make sure to tell myself: I did this and it is good. Reminding myself of my worth and accomplishments means that I waste a lot less time worrying about the PhD police coming to take my diploma away from me. It also reminds me to congratulate co-workers and students on their own achievements because they might be dealing with similar issues.

Concluding Thoughts

In this chapter, I outlined the five things that I think I did well in my PhD program that allowed me to complete the program with a strong CV. Those are the five things I would do again if I had to do it all over again. I also presented the five things that I would do differently if I knew then what I know now. My hope is that these nuggets of experience will help people who are considering entering a PhD program or students already in a PhD program to perform at their optimum or at least help them navigate some of the pitfalls that can be part of the experience.

Key Takeaways

1. Things I got right
   i. Worked on many projects, but only within a few streams
      a. Use every course with a paper requirement to further your primary research focus
      b. Develop papers across multiple classes
   ii. Advanced the portfolio: Never wasted an opportunity
      a. Submit class papers to conferences
      b. Take every opportunity to work with senior students and faculty members
      c. If possible, convert work done on the comprehensive exams (e.g., a paper or grant proposal) into conference or journal submissions or use it in your dissertation
      d. Consider external sources of training, such as working for the National Science Foundation
   iii. Worked with organizations
      a. Working with organizations can help with research productivity as well as round out your education
      b. Like any battle, original battle plans never survive the first encounter with the "enemy"
      c. Learning to deal with organizational data collection issues provides greater insight into problems organizations face, ways organizations operate and can provide ideas as to what future directions one's research might take

      d. Working with organizations also affords opportunities to network with managers and employees that can be mined as sources of information or future research opportunities

  iv. Kept a big book of ideas: Creative ideas can come at any time

      a. Keep a small notebook with you so you can capture these ideas when they come

  v. Didn't allow myself to get discouraged

      a. Keep yourself focused on what you're there for—i.e., the PhD degree

      b. Be stubborn and defend your ideas but always be willing to listen and take advice from your mentors—if everyone says it's a bad idea, it probably is

      c. Don't be discouraged if everyone says an idea is bad—find ways to re-tool it into something that is more acceptable

2. Things I'd do differently

  i. Dealing with the perfection-procrastination paradox

      a. Don't get mired in trying to achieve perfection before you allow your work to be reviewed—you will avoid your work, knowing that you cannot achieve perfection

      b. Let go of your work (for peer/faculty member/co-author review) sooner—if you are working with co-authors, make sure you have something tangible on which they can comment

      c. Editing is always easier than writing (composing)—worry first about getting something down on paper

  ii. Getting on top of time management/deadline issues

      a. Plan ahead by creating to-do lists at different levels of abstraction—monthly, weekly and daily

      b. Prioritize what you need to get done and break it into small modules

      c. Create contingency plans—schedule some time for "catch-up" work each day, knowing that you likely won't get to everything on your to-do list

  iii. Risking breadth for depth

      a. Avoid the risk of being labeled a "one-trick pony" by establishing multiple (2 or 3) streams early, rather than later, in the PhD program

      b. Breadth is important to show diversity and an ability to work in multiple distinct but related streams

  iv. Balancing work and life: Take some time to do something fun one night a week—doing so will help achieve some balance between work and life, helps relieve stress and avoids the danger of being labeled boring

  v. Getting over the impostor syndrome

      a. Impostor syndrome is a psychological phenomenon where people have difficulty internalizing their accomplishments

      b. Don't undermine yourself by not recognizing the hard work you do

      c. Recognize your weakness and identify ways to compensate for or correct them, but don't neglect to celebrate your strengths and accomplishments as well

CHAPTER 11

FOUR ESSAYS ON SUCCESS IN A DOCTORAL PROGRAM: A MODEL OF SUCCESS, AVOIDING MISTAKES, TAKING STOCK AND NETWORKING

Varun Grover

William S. Lee Distinguished Professor of Information Systems
College of Business and Behavioral Science
Clemson University
Clemson, SC
vgrover@clemson.edu

In having the good fortune of interacting with numerous doctoral students over the past 22+ years, I am always amazed by the exceptions. There are some doctoral students who are truly exceptional. They can contextualize, run data analysis, and write and package research. They can juggle multiple projects and manage their program well. They have a positive "can do" attitude. They get it—and they get it early in the program. These students are tremendous assets to faculty members as most of their learning comes through doing and not through micromanagement by faculty members. The other extreme also surprises me. These are students who are lost and flounder in a maze of projects and program requirements. Pushing them hard often backfires, as these students can't seem to get their work to the requisite level. Good programs weed these students out during or before the comprehensive exam stage—but some still make it through. Such students are difficult for faculty members who want them to do well but don't know how to deal with their lack of competence and/or motivation. Such students can sap energy and productivity. Most students, however, don't fall into the extremes (by definition) and evolve through the process.

Ideally, faculty preference would be to identify and nurture the "exceptional" students. However, I have always maintained that identifying these exceptional exceptions at the input stage is very tough. We can evaluate the quantitative performance metrics but we cannot assess the intangibles very well—like motivation, ability to deal with unstructured problems, ability to package and market ideas, and systematic thinking, among others. Often, we get it right through interviews—but occasionally, we get it wrong. Once entered into the program, there is a dual responsibility of the student and faculty to culminate the process in a "win-win" outcome for all involved. Doctoral programs can have significant multiplier effects on institutions, their research culture and reputation. There is a tipping point that can spawn a virtuous cycle with lots of the "good" students or a vicious one with lots of the "not so good" ones.

This chapter focuses on some guidelines for doctoral students to push themselves up the exceptional scale. It can also serve as a guide to faculty members on how best to direct doctoral students so that the relationship may be mutually beneficial. There are four essays. These were done at various times over the past decade and reflect my thinking regarding doctoral study. They were published in *Decision Line* (a newsletter of the Decision Sciences Institute). The first essay[161] represents a "model" of success for doctoral students, which identifies the core aspects of a successful student. The second essay[162] identifies 10 common mistakes made by doctoral students in managing their program. The third essay[163] provides a stage model and a checklist that might allow doctoral students to take stock of how well they are doing. Finally, the fourth essay[164] deals with a topic not often discussed, namely networking, and offers suggestions on how doctoral students should go about doing it. Collectively, these essays focus on guiding the doctoral student up the exceptional scale—so that they can be an asset to their institution, successful in their career and go on to be outstanding stewards of the field.

Essay 1: A Rough Model For Success In Doctoral Study

What makes a doctoral student tick? Figure 11-1 shows a rough but integrative model for success in doctoral study, the crux of this essay.[165]

Figure 11-1. A Rough Model For Success In Doctoral Study

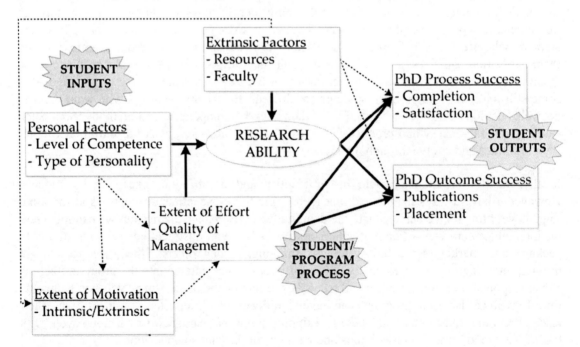

After having had numerous delightful experiences with doctoral students, I still find the answer to that question somewhat elusive. I can recall the case of an applicant for admission to a premier doctoral program. The applicant came across well in the interview, but the review board voted against financial aid (which is tantamount to denying admission for doctoral programs). The reason given was the candidate did not pass the litmus test for GMAT scores. Further, that year's applicant pool was very strong—relegating this candidate to the bottom of the list. One committee member who voted for the candidate did so because he saw something during the interview process that gave him a "good feeling." Unfortunately, good feelings are not good enough for bureaucratic committees. After all, standards and metrics are established to sustain quality. The outlying committee member in this case decided to be vociferous and champion the student. Grudgingly, the committee decided to give the candidate admission without aid. After one year in the program, the candidate wowed everyone with top notch grades, diligence, and quality of interaction with faculty members and peers alike. The student then turned out to be one of the best students in the program, and has since gone on to write seminal papers and become a highly productive academic. If the committee member in this case didn't act, the institution would have lost their best student and if the student gave up on trying for a doctorate, the field would definitely be intellectually poorer. So, that brings me back to the original question. What makes a doctoral student tick?

Many times during my job, the issue of success in the doctoral program comes up. Sometimes, it is at the input stage, when we evaluate applications and interview candidates. At other times, it is during the process of interacting with students during their coursework, comprehensive examinations, dissertation or research projects. Sometimes, it is at the output stage when we are evaluating how to better place our candidates or recruit from good programs. In general, I find that our measurement instruments are fairly blunt when it comes to evaluating candidates at the input stage. We might be able to get a general feel for competence (GMAT scores, GPA, achievements, communication skills) and make broad assessments of personality (outgoing, seems conscientious, aware)—but we can never really predict with tremendous confidence how successful the student is going to be in the program and later in their academic career. Doctoral study is different from other levels. It requires a special kind of person who has the motivation to work hard, beyond mere coursework, and pursue the unstructured process of knowledge creation even though it is replete with dead-end paths and frustrations. It requires competence to absorb and integrate knowledge, apply tools and communicate knowledge effectively. While a minimum threshold of motivation and competency is needed, there is one more ingredient: namely, the ability to manage their program. In essay 2 ("10 Mistakes Students Make In Managing Their Program"), I argue that students often do a poor job in managing their resources including their time, competency, projects, peers, faculty and even their advisor.

This brings me to the issue of "success" in the doctoral program. At the simplest level, I believe that motivation and competence work synergistically, and when complemented with good management, students could be well on their way to a successful program and career. To formalize this, I propose (below) a rough model of success in doctoral study. I call it rough because it probably will not withstand (at least at this stage) rigorous academic scrutiny. However, I believe that it does reflect the core components of a successful student. The only caveat here is that this model focuses on the research/dissertation aspects of success—which is a core attribute of all doctoral programs—but more important for some than others.

In the initial stages, I believe that competence and certain kinds of personalities are more likely to develop the research abilities that we try to create. Competence refers to knowledge and communication skills that we broadly assess through the application process. Certain personality traits, such as reflective observation and conscientiousness, are also desirable, but they are much harder to assess *a priori*. These characteristics are related to motivation with respect to the program. Ideally, we'd like motivation to be intrinsic—students involved in research for the innate excitement of creating and exchanging ideas and the possibility of the *eureka* moment. However, in some cases, extrinsic motivators are the primary drivers (the stamp of credibility or the hope of financial rewards). The support infrastructure at the institution, including the faculty and other resources, could inculcate both the intrinsic (excitement about research) and extrinsic (prestige of institution, financial support, infrastructure) motivations for the student. Highly motivated students in turn manifest that attribute into effort toward their work as well as effort in managing their program. I see the level of effort and quality of program management as moderating the relationship between competence/personality and research ability. Competent students with the right personality will translate those attributes into research ability but effort and management will strengthen that relationship. Research ability is also influenced by the institutional resources, particularly the faculty. Transfer of research skills through apprenticeship-like processes, student supervision, etc. can greatly enhance a student's ability to do research, particularly if the student has the desirable innate characteristics. This research ability will translate into process success (i.e., completion of program requirements) and outcome success (i.e., publications, placement). Of course, the outcome metrics will also be influenced by institutional resources (e.g., faculty assistance in placement). Finally, both types of success boxes are directly influenced by the student's effort and management of their program. For instance, networking and time management could directly influence placements. Needless to say, other attributes (e.g., luck, nature of marketplace) could influence the ability to publish or to be placed in a high-quality (research) institution.

In looking at the model, we can see the issues. At the input stage, we do a coarse assessment of competence and within this, a very coarse assessment of communication skills—usually in the form of an oral interview or admission essay. Other attributes like desirable personality traits, motivation and program management ability are left unassessed. However, those are the ones that manifest themselves during the program and are often the cause of low success or failure. To offset this issue, most institutions have a trial period (qualifier)—after which doctoral students who don't make the grade can be asked to leave the program. Such students cause frustration and dissipation of tremendous energy and (faculty) resources. Ideally, we should try to develop more structured forms of *a priori* assessments. At the minimum, questions that try to root out whether the student has certain traits for doctoral study should be assessed (e.g., Do you enjoy reading? Discussion? Debate? Thinking about areas in the field? Writing? How are your organizational skills? Time management skills? How would you handle unstructured situations? The following scenario? Etc.). These questions are not uncommon (e.g., situation analysis) in corporate interviews and they could prove useful for doctoral study. However, I suspect that these questions are not an integral part of many admission processes.

While the model is not very profound, it does offer a rough structure for examining doctoral success. Adding more granularity to each of the boxes might be useful in creating diagnostic/prescriptive tools for doctoral study or at the minimum stimulating more debate. These programs usually have high resource inputs including tremendous investments of faculty time and few students. The payoffs can also be significant. A good doctoral student can be a tremendous asset to the faculty and institution and create a positive multiplier effect when he or she becomes a top notch researcher. In contrast, a poor choice can be a liability—consuming time and opportunities from faculty members. Therefore, errors of admission (both type I and II) can be far more expensive than it is (say) in the case of an MBA student. I think we need more vigilance. The rough model presented is a start.

Essay 2: 10 Mistakes Made By Doctoral Students In Managing Their Program

In my dozen or so years at the University of South Carolina, I had the privilege of working with numerous doctoral students in various roles. Each one of these experiences has been rewarding in its own special way. Every doctoral student has been unique in his or her attitude and ability, and consequently in the management of their tenure through the program. I have often been asked that between motivation and competence, which characteristic better differentiates successful from unsuccessful students. My answer is that while one might compensate for the other, a minimum threshold of both is needed. In my mind, there is clearly an interaction effect between motivation and competence. Motivation is required in order to be willing and enthusiastic about engaging in the unstructured process of knowledge creation, particularly when many avenues of pursuit reach frustrating dead ends. Competence allows students to be efficient in knowledge absorption, integration, deployment of tools and ultimately, delivery of a quality product. Together, they form a powerful combination. However, one underemphasized predictor of success in my mind is the ability of students to effectively manage their doctoral education.

In reviewing my experiences, I have compiled a list of what I believe to be "mistakes" that students make in managing their doctoral program. These risks are not mutually exclusive, but can hopefully provide guidance on what should be avoided as well as what ought to be done proactively by a PhD student in managing their education.

1. Doctoral Students Do Not Create Synergy

Doctoral programs offer students a variety of opportunities to create pedagogical value. These could be in the form of teaching experiences, course research projects and individual projects with colleagues or faculty members, and reviews of articles and topics. Many students often take a piece-meal approach to these opportunities, doing what is practical, expedient or expected. While I believe that it is useful for students to have a breadth of knowledge of the field and for them to create their own "schema" or understanding of key areas and their relationships, it is just as important to start building depth in an area. Students who consciously manage their opportunities and attempt to create synergy between them, are often successful at honing in on an area of research interest. For instance, creating synergy between course projects that require a research paper, can facilitate the creation of better products, enhance in-depth study of literature in an area, help in time management and possibly, give students a head start on a dissertation topic.

2. Doctoral Students Are Too Reactive

Doctoral Students need to recognize early that *they* are in charge of their program. It is not their advisor or their colleagues but the student who has to earn the degree and create the foundation for his or her future. The degree is more than just taking a series of courses and checking off boxes on a list. It forms the fundamental grounding for a career. Students who go through the program in a reactive mode by merely reacting to program requirements tend to get less out of their doctoral education than students who are proactive. By that, I mean taking actions that keep the broad objective of learning, and cultivating research and teaching skills, while simultaneously focusing on program requirements. Some of the most successful students I've had took the time to build an evolving reference set, did not avoid challenging courses, read copiously, exposed their work in conferences, and sought opportunities to work with colleagues and faculty members. Yes, doing these things requires motivation and competence, and also accelerates their maturation process as researchers. In doing so, they command respect in the eyes of their colleagues and mentors. In a reactive mode, a student might successfully meet the program requirements and (in the case of a well-designed and structured program) be a pretty good candidate on the market. However, those students who proactively (but judiciously) leverage their time in the program tend to be more successful in their careers.

3. Doctoral Students Do Not Carefully Evaluate Opportunity Costs

In general, I've observed that students who are noted for their competence and motivation tend to have more demands on their time from their colleagues and faculty members. However, with every opportunity comes corresponding costs. For these students, *prioritization* is key. Rather, saying yes to every opportunity (whether it be a research project, review, consulting assignment or technology seminar) could be counterproductive. Spreading themselves too thin could detract students from moving forward programmatically and some often find themselves in the bowels of a project that is not pertinent to their area of interest. Yet, they continue to do it. To the extent that students have control over their opportunity set, every opportunity should be evaluated strategically. Pertinent questions could be: Does this (new) project contribute to my doctoral education? Is it an appropriate use of my time in lieu of other uses (e.g., getting done with my series of incomplete grades)? Am I getting into something that could keep expanding like a black hole? I'm not suggesting that risks should not be taken... but they should be measured. There are tactful ways of managing political pressures of opportunities. If not done, it could delay candidacy in the market by one recruiting cycle and have real dollar opportunity costs.

4. Doctoral Students Fall Into A Lull Period

I've seen this one too many times. Particularly, after successfully going through the stress and the psychological hurdle of comprehensive exams, students feel relieved and take a month off. That month becomes two months. Then, three months. Then, it is a slow process of getting back into the dissertation mode. I've observed that the duration between post-comps and the dissertation proposal is often the most poorly managed time. Yes, by all means take that well-deserved break. Go to the beach. But, be cognizant of the program. I've seen advisors lose interest in non-responsive students, which at the minimum results in loss of continuity and tremendous start-up costs in every interaction (i.e., what were you working on?) and ultimately could prove fatal. Students who have planned their program well by creating synergy and thinking of topics while studying for comprehensive examinations can and should quickly hone in on their topic and work on developing it with their advisor. There is no substitute for continuous interaction, even if it is for minor updates.

5. Doctoral Students Do Not Manage Their Advisor

Many students don't consider the duality of their relationship with their advisor. Despite their best attempts at choosing an advisor who is available, supportive, knowledgeable and responsive, in reality, there will be different profiles of advisors along these and other dimensions. For instance, some advisors have good intentions and do care about the student but are so busy that they cannot be as responsive or available as the student might want. In that case, the student should be proactive in managing his or her advisor. For instance, students should not go into a meeting with an open-ended question that they have not thought through. This will result in a discussion that might soak up a precious hour or two and not be effective use of time. Instead, if they go in prepared with the issues, their possible solutions and solicit their advisor's *advice* (that's what advisors are supposed to do: give advice) in resolving the issue, the limited interaction time can be more efficiently managed. Similarly, seek guidance on major issues, while taking a leadership position on the minor ones. If an advisor is "hands-on" by meeting regularly and keeps the student on track with substantive advice and encouragement, then the student is truly blessed and should leverage their advisor. If an advisor is pushing a student in a direction that seems like too much work for the return, then they should present persuasive arguments against that advice and do so cogently. Most advisors will appreciate the thought and preparation students put into meetings and will be open-minded about alternative approaches. Students should never hide from their advisor. Hiding is a pathological behavior in which students indulge, particularly if they cannot deliver on a product. However, hiding is delusional in that the problem (whatever it might be) gets compounded. If there is something amiss, communication with the advisor is a prerequisite to getting it resolved. Ultimately, a symbiotic relationship between student and advisor is the most productive one.

6. Doctoral Students Do Not Seek Help

If a student is in a program with a lot of colleagues and faculty members with expertise, they have tremendous resources at their disposal. They should use them. I occasionally see doctoral students invest inordinate amounts of time on topics or methods for which expertise is already available. However, they try to resolve their problems through their own means rather than ask for guidance. While there is no substitute for perseverance, remember, in many cases, guidance can save hours of fruitless work. For instance, if there is a methodological concern that is consuming a lot of time, they should seek help. Maybe a faculty member in another department is well-versed in the technique and can help or even a colleague who might know of a relevant book (or some other source of information). Even an e-mail to someone whose article uses the same technique can compress the frustration cycle. In a related vein, doctoral students should not be afraid of criticism. In fact, they should actively seek it. Sharing and critiquing each other's ideas is the essence of research development. If the student surrounds themselves with good people who are excited about their work, their enthusiasm will rub off. Research can actually be fun.

7. Doctoral Students Do Not Build An Asset Base

In their career as researchers, doctoral students will have the opportunity to work with a number of research groups. However, never will they have devoted time to learn as they do in their doctoral program. While lifelong learning is a noble goal, we often don't have the time or inclination to learn as much as we'd like in our jobs. Therefore, doctoral students should use the time in their program to build their value. Relevant questions for a student are: If I work on a joint project, what do I bring to the table? Can I cultivate those skills while in the program? For instance, I have often seen doctoral students solicited for their expertise in a certain area or methodology or even for their writing skills. Cultivating these assets while in the doctoral program creates value on joint endeavors down the road. Therefore, doctoral students should assess their assets and how they can leverage the "learning" in the program in order to create unique (inimitable) value for themselves. Students who do not build an asset base tend to be "followers" and cannot sustain the joint research relationships that are so critical for success.

8. Doctoral Students Are Too Ambitious

"The best dissertation is a done dissertation" is an oft-heard saying. While partially facetious, there is an element of practicality in the statement that needs to be noted. I have observed competent and motivated students investing tremendous amounts of time in proposing projects that are extremely ambitious. In some cases, they draw from multiple theoretical lenses, include a plethora of variables and require an ambitious methodology. Often, I see my role as an advisor as simply to narrow down their topics into a project that is not only interesting and relevant, but also *defensible and feasible*. The dissertation process is also a learning process and not necessarily the most significant project the student will ever do. Also, feasibility (i.e., completion of a project within a reasonable time frame) is as important a criterion as any other. I often advise students to evaluate their ambitious changes in terms of costs and benefits: What is the cost in time and effort to make these changes? Would some people disagree with the importance or need for the change? How do the benefits translate into probability of publication in a major journal? This kind of analysis often suggests that reasonable imperfection is acceptable.

9. Doctoral Students Are Not Politically Astute

Unlike most masters programs, the doctoral program involves a higher level of dependence on faculty members. An unfortunate reality is that some faculty members tend to be parochial and egocentric. Therefore, it is important for students to be politically astute when managing their program. I have heard of cases in which confrontation among faculty members during a PhD oral examinations or defenses denigrated to a no-win situation for the student caught in the middle. In general, students should be friendly, receptive and responsive to faculty members, professional in their demeanor, avoid taking unilateral actions that can create potential conflicts (without protection from other faculty members), and carefully choose their committees based on their (members') contributions, interests and local (departmental and school) politics.

10. Doctoral Students Leave Too Early

This one is fairly pervasive. While we generally discourage our students from leaving before their final defense, the pressures of getting a head start in their career often takes precedence. I have generally observed that a dissertation with one month of pending work on-site, sometimes takes months or even years off-site. In a new job, a year goes in settling down, preparing courses and establishing new relationships. The dissertation tends to get squeezed out. In the long-run, that one-month investment can save the student many times over in tension, anxiety, as well as risk in losing continuity of the dissertation process and interest (or even physical presence) of the committee.

In sum, I believe that while doctoral education is challenging, motivation and competence can work synergistically to alleviate the risk of failure. However, students can extract the most value from their program by carefully considering program management issues as the third crucial factor. Students who create synergy, are proactive in their approach, evaluate opportunities carefully, avoid a deep lull period, manage the interaction with their advisor, seek help and criticism of their work, build a particular skill set, temper ambitious projects with reasoned reality, consider political realities, and don't leave the program prematurely tend to be successful in the program. Moreover, I believe that this success will translate to their professional career.

Essay 3: How Am I Doing? A Checklist For Doctoral Students At Various Stages Of Their Program

Most doctoral programs inherently have a lack of structure associated with them. It's the nature of the business. While there might be course requirements and program guidelines, the process of developing competent candidates for the doctoral market is not well-defined and is highly idiosyncratic for every student. Faculty members are often asked by doctoral students: "how am I doing?" Their response usually stems around the administrative components of doctoral study: "you seem to have your coursework in order," "you are on schedule for your comprehensive exams," or "why don't you consider taking this course?" Such responses are necessary but incomplete. They do not reflect how the doctoral student is doing as a budding researcher (or teacher) at their current stage of the program.

I came across this amusing analogy between stages of doctoral study and the seven dwarfs (in the *Snow White* fairy tale). Doctoral students are like all seven dwarfs at different stages of their program. At first, they are Dopey and Bashful. In the middle, they are usually sick (Sneezy), tired (Sleepy) and irritable (Grumpy). But at the end, they're called Doc and then, they are Happy.[166] While this may get a chuckle, I think the idea of stages of development in a doctoral program has merit. I have had the delightful experience of working with dozens of doctoral students in various capacities and in various stages of their program. I have observed students go through a maturity cycle of sorts as they develop their research and teaching skills. The pace and acuity of development might vary by student based on their capability, motivation and ability to manage their program (see essay 2) or manage their advisor.[167] But, the stages generally remain the same.

In my observations, students go through four stages, roughly reflecting the four years of a typical doctoral program. I call these stages: exploration, engagement, consolidation and entry.

The stage of exploration epitomizes first-year students. Despite the plethora of voluminous research that many students do when searching for the right program, it doesn't really hit them until they are actually in the program. Here's when they realize that doctoral study is different—really different—from (say) a professional master's program. Here's when they hear senior students tell them how hard they need to work, the battles of the job market, comprehensive exam pressures and the importance of working on research outside the classroom. Many of these concepts are new to the students and they have to battle this noise, as they deal with seminars and research articles not written for the lay person, and statistical techniques that they never knew existed. It's tough—and to succeed, they need to take a deep breath and explore, question and learn about where they are, what they are doing there, and where they are going.

The stage of engagement is further up the value-added axis. This is exploration with a purpose. Students begin to have a sense of doctoral study and their position in their institution and (perhaps) their chosen profession. This is the stage where students engage with faculty members, with published work and with research ideas. They also begin to sense their path of success through the program—the colleagues and faculty members who they will need to interact with, and research areas and methods that they particularly enjoy. While it's still a struggle for many to prioritize—because these opportunities are increasing and time is becoming increasingly scarce as students are straddling both the broad view and the more narrow personal view of research.

The stage of consolidation is when ideas crystallize. Students in this stage are engaged tightly with the institution. They are committed. The institution is committed—irreversibly, if the students pass their comprehensive examinations. Students here should have a very good sense of their field and its structure, and the ability to position research within that structure. The student should be able to traverse up and down between the supra-system (the broad field) and the sub-system (individual research). Dissertation ideas should be developed in this stage, as the personal view of research dominates the latter part of this stage. The student should also develop their engagement with the broader profession as they package themselves for the job market.

Finally, *the stage of entry* is the final thrust before the student formally enters the profession as a peer. This could be a particularly challenging stage as the student has one foot in the home institution and another foot trying to move outside it. Broader notions of career, research stream and tenure enter the student's consciousness, as do family, location and job satisfaction. The "light at the end of the tunnel" keeps the student going as the process culminates with a doctoral degree.

Below, I have put together a checklist of the four stages that might be useful for students and faculty members to respond to that tricky question: "how am I doing?" The stages roughly correspond to the four years of a typical program, although there could be variance in the nature of the programs themselves, the student's acumen and approach, and the alignment between time and stages. It's important to note that motivation is critical to keep going through these unstructured processes and much of this stems from the excitement of a knowledge-centric career.

I would like to add that while the maturity cycle might be complete within the administrative framework of the doctoral program, it is far from complete when one considers that we continue to evolve and learn as we mature as academics in our careers.

In Table 11-1, I present a checklist for doctoral students at various stages of their program. The goal of this table is to provide students with diagnostic information to assess if they are on course, lacking in some areas or if they should call it quits!

Table 11-1. Checklist For Doctoral Students At Various Stages Of Program

End of Year 0 (Just Before Entering the Program):
Are you motivated to do this…
☐ Does a research and teaching career appeal to you?
☐ Does the idea of generating and disseminating knowledge excite you?
DIAGNOSTICS: If you answered NO to these, QUIT NOW!
End of First Year in the Program
☐ Are you motivated to do this…
o Does a research and teaching career appeal to you?
o Does the idea of generating and disseminating knowledge excite you?
☐ Do you have a sense of research in your area by reading articles in major journals in your field?
☐ Have you tried to write an original proposal or engage in a research project?
☐ Are you getting a sense of the variety of research methods and getting in-depth knowledge in a few?
☐ Are you beginning to develop a local network of faculty members and students with whom you think you can collaborate?
☐ Are you drifting toward areas that are more exciting to you?
☐ Are you organizing your program and developing plans of action for each year of doctoral study?
DIAGNOSTICS: Work on remedying NO responses
End of Second Year in the Program
☐ Are you motivated to do this…
o Does a research and teaching career appeal to you?
o Does the idea of generating and disseminating knowledge excite you?
☐ Have you completed a research paper for submission to a conference (or a journal)?
☐ Have you had the opportunity to present your ideas in a group setting?

Table 11-1 *Continued.* **Checklist For Doctoral Students At Various Stages Of Program**

☐	Are you getting a good understanding of a variety of research methods and tools?
☐	Can you see the integration of articles that you read as you begin to create your schema (structure) of the field?
☐	Have you established a small portfolio of projects with peers and faculty members that are important to you?
☐	Are you converging through your readings and topics on an area that could be the foundation for a dissertation?
☐	Are you prioritizing your time and managing your various activities well?

DIAGNOSTICS: Work on remedying NO responses

End of Third Year in the Program

☐	Are you motivated to do this…
	o Does a research and teaching career appeal to you?
	o Does the idea of generating and disseminating knowledge excite you?
☐	Have you experienced a review process with your submissions?
☐	Have you had the opportunity to present your ideas at a regional/national conference?
☐	Have you had the opportunity to review a submission to a conference or a journal?
☐	Can you read articles more efficiently and rapidly integrate them into your stable schema?
☐	Have you passed your comprehensive examination?
☐	Have you developed an idea for your dissertation and defended your proposal?
☐	Are you very comfortable with your proposed methodology?
☐	Have you honed your presentation skills, particularly for the proposal?
☐	Have you entered the job market?
☐	Have you identified your dissertation chair/committee that is on-board with your topic?
☐	Have you had the responsibility for teaching a course?

DIAGNOSTICS: Work on remedying NO responses

End of Fourth Year in the Program

☐	Are you motivated to CONTINUE TO do this…
	o Does a research and teaching career appeal to you?
	o Does the idea of generating and disseminating knowledge excite you?
☐	Have you got articles accepted in conferences or journals?
☐	Have you attended a national conference in your field?
☐	Have you defended your dissertation?
☐	Have you structured a research program from your projects and dissertation?
☐	Have you developed a set of competencies that you can bring to collaborative efforts?
☐	Have you interacted with peers outside your institution who share your interests?
☐	Have you got a job?

DIAGNOSTICS: Work on remedying NO responses

Essay 4: "Hi, I'm Me": Judicious Networking For The Doctoral Student

We've all known someone like him. He surveys the room, evaluating every person. Some are discounted off the bat. Some are placed at a premium. Where can he get the biggest return? Who needs to know him? Who does he need to know? After careful assessment, he smoothly snuggles into an ongoing conversation. They accommodate. They chatter. He thinks nothing of moving to another group—when he sees a higher return on his investment. It doesn't matter with who he is. It doesn't matter why he is there. What matters is who he knows and with whom he is seen. He is the *networker*.

As someone who generally abhors people who behave like the networker above, I am perhaps not the best person to be talking about networking. I am perhaps closer to the other extreme; working on the arguably naïve assumption that putting your head down and working hard to get your work out is the best avenue for success. I don't network. I've been known to hide my nametag and actively avoid it at conferences. However, over the years, I've come to realize that networking is not necessarily a bad word. If done judiciously, it can serve as a catalyst to enhance relationships, contribute positively to the quality of your work and enhance your position in the academic community. However, selfish networking, epitomized in the vignette above, might work temporarily. Ultimately however, the selfish networker—will be known as just that—selfish. If networking is all the person has to offer, the house of cards will collapse. Selfish networking is not sustainable.

So, what is judicious networking? How should a doctoral student network judiciously? If we look at the stages a doctoral student goes through in the program (see essay 3), we can contextualize these questions. Most doctoral students come into their program rather naïve about research and the institutions supporting it. Let me briefly revisit the stages and what they mean. This is the "stage of exploration" where to the wonderment of some, they are exposed to knowledge in their field, its basic structures and the prominent people behind the knowledge and structures. In the next year, the "stage of engagement," students engage with research projects and faculty as they sense their path through the program. The "stage of consolidation" is where they have a sense of both their personal research as well as a schema of the broader field and its constituents. Finally, in the "stage of entry," students leverage the previous stages as they seek formal entry into the profession. Where does networking fit into all this?

In general, students need to begin their networking within their home institution. During the stage of exploration, and particularly the stage of engagement, it is important that students get to know the faculty members at their institution. It would be most appropriate for students to approach faculty members, particularly those in their major area, and introduce themselves. At the minimum, having faculty members aware of their existence and better still, cultivating institutional (faculty) support for their candidacy is an important goal of networking. While it may not be practical for a student to work on projects with every faculty member, engaging faculty members on content by seeking advice helps achieve this goal. As we discuss later, students should build relationships, not mere contacts. In order to avoid getting pulled in too many different directions, students can establish special kinds of relationships with different faculty members. From faculty members that might eventually serve on their committee, they might try to get content-based advice. From others, they can obtain process-based advice on navigating the program, or advice on a methodological issue. Ultimately, if faculty members get to know a student as motivated, competent and one who does not shy away from hard work, this will hold the student in good stead during the later stages of the doctoral program.

In the later stages of consolidation and entry, students will need to straddle the line between their internal institution and the broader professional context they are about to enter. External networking can help in this regard. There is a good chance that if students can develop some strong external relationships at this stage, they will likely sustain them through a good portion of their professional career.

Below, I add some granularity to the concept of "judicious" networking. I organize this subtext in the form of five rules:
1. Network on content
2. Network when you don't have to
3. Network online
4. Network gently
5. Network prepared

While some of my colleagues may find these rules too conservative, I think students need to network carefully lest they be viewed as the selfish networker that forces his way onto others. Underlying these rules is the assumption that networking is a two-way street and relationships are built on mutual benefit.

1. Network On Content

When doctoral students attend professional conferences, they often seek introductions to well-known people. In my experience, this rarely leads to anything other than (perhaps) a casual exchange of names (which the well-known person usually forgets). It is nice when a doctoral student finds themselves in a social situation at a conference. Going out for dinner with some bigwigs can be an illuminating experience. If the student has a dazzling personality, associations can be forged and this could lead to good outcomes. However, in most cases professional associations might have non-professional discussions as conversation starters but are usually sustained on professional content and common interests. Purely social relationships are nice and enjoyable but they usually remain at that level. So, the best networking is based on discussing common professional interests. If, for instance, a doctoral student is working on a thesis that builds on someone's work, it is entirely appropriate to touch base with that person and discuss how their work is being used. This is better done with a pre-arranged meeting but, on occasion, even approaching the person in a conference might work. In the latter case, it is important for doctoral students to recognize that social gatherings at conferences might not be the right setting for a detailed academic discussion. The key point is that by focusing on content—in a manner that is interesting to the other party—the student comes across as *interesting*. At the minimum, the approached party is now aware of the student and their work. Better still, they can provide useful feedback. More importantly, with appropriate follow-ups, a professional relationship can be built. Social interactions can lead to or leverage professional associations but for sustainability, the latter is critical.

2. Network When You Don't Have To

Network to give without expecting anything back in return. If a doctoral student is on the job market, casual interactions with attendees at a social gathering rarely lead to positive outcomes and, in some cases, can even hurt candidacy. In these settings, the approached party is not necessarily in a working mode. If they are recruiting, they probably spent time going through resumes and interviewing numerous candidates already. They probably have many satisfactory candidates for the position. Unless a doctoral student can "wow" them under such unfavorable conditions, the student is more likely to be viewed as anything from unfortunate to a downright pest. Similarly, approaching an editor of a journal and asking for detailed feedback on a paper on which the student is working should be done carefully. Be aware of the setting. Try not to come across as a taker. For instance, it is entirely appropriate to ask an editor about the fit of a paper. But to demand more than that in a casual setting, with the idea of building a relationship is not apropos. It is far better to network when you don't have to. When there is a genuine interest in the other person's work or advice, you are giving respect, exchanging interesting ideas and perhaps, at the embryonic stages of building a relationship. In cases where the person has graciously responded, students should be equally gracious in return—perhaps offering to help them with something they might need in the future. This shows that the student is concerned about the responder as a person and not just what they can do for them.

It is important to network not only with faculty members, but also with fellow doctoral students. Cultivating such relationships through doctoral forums (e.g., consortia, blogs) can be important as students and their peers grow together professionally. Given the common career stage of peers, some of these relationships could turn out to be very strong and sustain for years. They could also lead to important relationships with faculty members at the peer's institution. At the minimum, good peer networking can help doctoral students benchmark themselves and gauge their competition as they prepare for placement.

3. Network Online

In today's environment, there is no need to network physically. In fact, the relatively non-invasive nature of email allows students to communicate and exchange documents with unknown entities. It is a great tool for establishing a solid content-based foundation for a relationship. In this medium, a carefully worded request or exchange of ideas, or feedback on a paper can go a long way in establishing awareness, credibility and even fostering a working relationship. I know of many researchers who have successfully published papers with people they have never even met! It offers a great social opening when two co-authors actually see each other face-to-face. Doctoral students should avail of this resource and not hesitate to contact others in the field regarding work-related questions. Perhaps a clarification is needed on a statement made in a paper? Perhaps advice is needed on a certain methodology? Perhaps an opinion is needed on a completed paper? In each case, the requestor should be cognizant of the recipient's time and try to ensure that there is benefit to the recipient in doing this. The requestor should also be sensitive to cues in the exchange—to see whether any mutual benefit is evolving into a sustained series of interactions. Also, doctoral student blogs and online communities are springing up—and offer a great resource to forge relationships with other doctoral students or faculty members who are in similar positions or share the same interests.

4. Network Gently

A pushy networker like the one in the opening paragraph of this essay is more often than not viewed as intrusive and unwanted. People are generally polite—particularly academics—and may not give out obvious cues as to their true disposition. In some cases, the networker is not even aware of their pushy propensity. I would generally advocate that doctoral students should figuratively have their antenna out. They can control their behavior—and "barging into" an ongoing group conversation should be one behavior to control. Worse is barging in and monopolizing the conversation, without being fully contextualized as to what was being discussed. A better practice is to be invited into a group or to gently make one's way into a group that has not established tight cohesion. It's generally good form, particularly as a doctoral student, to be a good listener and offer insights only on topics where the student has had some experience. Shooting from the hip in order to impress a crowd usually has an opposite private reaction. Some doctoral students (particularly those on the job market) tend to stalk their target. I doubt that stalking works—and again, it has the danger of backfiring.

5. Network Prepared

Whether a student is networking online or in person, it always helps to be prepared. The quality of the content exchanged will be far superior if the student is well aware of the person being approached and what they can and cannot do. For instance, requesting detailed information on the data from a 20-year old paper may not be a good request. Awareness of the methodologist on a 3-person paper can ensure that the request is targeted to the right person. Even in physical networking, awareness of the other party's work will lead to a far more substantive content-based conversation and a higher likelihood of a more sustained relationship. Also, students must be responsive and follow-up with their contacts. Sustained relationships are built and are not formed overnight. This requires work and a willingness to invest in building the relationship.

Summary

Judicious networking is a far cry from our vignette. Much of it involves good social etiquette, tact and basic decency. I suggest that students who network based on mutual interests and professional content, do it in an altruistic manner, establish and nurture communication links online, are diplomatic and non-intrusive, and work hard to build and cultivate contacts will be able to use networking to increase the quality of their work and their opportunity set in the profession. In contrast, the consummate networker will not sustain.

I reiterate that networking is about building relationships. Having hundreds of weak ties might not be as fruitful as having a few strong ties in the discipline. Most initial contacts fizzle out due to a lack of substance in the interactions. The ones that do sustain help establish a sense of belongingness in the community and can contribute greatly to success in the profession.

Concluding Thoughts

Life in academia is very satisfying but getting there first requires successfully navigating the doctoral program. These four essays provide doctoral students in various stages advice and tools about how to gauge their progress, steps to take to ensure adequate progress and ways in which they can take corrective action. I hope these essays will help you on your road to success.

Key Takeaways

Essay 1: A Rough Model For Success In Doctoral Study
1. Doctoral study requires four key ingredients:
   i.   Motivation to work hard
   ii. Pursuing the unstructured process of knowledge creation despite dead-end paths and frustrations
   iii. Competence to absorb and integrate knowledge, apply tools and communicate knowledge effectively
   iv. The ability to manage the PhD program
2. Motivation and competence work synergistically—when complemented with good management, students can be on their way to being successful in their program and career
3. Student inputs (e.g., competence and personality) and program processes (e.g., extrinsic

factors, such as resources, faculty and quality of management) work to produce student outputs (i.e., process success through program completion and satisfaction, and outcome success through publications and placement)

Essay 2: 10 Mistakes Made By Doctoral Students in Managing Their Program

1. Doctoral students do not create synergy: Students who consciously manage their research and teaching opportunities, and attempt to create synergy between them, are often successful at honing in on a research area of interest
2. Doctoral students are too reactive: Students need to recognize early that *they* are in charge of their program—they should make efforts to build an evolving reference set, not avoid challenging courses, read copiously, expose their work in conferences, and seek opportunities to work with colleagues and faculty members
3. Doctoral students do not carefully evaluate opportunity costs
   i. With every opportunity comes corresponding costs—*prioritization* is key (to the extent that students have control over their opportunity set, every opportunity should be evaluated strategically)
   ii. Pertinent questions about whether to take on a new project/task could be:
      a. Does this (new) project contribute to my doctoral education?
      b. Is it appropriate use of my time in lieu of other uses (e.g., getting done with my series of incomplete grades)?
      c. Am I getting into something that could keep expanding like a black hole?
4. Doctoral students fall into a lull period
   i. Students should take that well-deserved break after the comprehensive exams but be cognizant of the program—beware of letting that that break expand into one, two or three months of no progress
   ii. Students need to keep their advisor informed of their progress, even if it is for minor updates—accountability is important to keeping a program on track
5. Doctoral students do not manage their advisor
   i. Many students don't consider the duality of their relationship with their advisor
   ii. Students should prepare for interactions with their advisor—if they go in prepared with the issues, their possible solutions and solicit their advisor's *advice* in resolving the issue, the limited interaction time can be more efficiently managed
   iii. Seek guidance on major issues
   iv. Student should never hide from their advisor—a symbiotic relationship between student and advisor is the most productive one
6. Doctoral students do not seek help
   i. Students should recognize the wealth of resources and expertise available, rather than spending time on topics or methods with which they are not familiar
   ii. Consult with faculty members or email the author of a journal article to help compress the frustration cycle
   iii. Don't be afraid of criticism—actively seek it out

7. Doctoral students do not build an asset base
    i. Students should use the time in their program to build their value—relevant questions for a student are:
        a. If I work in a joint project, what do I bring to the table?
        b. Can I cultivate those skills while in the program?
    ii. Students who do not build an asset base tend to be "followers" and cannot sustain the joint research relationships that are so critical for success
8. Doctoral students are too ambitious
    i. Student should narrow down their topics into a project that is not only interesting and relevant, but also *defensible and feasible*
    ii. Evaluate ambitious projects in terms of costs and benefits:
        a. What is the cost in time and effort?
        b. Would some people disagree with the importance or need for some change?
        c. How do the benefits translate into probability of publication in a major journal?
    iii. Reasonable imperfection is acceptable
9. Doctoral students are not politically astute: Students should be friendly, receptive and responsive to faculty members, professional in their demeanor, avoid taking unilateral actions that can create potential conflicts (without protection from other faculty members), carefully choose their committees based on their (members') contributions and interests, as well as the local (departmental and school) politics
10. Doctoral students leave too early
    i. Avoid leaving the program before you have finished your dissertation
    ii. In the long-run, an investment in finishing the dissertation before taking a job can save the student many times over in tension, anxiety, as well as risk in losing continuity of the dissertation process and interest (or even physical presence) of the committee

Essay 3: How Am I Doing? A Checklist For Doctoral Students At Various Stages Of Their Program
1. Doctoral students go through various stages in their program:
    i. Exploration: This is the stage in which they are exposed to knowledge in their field, its basic structures and the prominent people behind the knowledge and structures
    ii. Engagement: This is the stage in which they engage with research projects and faculty mentors as they sense their path through the program
    iii. Consolidation: This is the stage in which they should have a sense of both their personal research as well as a schema of the broader field and its constituents
    iv. Entry: This is the stage in which they can leverage the previous stages as they seek formal entry into the profession
2. Use the checklist tool provided in this essay to monitor progress and take corrective action at every stage of the doctoral program

Essay 4: "Hi, I'm Me": Judicious Networking For The Doctoral Student

1. Network on content: The best networking is based on discussing common professional interests
2. Network when you don't have to: Be gracious and don't expect anything in return
3. Network online: Email, websites, blogs and online communities provide opportunities to network with those you have never or may never meet face-to-face
4. Network gently: Be polite, not pushy—make sure you listen and don't monopolize a conversation
5. Network prepared: Inform yourself about the person you may be talking to and familiarize yourself with their work

CHAPTER 12

NAVIGATING ASSISTANT PROFESSOR LIFE: YEARS 1, 2 AND 3

Starting as a new assistant professor in a new school in a new city creates many challenges. Except for a fortunate few who are returning to the city where they grew up, a city where parents or other relatives live, a city where one went to college, etc., most of us will have to relocate to an entirely new city, learn where the grocery stores are, get set up at home, meet new neighbors, and the list goes on and on. In many ways, the first year of relocation has a way of being extremely time consuming and for all the wrong reasons. These are just a few of the many reasons to give serious consideration to the tips below—some of these are from personal experience based on what worked for me and what I did wrong, which, of course, I realize with the benefit of hindsight. Some of these tips were handed down to me and I benefited greatly from following the wise counsel of others.

Before I begin discussing strategies, let me note that I am addressing the issue of a standard 6-year tenure clock where the evaluation for promotion and tenure happens at the end of the fifth year (or start of the sixth year). There are a few institutions that employ a longer tenure clock, e.g., 9 years. Obviously, the strategy in approaching such a situation would be somewhat different from what I recommend here. Given that my experiences do not permit me to relate to such a situation, I am not directly speaking to such a clock. However, I do believe that most of the strategies I suggest here will apply to all early career researchers. In addition, I believe those with longer tenure clocks should pursue some high risk-high reward projects that could potentially have high impact because impact is also a factor that is relevant at such institutions.

Following a move, there is an enormous amount of coping that is necessary in various aspects of one's life depending on one's personal situation. I am not addressing these issues here as there are other sources that provide great advice to help with coping. I will instead focus on specific ideas related to research and the broader issues related to the first workplace one goes to after a PhD program (assuming it's an academic institution). Specifically, I will provide advice using the following 7 topics as a guide:

1. Keep within a research program
2. Dyads and triads
3. Opportunity of a lifetime
4. Don't just co-author with your advisor
5. Some things not research
   i. Don't screw up teaching
   ii. Don't screw up service
   iii. Have few opinions
   iv. Be a team player
   v. Be a good citizen

6. Institution-specific versus institution-independent capital
7. Having your papers and ideas peer reviewed

1. Keep Within A Research Program

It is important to stay within an overarching question. This point is anchored to my comments in earlier chapters, particularly chapter 2, about staying the course with a research program. If you are someone who did not necessarily think about having a research program while in the PhD program, you should start when you begin your career as an assistant professor. One of the best ways is to build on your dissertation work and look at ways that it can be extended. The first three years are far too critical to not take advantage of what you already know and a topic where you have invested plenty of time already. Chapter 2 provided information on building and sustaining a research program. Much of the advice provided there is pertinent here. Electing to start something afresh is not a bad idea at all but it should not be at the expense of pursuing the general dissertation topic area further. For instance, while you wait on a co-author or wait for time to elapse between data collection points, you can always develop work in your second or third research streams.

2. Dyads And Triads

I raised and discussed this issue in chapter 7. But this particular point is worth discussing, especially in the context of what assistant professors should do to achieve success. All too often, in the excitement from the prospect of working with colleagues at one's new school, assistant professors start forming many combinations of dyads and triads for collaborative work. While collaborating with faculty members at the new workplace is certainly not a bad idea, it becomes counterproductive when the collaboration is more about creating relationships than it is about pursuing research projects. There are three types of collaborations that ensue in such new environments: (1) effective; (2) efficient; and (3) contrived. *Effective collaborations* are those that occur when the topic pursued is one that any member of the collaboration team would be able to pursue independently due to the lack of topical or methodological expertise that is, in fact, what each collaborator brings to the table. *Efficient collaborations* are those that are pursued simply to complete something quicker than any one collaborator could have done independently. Either of these scenarios is fine. Effective collaborations create better papers than what any one person can achieve independently. Efficient collaborations create more papers. Ideally, effectiveness *and* efficiency can result simultaneously over time as collaborators learn more about one another's expertise. The worst type of collaboration is one that is *contrived* in order to establish and build relationships. Two new assistant professors arriving at the same time at a new school may begin collaborating because they share a lot in common, not necessarily in terms of research interests, but career stage and newness to the location. It can help the assistant professors get comfortable with each other. However, I think such collaborations are a very bad idea. In my first two years as an assistant professor at Maryland, I did not collaborate with anyone at Maryland because there was no obvious fit (but

I was having conversations to find overlapping interests). If you want to build relationships, get together for a drink after work, go to lunch together and/or meet outside work for fun activities over weekends or holidays. Dyads and triads for collaboration should be formed only for the right reasons.

3. Opportunity Of A Lifetime

I have had many people talk about the opportunity of a lifetime in terms of research projects. Earlier in chapter 2, I had noted that people often will come to you twice a day with opportunities of a lifetime! By this, I mean: you are likely to have people coming to you to discuss absolutely can't-miss projects about twice a day! So, you have to be careful and mindful of what fits within the scope of your work. Just like not forming dyads and triads just for the sake of forming relationships, I strongly advise against jumping into these purported opportunities of a lifetime that will likely come by twice a day!

4. Don't Just Co-author With Your Advisor

On the one hand, I am suggesting keeping the focus to the research program that typically relates to the dissertation topic. On the other hand, I am now saying you should write with others besides your advisor. While I am suggesting having other co-authors besides the advisor, it is important to pick those collaborators cautiously. As already stated, pick them for the right reasons. One of the important reasons to have co-authors other than your advisor is to demonstrate some broadening past the dissertation and to show that you weren't being carried by your advisor—something that becomes pertinent at the time of promotion and tenure evaluation.

5. Some Things Not Research

I have five suggestions unrelated to research but important nevertheless for the survival of assistant professors. I note that not all of these are based on personal experience!

i. Don't Screw Up Teaching
Recently, teaching has received much greater emphasis in universities. However, in research schools, teaching excellence and/or teaching several different courses (many new preparations) will seldom lead to tenure. It is important to be a good, but not necessarily a great, teacher. Chapters 14 through 16 provide counsel on how to be an effective teacher.

ii. Don't Screw Up Service
Most universities protect their junior faculty members from excessive service. More important than how many committee assignments you receive each year is how much time you have to spend on the committees. It is important to do some service. However, for the most part, it is likely that the senior faculty members will take the lead. Just follow their lead.

iii. Have Few Opinions

This is perhaps one of the hardest things to do, as assistant professors frequently come to their first job with hopes of changing the world and doing so in one day. Soon, you will come to realize that the wheels of academia turn slowly. Having strong opinions and expressing them early and often serves only to: (a) upset someone; and/or (b) lead to someone knowing that you have no experience. It is unlikely that you can push your point of view. Even if you did succeed in getting your way and you had a stellar idea, little is gained—no one ever got promoted for stellar service, not in a research school, not that I am aware of anyway. Your time to have opinions, express them and act on them will come—after you receive tenure. Until then, back to research!

iv. Be A Team Player

This point is related to (iii) above. As I write this, the football season is in full swing, the baseball season is winding down. We hear about team players—good ones and bad ones. Good ones are loved even if they aren't very good performers and bad ones are hated even if they are great performers. Being a team player means many different things. Most of all, it means being deferential, seeking advice, taking advice, playing your part in the mission of the department and school, and keeping your opinions under wraps.

v. Be A Good Citizen

Being a team player is part of being a good citizen but when I speak of being a good citizen, I am referring to performing key activities. This involves showing up to faculty meetings, showing up to research workshops, showing up to some college banquets, showing up to some graduation ceremonies, etc. By and large, it involves being around, reaching out to faculty members within and outside the department for a coffee or a lunch, and not annoying any of these people you meet.

The ideas discussed above particularly emphasize aspects of how you should act within the workplace. There are broader issues, particularly networking and reviewing, that are discussed elsewhere in this book (see chapters 11 and 17).

6. Institution-specific Versus Institution-independent Capital

I want to address one important aspect related to the capital an assistant professor might build through their choice of activities. Institution-specific capital refers to favors, respect and leverage one creates within one's own department, school and university. Institution-independent capital refers to creating the same elements in the field. Both of these types of capital are important and useful.

It is tempting while being a good citizen and team player to build solid social capital within the institution so that when it comes time for your promotion and tenure evaluation, a favorable outcome will follow. Nothing could be farther from reality. People easily forget how much time you invested in a committee or a teaching preparation. Teaching and service comprise institution-specific capital that will seldom put a tenure case over the top. Worst of all, they are institution-specific and will not garner recognition in your attempt to get a job elsewhere. While the effort required to successfully get a paper accepted at a premier journal is clearly understood, the effort invested in preparing for a class or serving (or chairing) a committee varies greatly and is subjective. If you want to do things that are institution-specific beyond the basic investment in teaching and service, I recommend the university or school coffee mug for your morning coffee and the university or school shirt for casual Fridays.

The capital that is institution-independent is research. It is portable value that every school recognizes and craves. Here too, I want to emphasize the institution specificity that could envelope one's decision-making. Frequently, assistant professors are driven by internal journal ranking lists. Journal ranking lists cannot really be internally driven. Internal lists are, at best, a guide. Real lists are driven by perceptions of the field, perceptions of leading scholars in the field and not by departmental fiat. The best journal ranking list is the least common denominator as recognized by the field. In information systems, this would mean *Information Systems Research* and *MIS Quarterly*. As pointed out by Dennis et al. (2006),[168] *Journal of Management Information Systems* does not receive the same recognition for a variety of reasons: "it is published by a private, for-profit organization (as opposed to other elite journals that are traditionally sponsored by academic societies), since a noticeable proportion of its articles come from special issues that *fast track* conference papers through review processes that prevent nonconference papers from consideration, and since its editorial board is relatively static" (p. 7).

One other approach to building the institution-independent capital of research is to publish papers in leading journals in different fields. For information systems researchers, these tend to be management journals—e.g., *Academy of Management Journal, Strategic Management Journal* and *Organizational Behavior and Human Decision Processes*—or psychology journals—e.g., *Journal of Applied Psychology, Journal of Personality and Social Psychology* and *Personnel Psychology*—or marketing journals—e.g., *Journal of Marketing Research, Journal of Marketing* and *Journal of Consumer Research*. This advice applies to those in any field. This is beneficial for a few different reasons. First, research conducted such that it can be published in journals in different fields will have the greatest impact. Second, and somewhat more practically speaking, when a promotion and tenure case is examined, especially if it is evaluated by the entire school's tenured faculty (or the school committee), a case with publications in premier journals in different fields will likely fare better and could potentially have advocates in favor of the case in a field other than the candidate's own. Third, and also practically speaking, some journals have much faster turnaround times and fewer rounds of review before a decision. Information systems and marketing journals tend to have review cycle times upwards of four months and three or four major rounds in most cases, while management and psychology journals tend to be quicker and have fewer rounds.

7. Having Your Papers And Ideas Peer Reviewed

One of the hardest things to do early in one's career, with little experience, is to simulate the review process without the pain and suffering of rejection, not to mention all the time lost due to a review process that culminates in rejection.

Using the review process as a way to get feedback is a bad idea. For one thing, a good journal outlet is wasted. More importantly, your reputation is tarnished before you even get out of the gate. Not because you received a rejection but because you sent a paper that was quite sub-par (often through a peer review process, many issues can be fixed that will result in a fairly good paper being submitted). We do frequently talk about having papers workshop-ed and peer reviewed. I would take that a step further and say, you should have ideas peer reviewed. Present and discuss models in their formative stages. Sometimes, adjustments and repositioning can be done through the addition of a few constructs and related adjustments in the data collection that can produce a paper that will be liked by editors. I recall stumbling into one such situation where the then-editor of *Personnel Psychology* was clamoring for an article related to technology use and age differences. While we didn't modify the research project for this purpose, my co-author, Mike Morris, and I produced a paper that was exactly what the editor wanted by making some adjustments to the framing.

I categorize the peer review process into two types. The first type of review comes from senior colleagues who can see the forest for the trees and suggest framing adjustments, identify relevant seminal papers and suggest doing things that will make a paper more likely to survive a grueling review process. The second type of review comes from junior colleagues or even PhD students—the profile of the likely reviewer—who may not always see the forest for the trees but can help see the paper through the critical (perhaps even overly critical) eyes of a reviewer. Such a person may need to be persuaded differently and likely looks for different things. Both types of reviews are very useful.

In any case, make sure your ideas and papers are carefully reviewed by friendly eyes before they encounter reviewers. Additional thoughts and ideas that are relevant here include the discussion of reviews by co-authors in chapter 7 on collaboration and also the discussion of the hat trick in chapter 4.

Concluding Thoughts

I sought to share some thoughts related to how to cope with the transition to a new workplace. I didn't seek to address coping related to a junior faculty member's personal life. The crux of my message is to keep the focus on the chosen research path and doing things to be seen as a good citizen within the department and college. I also raised points related to building collaborations and not sending papers to journals without adequate peer review.

Key Takeaways

1. The first year of relocation for a new job is extremely time consuming
2. Keep within a research program (see also chapter 2)
   i. Stay within an overarching question—the first three years are far too critical to not take advantage of what you already know and a topic where you have invested plenty of time already
   ii. Ensure that you pursue your dissertation topic, while beginning to branch out into other research streams
3. Dyads, triads
   i. Don't let your excitement about working with colleagues at your new school cloud your judgment when it comes to managing collaborations
   ii. In the beginning, collaboration should not just be about establishing new relationships but about pursing research projects within your areas of expertise—if you want to build relationships, get together for a drink after work, go to lunch together and/or meet outside work for fun activities over weekends or holidays
   iii. Collaborative relationships can be:
      a. Effective—collaborations that occur when the topic pursued is one that neither collaborator would be able to pursue independently due to the lack of topical or methodological expertise that is, in fact, what the other person brings to the table
      b. Efficient—collaborations that are pursued simply to complete something more quickly that either person could have done independently
      c. Contrived—collaborations that are pursued to establish and build relationships
   iv. Collaborative relationships should be effective, efficient or both—it should not be contrived
4. Opportunity of a lifetime
   i. They will come by twice a day—as with your collaborations, be judicious about which opportunities you choose
5. Don't just coauthor with your advisor
   i. It's important to demonstrate some broadening past the dissertation and to show that you weren't being carried by your advisor
   ii. Be selective in choosing your collaborators
6. Some things not research
   i. Don't screw up teaching—it is important to be a good, but not necessarily great, teacher
   ii. Don't screw up service—more important than how many committees you serve on each year is the time you have to spend on the committees; on most committees, senior faculty members will take the lead on committees (just follow the lead)
   iii. Have few opinions—having strong opinions and expressing them early and often serves only to: (a) upset someone; and/or (b) lead to someone knowing that you have no experience

    iv. Be a team player—being a team player means being deferential, seeking advice, taking advice, playing your part in the mission of the department and school, and keeping your opinions under wraps

    v. Be a good citizen—this involves showing up to faculty meetings, showing up to research workshops, showing up to some college banquets, showing up to some graduation ceremonies, etc.

7. Institution-specific versus institution-independent capital

    i. Institution-specific capital refers to favors, respect and leverage one creates within one's own department, school and university—usually created through teaching and service

    ii. Institution-independent capital refers to creating the same elements in the field—usually created through research

    iii. Both types of capital are important and useful, however institution-independent capital is more important because it will gain you recognition and respect in the field. It is the portable value that makes you more mobile, and is value that every school will recognize and crave

    iv. Institution-independent capital is particularly important for external recommendation letters sought at the time of tenure

    v. To build institution-independent capital, publish in highly regarded journals that are clearly elite in your field and not just those that may be on the list for tenure requirements at your school

    vi. Publishing in top journals in reference disciplines also helps to establish institution-independent capital

        a. Research conducted such that it can be published in journals in different fields will have positive impact

        b. When a promotion and tenure case is examined, a case with publications in premier journals in different fields will likely fare better and could potentially have advocates (on college and university committees) in favor of the case in a field other than the candidate's own

        c. Some journals have much faster turnaround times and fewer rounds of review before a decision

8. Having your papers and ideas peer-reviewed

    i. Don't use the journal review process as a means to vet your ideas—the journal outlet will be wasted and your reputation may be tarnished

    ii. Present and discuss models with peers when the ideas are still in their formative stages

    iii. Peer review can come from a senior faculty member who can see the forest for the trees and suggest framing adjustments, identify relevant cites and suggest doing things that make a paper more likely to survive a grueling review process

    iv. Peer review may also come from junior colleagues or even PhD students who may not always see the forest for the trees but can help see the paper through the eyes of a reviewer

CHAPTER 13

NAVIGATING THE ASSISTANT PROFESSOR LIFE: YEARS 4 AND 5

This chapter is intentionally short. Most major activities that lead to a successful tenure case have likely already been undertaken in the first three years. The last two years are *merely* a push toward the finish line. Of course, it is often in the last two years when many of the papers you've written since the beginning of your time as an assistant professor may get accepted. The last two years before tenure is also frequently a blur. The days go by quickly and the semester goes by even more quickly, if that's possible. Often, the mad scramble in the final stages of the hunt for tenure can lead to many mistakes that can be avoided with three strategies:

1. Move papers to closure
2. Show life in other streams
3. Reviewing and networking

I repeat the caveat I discussed in Chapter 12. Before I begin discussing the three strategies, let me note that I am addressing the issue of a standard 6-year tenure clock where the evaluation for promotion and tenure happens at the end of the fifth year (or start of the sixth year). There are a few institutions that employ a longer tenure clock, e.g., 9 years. Obviously, the strategy in approaching such a situation would be somewhat different from what I recommend here. Given that my experiences do not permit me to relate to such a situation, I am not speaking to such a clock. However, I do believe the advice provided here should apply to the last two years before tenure evaluation for a 9-year clock.

1. Move Papers To Closure

While there will be heightened interest in starting many projects/papers during the last two years in the hope that one or more will hit prior to the promotion evaluation, this can be detrimental as it can create distractions. Instead, the approach should really be to focus on moving mature papers—papers that have been invited to be revised—to closure. Also, papers that have been rejected at one journal, even if after multiple rounds, are worth pushing forward. Such papers have the benefit of enormous feedback and often, reviewers may have been biased against the paper whereas the paper might fare better with a new panel. The bottom line is that papers should be moved to closure rather than starting up many new projects and papers in the hope that something will get accepted.

Related to the above point, do take the quick hits. Some papers may simply not have the potential to be published in a premier journal, but they may have an interesting empirical point within your stream of research. Such papers can be quick hits in second-tier journals. While I do not advocate a major focus on second-tier journal articles, a small number of them will increase your total number of publications and some second-tier journals may be perceived favorably by some external evaluators. Also, such articles will allow your work to have a cumulative contribution to a stream such that the whole (total contribution of your papers) is greater than the sum of the parts (contributions of individual papers).

2. Show Life In Other Streams

The reality of a six-year tenure clock makes it quite difficult to show success in several unrelated streams of research. So, I return to my earlier point about continuing research in the major stream related to the dissertation. As I mentioned when discussing a research program, in my work, my second stream of research on technology in society leveraged my first stream of research on technology in organizations. It is good to have some work in this second stream of research and show some activity—i.e., papers in 2nd round of review, initial submissions and working papers. In a five-year window, before your tenure packet has to be submitted, seldom is there an expectation that the second stream of work will have as many papers published or in the pipeline as the first stream. However, the second stream becomes important to show some separation from your advisor. As you are scrambling to find potential papers to work on that may hit (i.e., get accepted) before the tenure evaluation, try to work on those that fall into a coherent second stream. Of course, a published paper in a premier journal is always a plus. But, even if it is still under first or second round of review, it shows life and future potential that is an important criterion to evaluators.

3. Reviewing And Networking

The topic of reviewing and networking are addressed in other chapters, including chapters 11 and 17. These are key factors that can help an assistant professor get noticed by scholars who may write tenure evaluation letters. Doing good reviews in a timely manner is important. Good reviews and good reviewers tend to be noticed by editors. Tenure evaluation letters frequently contain the information about the senior scholar's experiences with the junior scholar when the latter served as a reviewer. Networking can thus be accomplished by reviewing and also by meeting key players in conferences. Both reviewing and networking are important throughout an assistant professor's life. In years 4 and 5, both reviewing and networking assume even greater importance due to the proximity to the tenure packet going out for evaluation.

Concluding Thoughts

The focus of this chapter was really to identify three simple, relatively rational strategies to help an assistant professor make that final push toward putting together the best tenure packet possible. I discussed moving papers to closure, showing life in streams other than the dissertation, and reviewing and networking. This chapter did not seek to address issues of politics and how that may relate to tenure processes, and such politics may be important as well, but is best discussed with senior colleagues and not written up!

Key Takeaways

1. Most major activities that lead to a successful tenure case have likely already been undertaken in the first three years—the last two years are *merely* a push toward the finish line
2. Move papers to closure
    i. Focus on moving forward mature papers or papers that have been invited to be revised—avoid the temptation to start many new projects that may distract you from your more mature projects
    ii. Do take the quick hits—some papers may simply not have the potential to be published in a premier journal but they may be an interesting empirical point within your stream of research and publishable in second-tier journals, thus helping you grow your overall contribution in your topic
3. Show life in other streams
    i. The reality of a five-year clock for tenure makes it quite difficult to show success in several unrelated streams of research—if possible, leverage this primary stream to demonstrate activity in other streams
    ii. Even if a paper in another stream is under first or second round of review, it shows life and future potential that are important to evaluators
4. Reviewing and networking
    i. External letter-writers are often sought for promotion and tenure evaluations—doing good reviews and networking at conferences and professional meetings is important, and can help create a favorable impression on senior scholars who may write your letters

CHAPTER 14

TEACHING PHILOSOPHY
Dr. Susan A. Brown

Associate Professor and McCoy-Rogers Fellow
Eller College of Management
University of Arizona
Tucson, AZ 85721
suebrown@eller.arizona.edu

Teaching is an important aspect of what we do as faculty members. Many doctoral programs assume that people will learn to teach by watching teachers. After all, we have many years of observation under our belts by the time we complete a doctoral program. Whether we realize it or not, we have kept track of the things we liked and didn't like about our teachers over the years. We might not have written them down, but the things that worked have a lasting impact. Likewise, the things that didn't work, like the class I was in where the instructor read the news to us, also have a lasting impact. Many of us graduate not wanting to be "that teacher." We also graduate with little, if any, formal training on how to teach. Depending on the type of school in which you work, failing to teach well can, at a minimum, have a negative impact on merit evaluations and, in the worst case, stand in the way of getting tenure. With such potentially high stakes, it is clear that teaching should not be ignored.

In a series of three chapters, starting with this one, I will take you through some basic, but important, steps that you can follow to improve your teaching and your documentation of it. Specifically, in this chapter, I will discuss developing a teaching philosophy statement. This is a very important statement that, once developed, will provide a solid foundation for how you approach teaching in the future.

A teaching philosophy is a statement of who you are as a teacher. It can be a fairly personal statement that highlights what you value with respect to teaching and learning. It is also a very useful statement that can be used in job applications, tenure portfolios and teaching award applications. Giving thought to this early in your career can save you a lot of time down the road. There are several additional resources that can help with a teaching philosophy statement and other aspects of your teaching in Table 14-1.

There are a number of ways to approach writing a teaching philosophy. In fact, if you search the web, you will come up with thousands of suggestions. Here, I will offer a handful of suggestions that should get you on your way. One additional source that may be helpful is: http://www1.umn.edu/ohr/teachlearn/tutorials/philosophy/start/prompts/index.html.

Table 14-1. Recommended Teaching Resources

Assessment: Angelo and Cross (1993)[169]

Cooperative learning: Johnson, Johnson, and Smith (1991).[170] The Johnsons are known for their work on cooperative learning. They have a number of books. This one has tools you can use in class.

Course portfolios: courseportfolio.org. This is the "Peer Review of Teaching Project" web site. It has sample portfolios as well as resources.

Learner-centered instruction: Huba and Freed (1999).[171]

Teaching portfolios: Seldin, Miller, and Seldin (2010).[172]

Teaching tips: Boice (2000);[173] Davis (1993);[174] Fink (2003);[175] McKeachie (2006);[176] Walvoord, Anderson, and Angelo (1998).[177]

Other resources: Wiley Periodicals (Jossey-Bass): *New Directions for Teaching and Learning;*[178] IDEA papers at The IDEA center: theideacenter.org/.

I ask you to think about seven questions so you can develop and understand your teaching philosophy:
1. What makes a teacher effective?
2. What is your role as an instructor?
3. What are your goals for your students?
4. What are your methods and techniques in the classroom?
5. How do you evaluate your effectiveness?
6. How do you connect research to teaching (if applicable)?
7. What will the obituary to your class say?

I discuss possible ways to formulate answers to these seven questions, with a view toward helping you build a teaching philosophy statement.

1. What Makes A Teacher Effective?

One way to begin writing your teaching philosophy is to reflect on all of the teachers you have had over the course of your learning career. Which teachers were most effective and why? Which teachers were ineffective and why? If you were teaching those classes, what would you do differently? Answering these questions will help you to see what you appreciate as a learner. It's important to remember though, that, as a learner, you are different. Most people will not go on to complete an advanced degree, let alone a PhD. So, when thinking about what you appreciate in a class, think about the student for whom school is a challenge and what does *that* student need? This idea has had a profound impact on how I think about my classes.

2. What Is Your Role As An Instructor?

As you work on your statement, it's important to reflect on why you want to teach. What is it about teaching that excites you? What are your beliefs and values with respect to teaching? What kind of teacher are you? Some people might feel that their role as a teacher is to impart knowledge—give the students what they need to know. Others might see themselves as coaches who help guide students to get to the knowledge. Still others might feel that the key to student learning is to be an entertainer—provide an environment where students don't realize they are learning. It's important to think about how you see yourself in the learning process.

3. What Are Your Goals For Your Students?

Along with considering your role in the learning process, it's important to determine your goals for students. Is there something that students should get from all of your classes? Perhaps you have students engage in projects that are specifically designed to help them become better writers or better team members. These are important goals to consider. If you have specialized in teaching a particular class, you might have very specific goals for that class. If you have taught multiple courses, think about the themes that run across your classes. This is a very good indication of your goals, even if you haven't previously articulated them. If you haven't taught much, then thinking about the good and not-so-good classes you have taken can help you begin to formulate your goals.

4. What Are Your Methods And Techniques In The Classroom?

As your beliefs start to become clear(er), it's important to consider how you enact them in the classroom. What specific methods or techniques do you use to reinforce them? If you are a coach, how do you guide students to obtain the knowledge they need? Once you have taught and used some of these techniques, you can leverage them as examples in your philosophy statement. For example, if you say that student-student interaction is important and you provide an environment that fosters it, you should provide an example of a technique that you use that fosters such an interaction. Try to provide concrete examples to tie things together.

5. How Do You Evaluate Your Effectiveness?

Now that you've thought about your role, the students' roles and the techniques you use, it's time to consider how you will know if you have been effective. How will students behave if they have learned what you want them to learn? What will they be able to do if you've done a good job? How you will deal with (or have dealt with) a negative outcome? How do you deal with student feedback? If closing the feedback loop is important to you as a teacher, you should discuss that in your philosophy statement. What do you do with the end-of-semester feedback?

Have you made changes because of it? If you have, then they provide nice, concrete examples for you to include in your portfolio.

6. How Do You Connect Research To Teaching (If Applicable)?

Another aspect of your teaching can be how you incorporate your research into your teaching. This can be based on topics and how they map to the courses you teach or it can be how you invite students to participate in your research to augment their learning. Both aspects of connecting teaching and research can be meaningful in the teaching portfolio.

7. What Will The Obituary To Your Class Say?

We can also take a page from *the popular book on 7 Habits of Highly Effective People* (Covey 1990),[179] where writing your own obituary is seen as a way to spur you to where you'd like to be. Although we won't be writing *your* obituary, we will write an obituary for *your class*! Imagine that the semester is over and people are writing reviews of your class. Who are the people who would be writing these obituaries? Most likely it would be your students, your peers and your department head. Think about what you would like the students to say. How would they describe the class? What would they say about what they learned? How would they describe you as a teacher? Why would they tell other people to take your class? If a peer was observing your class, what would he or she say about it? Likewise, what might your department head say about your class? Envisioning what you would like people to notice can help further highlight your values.

Below is an example using my teaching philosophy. Writing a teaching philosophy statement is not a one-time event. I encourage you to revisit it from time to time. Over time, your beliefs may evolve and your teaching techniques may change accordingly. The simple act of keeping your teaching philosophy at the forefront in your awareness can have a significant impact on your teaching. Table 14-2 shows a sample of my philosophy statement dating back to when I was an assistant professor.

Table 14-2. Teaching Philosophy

My teaching revolves around three beliefs. First, I believe that students must actively participate to learn. Second, I believe that students will actively participate when they feel it is "safe" to do so, and perceive that the instructor is interested in them, their learning and the topic. Third, I believe that learning must be challenging but fun. My primary goal is to provide a classroom environment where even the most reticent students participate in some manner and wrong answers are seen as learning opportunities. To do this, I rely on active learning techniques, critical thinking exercises and cooperative learning groups.

There is a significant body of research that supports the importance of active participation in the learning process. My class notes are "fill-in-the-blank" so that students cannot passively

Table 14-2 *Continued*. Teaching Philosophy

listen to me or simply print my notes and avoid the class all together. I rely heavily on in-class activities that provide opportunities for students to *apply* what we have been discussing. For some portion of nearly every class, students work individually, in pairs or in groups to work through a problem. I particularly like to use cooperative learning groups that make the students responsible for each other's learning. They often find, as I have, that it is when we have to teach something to others that we truly learn it. I am also very diligent about providing multiple avenues for participation. I rely on electronic mail, listservs and small group activities to elicit participation from the less out-going students. My goal is to provide a non-threatening environment in which all students actively engage with the material.

To encourage participation and help students feel "safe," I try to create a non-threatening environment in which I get to know the students on an individual basis. Some students are happy to take risks and talk in class, while others sit quietly hoping I won't ever call on them. As a teacher, it is important to me that I build relationships with my students. I take pictures of the students and try to learn their names as quickly as I can. I have found that when I get to know something about the students, they react to me as a person, open up to my ideas and actually learn more in my classes. As they get to know me, they realize that I am most excited when they "get it." I honestly don't think there is anything more gratifying in the classroom than when a struggling student finally sees the light! I care that they learn the material and I believe my students know that. In addition, I think many of my students want to learn because they see how excited I am about their learning and about the topic—excitement breeds excitement (or at least interest).

To foster excitement, I aim to make my courses challenging and fun; it's not always easy to have both. I do have a reputation for being a hard grader and for expecting a lot from my students. To me, that is good because it means that many of the students will rise to my expectations. To balance this out, however, I constantly stress the importance and value of *wrong* answers *in the classroom.* I try to make students feel at ease when they attempt to answer a question and mention how helpful that wrong answer was to everyone else in the class by pointing out the learning as well as the fact that others were likely thinking the same thing. I also offer "anonymous" opportunities for students to go to the board with their answers and encourage them to leave their mistakes out there for everyone to see...and from which everyone can learn. Finally, I try to use as many different techniques as possible in the hopes of capturing everyone's interest.

I have incorporated a number of active learning and group exercises into the course. I have increased the number of in-class active learning exercises, added cooperative learning exercises, used crossword puzzles to review concepts and modified a jeopardy game to use as a tool to engage students in reviews of course material. I have received very positive feedback about these activities. The active learning exercises provide opportunities for the students to

Table 14-2 *Continued*. Teaching Philosophy

apply the material they have read (and we have discussed). The cooperative learning group exercises are used to review particularly difficult material—and are always given rave reviews! The students are organized in groups, given an assignment (for which they can receive a certain number of homework points) and told that everyone in the group must understand the answer. When they are ready to answer, I go to the group and select the "explainer"—if the person can explain the answer, the whole group gets the points—if not, I go away while the group teaches this person the concept they have missed. The crossword puzzles help students to learn the important terminology of the course, while the jeopardy game is used to review for the final exam. The game highlights the main topics and provides a way for the students to check their own learning. Finally, I use a semester-long project that provides an opportunity for students to apply their newly learned knowledge and integrate it in order to understand the bigger picture. There are not very many good projects of this sort in existence so I have had to modify and write my own for use in this course. These projects are extremely important for the students because they help them move away from thinking about the course in terms of chapters and move toward an understanding of the big picture, i.e., how this works in the real world.

Concluding Thoughts

A teaching philosophy is a very important statement. If you have never thought about it, I hope this chapter spurred you to be reflective. Once you've got a statement together, it can serve as a roadmap for where you want to go and what you may want to change. The statement is not a static one—as you make changes, you can change it to reflect your current thinking. Ideally, at the time of your promotion evaluation, the statement captures how good and thoughtful a teacher you are!

Key Takeaways

1. A teaching philosophy is a statement of who you are as a teacher
2. In writing a teaching philosophy, consider the following questions:
    i. What makes a teacher effective?
    ii. What is your role as an instructor?
    iii. What are your goals for your students?
    iv. What are your method and techniques in the classroom?
    v. How do you evaluate your effectiveness?
    vi. How do you connect research to teaching (if applicable)?
    vii. What will the obituary to your class say?
3. Recommend teaching resources are included in Table 14-1
4. Revisit your teaching philosophy statement—your beliefs and approaches may evolve

Chapter 15

Course Syllabus
Dr. Susan A. Brown

Associate Professor and McCoy-Rogers Fellow
Eller College of Management
University of Arizona
Tucson, AZ 85721
suebrown@eller.arizona.edu

In this chapter, I will discuss the ingredients of a course syllabus and how to develop an effective course syllabus. Related to this, I will also talk about the importance of your course syllabus and how to write good learning outcomes. As more universities and accreditation organizations, such as the Association to Advance Collegiate Schools of Business (AACSB), are paying attention to assessment, it is critical that you write good learning outcomes and develop techniques to determine how well students have achieved them.

A course syllabus is an extremely important document. It describes the course and outlines what you expect students to learn from the course. It also lays out the requirements and the schedule for the course. The syllabus is essentially a contract between the students and you. You are agreeing to provide content within a specific schedule and if students participate in the class and the assignments, they should learn those things identified in the objectives. Davis (1993)[180] provides a nice outline of what to include in the syllabus, recommending that you include more information than less. In addition, you should consider the elements that are relevant to your particular institution. For example, most universities have statements that need to be included about students with disabilities. One university in which I worked had us include building and evacuation plans. You should follow your university's guidelines regarding the expectations for the course syllabus.

One of the most important aspects of the syllabus is the description of the course objectives. In the past few years, there has been a growing interest in approaching the objectives through the lens of learning outcomes. Learning outcomes are being used as the basis of assessment in many colleges and universities today as the importance of documenting student learning has been elevated by accreditation agencies, including the AACSB. By specifying learning outcomes, the focus is shifted to the student and what the student will take away from the course, rather than what the teacher will provide.

Huba and Freed (1999)[181] offer excellent suggestions for writing learning outcomes. I have found their suggestions very helpful and summarize three of their key points here:
1. Use action verbs

2. Focus on outcomes, not activities
3. Focus on key (not trivial) aspects of the course

Learning outcomes communicate what the instructor sees as important in the course. In writing learning outcomes, it is important to keep in mind that the focus is on the learner. It is not about what you will teach or how you will teach it; it is about what the students will learn and what they will be able to do as a result of taking this course.

1. Use Action Verbs

To begin, learning outcomes should be stated using action verbs. Some words and phrases, such as *be familiar with*, *understand* and *know*, do not truly communicate the knowledge and skills students will get from the course. Table 15-1 is a list of action words and phrases that can be used in developing learning outcomes.

Table 15-1. Action Words And Phrases For Learning Outcomes

accept	compose	employ	label	rate
analyze	compute	estimate	list	recall
apply	conclude	evaluate		recognize
appraise	construct	examine	manage	recommend
appreciate	contrast	experiment	measure	relate
arrange	convince	explain		reproduce
articulate	create	express	name	restate
assemble	criticize	extend		review
assess			operate	
associate	defend	formulate	order	schedule
attempt	define		organize	set up
	demonstrate	give examples		share
calculate	describe		plan	show
categorize	design	identify	practice	solve
challenge	diagram	indicate	praise	suggest
choose	differentiate	interpret	predict	summarize
classify	discuss	investigate	prepare	support
collect	dispute		propose	
compare	distinguish	join		tabulate
		judge	question	tell
			quote	translate

Using two statements, it is possible to easily illustrate some of the most common misconceptions about the way in which we, as instructors, think about learning objectives:

i.   *Students will understand how to create an entity-relationship diagram.*

ii.   *Students will be able to draw a conceptual model of the data requirements for a particular business problem.*

The first statement does not directly connect to what students will be able to do as a result of the course. How will you measure their understanding? If they understand how to create the model, then they should be able to draw one. Thus, while the first statement gets at important course learning, it does not connect directly to a specific outcome. By being more specific, it is easier to connect learning outcomes to assessments (i.e., measurements) that in turn makes it easier to demonstrate that students are learning.

2. Focus On Outcomes, Not Activities

Learning outcomes should focus on outcomes, rather than the activities that students will do. As an example, consider the difference between these two statements:
i.   *Students will be exposed to the terminology in the field of MIS.*
ii. *Students will be able to use and explain MIS terminology.*

The first statement focuses on the activity that will be used to achieve the learning outcome represented in the second statement. The difference is subtle but important. If you think about this in light of assessment, consider how you would determine whether or not the first objective was met. Perhaps you would look at how many lectures or assignments are in the course that exposes students to the terminology. But, in this example, the assessment is about what you, the teacher, are doing, not what the students are *learning*. In the second statement, you could evaluate the students' ability to use and explain the terminology through exam questions. In this statement, the focus is on the learning, not the teaching.

3. Focus On Key (Non-Trivial) Aspects Of The Course

Learning outcomes should reflect the critical aspects of learning in the course. In an attempt to create learning outcomes that are measurable, it might be tempting to focus on outcomes that are easy to measure. But, it is important to keep in mind that the learning outcomes of your course need to be meaningful to outsiders, including people in your field at other universities and people outside of your field within your university. Essentially, other people who teach this class should agree that these are the important things students should learn in a course of this type and they should make sense to potential external letter writers, promotion and tenure committee members, and potential employers.

Ultimately, the learning outcomes of a course are situated within larger curriculum and institutional settings. It is possible that the institution or program in which you teach has learning outcome targets. For example, in a business school, we might see a learning outcome along the lines of: "students will effectively communicate ideas in written and oral presentations." If oral or written presentations are an important element of your course, you might have a learning outcome that is directly connected to this.

Clearly articulating learning outcomes provides a valuable foundation for instructors who want to document student learning. Similar to your teaching philosophy, learning outcomes should be revisited regularly to be sure they are still relevant and the primary focus for your course. Table 15-2 is a sample course syllabus, using these principles.

Table 15-2. Sample Syllabus

S307 - Data Management
Course Logistics

Class Information:

Section:	4807
Time:	M, W 1:00-2:15
Location:	BU202
Web page:	(ADD SOCIAL MEDIA OF YOUR CHOICE HERE)

Instructor:

Name:	Sue Brown
Office:	BU 560E
Office Hours:	M 2:30-3:30 (other times by appointment, please)
Phone:	812.855.3484
Fax:	812.855.4985
Email:	suebrown@indiana.edu (please use this for communication with ME)

Required Text: McFadden, Fred R., Hoffer, Jeffrey A., and Prescott, Mary B. Modern Database Management. Fifth Edition, Addison-Wesley, 1999.

Suggested Supplemental Texts: Books about VB, Access, Oracle, SQL—anything that would be useful to you in completing the technology-based assignments in this class.

Course Description

Database management systems are at the heart of modern business information systems. They facilitate the sharing of data across the organization and therefore support the notion that data is a corporate resource. Data management, which focuses on data collection, storage and retrieval, constitutes a core activity for any organization. This course covers the basic concepts of data management, database systems and database applications in business. The goal of this course is to provide adequate technical detail while emphasizing the organizational and implementation issues relevant to the management of data in an organizational environment. Topics include: relational data modeling, logical database design, structured query language, client/server systems, data warehousing and database administration.

Table 15-2 *Continued*. Sample Syllabus

Course Objectives

Students in this course will learn about the design, implementation, use and management of database management systems. The course material is divided into three related components. During the first part of the course, we will focus on data models and logical database design. This component of the course will emphasize relational databases. At the end of this part of the course, you will understand the advantages and disadvantages of the database approach to data management, the components of a database system, the constructs of the entity-relationship model and the principles of normalization. You will be able to draw and discuss an entity-relationship model showing the structure and meaning of the data used in a business organization, and you will be able to apply the principles of normalization to the logical design of a relational database.

In the second component of the course, we will discuss physical database design and data retrieval using a standard database language (SQL). This component of the course continues the emphasis on relational databases. After completing this part of the course, you will understand how to use techniques, such as denormalization and indexes for enhancing the retrieval of data from relational databases. You will also understand the cost and benefit tradeoffs inherent in these techniques. Finally, you will be able to write SQL queries to create and retrieve data from relational databases.

The third component of the course addresses the administration of both centralized and distributed databases, database standards, planning for database systems, and a discussion of advanced concepts, such as transaction management, concurrency control, distributed and client/server database systems, data warehousing and object orientation in databases. After completing this part of the course, you will understand concurrency and database security problems as well as techniques for managing these problems. You will also have a basic understanding of client/server architecture and the options available for distributing data in organizations. You will understand the technical and managerial issues associated with the design and implementation of global client/server databases. Finally, you will have a firm grasp of the issues and terminology used in data warehousing.

Course Format

This class is designed to combine a variety of techniques to capture everyone's interests. The readings and lectures will provide a base of knowledge that participants can use in other components of the course. In-class exercises provide an arena for applying the knowledge base. Class discussions provide an opportunity for discovery (or a-ha experiences). This design can only work if everyone does the readings prior to class and everyone participates in the exercises and discussions. Practice makes perfect, particularly in the first two components of this course.

Table 15-2 *Continued*. Sample Syllabus

Course Requirements and Grading

Your performance in this course will be evaluated in four areas: class participation, homework assignments, a group project and two exams. Each will be weighted as follows:

Class Participation	10%
Homework Assignments	10%
Group Project	25%
Midterm Exam	25%
Final Exam	30%

Overall Grading Guidelines

The letter grading systems (ABCDF +/-) will be used in this course. The following interpretation of this grading scale will be used:

A = **Excellent work.** Assigned work is clearly presented, thoughtful, insightful and creative. The student has demonstrated that the course material has been thoroughly learned. The student has demonstrated the creative application of the course material to novel situations.

B = **Good work.** Assigned work is clearly presented and thoughtful. The student has clearly demonstrated that the course material has been learned.

C = **Acceptable work.** Assigned work is completed and the course standards are met. The student has clearly demonstrated that much of the course material has been learned.

D = **Marginally acceptable work.** Most of the assigned work is completed in a way that meets the course standards or all of the assigned work is completed in a way that almost meets the course standards. The student has clearly demonstrated that some of the course material has been learned.

F = **Unacceptable work.** The student has not clearly demonstrated that the course material has been learned.

All CIS courses have a target grade range. The range for this course (and all 300-level CIS courses) is 2.9-3.1. This target range was established by the CIS faculty.

Class Participation

In order for the design of this class to work, we all must be actively involved in the class. First, we must attend. Second, we must have read and thought about the material. Third, we must be willing to share our thoughts and ideas to enhance our own and others' learning. Please realize that it's OK to be wrong. What I mean by this is if you try to answer a question and your answer is incorrect, there is a good chance you are not alone! By seeing the wrong answers and understanding why they are wrong, we ALL learn. Of course, wrong answers on exams still carry a penalty (that's why they are so valuable in class!!). If you have any questions about your class participation, please see me.

One way of finding new and exciting topics for discussion would be to read the trade press

Table 15-2 *Continued*. Sample Syllabus

(e.g., ComputerWorld, Newsweek, Time, Wall Street Journal) or search the Web for articles related to the course material. As a CIS major (or minor), it's a good idea to stay informed about what is going on in organizations in terms of information systems in general and data management more specifically.

Homework Assignments

The effective assimilation of the technical course material requires repeated exposure and practice. The homework assignments are designed to encourage students to adopt the habit of working actively with the course material. The objectives of the homework assignments are to help students understand the course material and to help both the students and the instructor recognize any points that are not yet completely understood. You are encouraged to diligently attempt each homework problem. However, if you get seriously stuck on a problem, make a note of the specific difficulty you are having and move on. You may discuss the homework problems with your classmates before they are due. However, *you should work independently when you actually write up your work.* For instance, if two (or more) homework answers have the same typos, I have no choice but to assume you have not done independent work and this is a violation of the honor code and I will take appropriate action, ranging from a reduction in grade to reporting the violation. Even more important, it is essential that you individually understand the homework assignments in order to do well on the exams.

Group Project

The goals of the group project are: (1) to integrate and apply what you learn in this class; (2) to give you experience working in team situations; and (3) to enhance your communication and presentation skills. Teams, created jointly by you and me, will consist of four or five students.

The working system, a final written report and an oral presentation to the class will be the basis for the project grade. During the semester, you will be asked to provide feedback on your own and other team members' commitment and contribution. The objective of this peer evaluation is to encourage 100% commitment and performance from each team member throughout the semester. Your work should be of professional presentation quality. This means you would be proud to share it with business people or other faculty members. Indeed, we may invite other faculty members or business people to attend the presentations. More details will be provided.

Exam

There will be two exams in this course—the first one will count toward 25% and the second one toward 30%. The final exam will cover all of the course material, although material covered after the midterm will be emphasized. The exams will consist of multiple formats (i.e., multiple choice, short answer, problems, etc.). They will be designed to assess your basic understanding of the concepts and their application. Prior to the exams, I will provide a review sheet and example questions.

Table 15-2 *Continued*. Sample Syllabus

Possibility for Bonus Points

An opportunity for bonus points may be available for participation in a course-related research study. Students who participate in such a study will be awarded the equivalent of full credit on one homework (this means if you do really badly on one homework that you can still get full credit on it!).

Miscellaneous Grading and Course Info

Timeliness. If you want full credit for a written assignment, you will have to turn it in at the beginning of the class period on the day it is due. Late work will not be accepted. If you have obligations that conflict with exam or assignment due dates, you should make arrangements with the instructor as soon as possible. Feel free to email or fax homework assignments, if necessary.

Missed Exams/Assignment. Make-up exams will be given only in extraordinary circumstances. If you expect to miss an exam or to be unable to meet another requirement, please discuss this with the instructor before the scheduled date.

Score/Grade Appeals. It is important to recognize that a grade reflects another's judgment of your work. In this sense, all grading is subjective. Of course, any grade you receive on an assignment or quiz is subject to appeal. However, score changes are at the discretion of the instructor. It is important to understand that your score may go up or down based upon a complete review of the work in question. It is usually the case that changing a few points on an assignment rarely makes a difference in the final grade. Time is much better spent discussing and clarifying the information content presented in the course.

Incomplete Grades Policy. A grade of Incomplete may be awarded to students who have a legitimate reason for needing additional time to complete a course. Legitimate reasons include emergencies or extenuating circumstances that prevent a student from completing the course requirements within the normal time frame. Students must initiate the request for an incomplete prior to the end of the semester and must be in good standing in the course. In no case will a grade of incomplete be awarded to someone seeking more time to master the course material in order to improve their grade.

Withdrawal Deadline. The final day to withdraw from any School of Business course with an automatic "W" is Wednesday, October 24th at 4:00 pm. After that date, virtually no withdrawals will be permitted. This policy applies to all students enrolled in any School of Business course.

Academic Conduct. You are expected to abide by the Undergraduate Honor Code in this course. It is assumed that you have a copy, and have read and understand this code. If you need a copy, you may obtain one from the Undergraduate Office or from me. Further, you are

Table 15-2 *Continued*. Sample Syllabus

expected, especially as information systems professionals in training, to respect campus computer resources and to use them productively and wisely. For example, you should not illegally copy software and you should refrain from sending abusive electronic mail messages.

Accommodations for Students with Special Needs. Any student in this class who has a documented visual or physical impairment, hearing disability or any other disability covered by the University's Services for students with Disabilities should contact the instructor during the first week of class to discuss and arrange any instructional accommodations that may be necessary. Students who would like to serve as volunteer tutors, readers or note takers for students needing special assistance are encouraged to contact the instructor during the first week of class.

Course Schedule

Date	Topic	Reading	What is Due?
Aug. 27	Introduction to the course		Buy Book☺
Aug. 29	Introduction to database systems	Chapter 1	
Sept. 3	Entity-Relationship Model	Chapter 3	Subscribe to social media☺
Sept. 5	Entity-Relationship Model (cont.) and Enhanced ER Model	Chapter 4	
Sept. 10	More ER diagramming		
Sept. 12	Relational Databases and Normalization	Chapter 6	Homework assignment #1 (ER diagramming)
Sept. 17	Relational Databases and Normalization (cont.)	Appendix B	
Sept. 19	Relational Databases and Normalization (cont.)	Re-read chapter 6!	*This can be confusing material. Re-reading the chapter helps!*
Sept. 24	Relational Databases and Normalization (cont.)		
Sept. 26	*Group Day (interviews for conceptual Model, in my office)*		Homework assignment #2 (Normalization) **Due by 5:00 pm**
Oct. 1	ER and Normalization - *Pulling it together*		
Oct. 3	***Group Project Presentations***		*Project - Conceptual Model **Due** Conceptual Model Presentations*
Oct. 8	Review for midterm		
Oct. 10	**MIDTERM**		MIDTERM

Table 15-2 *Continued*. Sample Syllabus

Oct. 15	Physical Design (index and denormal) Return Midterm	Chapter 7	
Oct. 17	Data Retrieval	Chapter 9	
Oct. 22			Oracle /SQL Lab. Class held in BU419
Oct. 24			*Project - Logical Model **Due** Logical Model Presentations*
Oct. 29	Data Retrieval (cont.)		
Oct. 31	Data Retrieval (cont.)		Homework assignment #3 (Oracle)
Nov. 5	Data Retrieval (cont.)		
Nov. 7	Data Retrieval. SQL Challenge day		Homework assignment #4 (SQL)
Nov. 12	Distributed and Client/Server Databases	Chapter 8, 11	
Nov. 14	***Group Project Presentations***		*Project - Final Design Presentations Preliminary database systems due*
Nov. 19	*Group Day*		Work on Final designs!
Nov. 21	No Class Thanksgiving		
Nov. 26	Data Administration	Chapter 13	
Nov. 28	Data Warehousing	Chapter 14	
Dec. 3	Catch-up and wrap up of material		***All Projects Due***
Dec. 5	Review for Final		*Jeopardy!*
Dec 12	**Final Exam all sections**		

Concluding Thoughts

The course syllabus is a key document as it represents a contract between your students and you. It tells them what your expectations are, what they can get out of the course and where to turn regarding various course-related issues as the semester progresses. A key step in ensuring that you are an effective teacher is to have a comprehensive and comprehendible syllabus. I hope this chapter has you on your way to building such a syllabus.

Key Takeaways

1. A course syllabus outlines what you expect students to learn from the course, lays out the requirements and schedule for the course

2. Be aware of what your institution requires you to include in the syllabus
3. The syllabus should include learning outcomes. In writing learning outcomes:
   i. Use action verbs
   ii. Focus on outcomes, not activities
   iii. Focus on key (not trivial) aspects of the course
4. Revisit your learning outcomes from time to time to make sure they are still relevant and the primary focus of your course
5. The illustration provides information on what could go in various sections of the syllabus

CHAPTER 16

DOCUMENTING TEACHING EFFECTIVENESS:
COURSE PORTFOLIO

Dr. Susan A. Brown

Associate Professor and McCoy-Rogers Fellow
Eller College of Management
University of Arizona
Tucson, AZ 85721
suebrown@eller.arizona.edu

The teaching philosophy and learning outcomes serve as important foundation elements for the meat of this chapter documenting your teaching effectiveness. I'll talk about teaching and course portfolios, and walk you through the process of creating a benchmark course portfolio, preparing an inquiry portfolio to include leveraging the data for pedagogical publications.

Now that you have taken the time to think about who you are as a teacher and you have developed a syllabus with clear learning outcomes, it's time to deliver the class. We all want to believe that students will be hanging on to our every word; that they will soak up everything we tell them like sponges. And, sometimes they do. However, it is likely that at some point, someone will ask you for evidence that you're an effective teacher. The default is to provide the student evaluation score for the question that addresses how effective the teacher is. There are a number of variations on this question but the bottom line is to determine how happy students are with the instructor.

Documenting teaching effectiveness is valuable for both personal and professional reasons. From a personal perspective, understanding how your teaching is impacting students can lead to a better experience in the classroom for the students and you. Knowing what works and does not work can make going into a classroom a more positive experience. Professionally, having evidence that you are teaching effectively can be leveraged to get a job and to be promoted. But, when it comes to documenting teaching effectiveness, universities tend to rely on student evaluation scores and typically, the question regarding the quality or effectiveness of the instructor. Thankfully, student evaluations are not the only mechanism for doing this.

For decades now, we have known that many things can impact student evaluation scores. Courses that are required by all students are often rated lower than courses that are either elective or within a student's major area (e.g., Kulik and McKeachie 1975; Marsh and Dunkin 1992; McKeachie 1979).[182,183,184] Likewise, there are gender differences in teaching evaluations. For example, female teachers tend to receive lower evaluations if they do not fall within a traditionally female stereotype, such as sister or mother (Anderson and Miller 1997).[185] Some instructors take a risk by trying something innovative in their classes. If the students like the innovation, there is no harm. However, if the students do not like this creative endeavor, the evaluations will reflect it. Should the instructor be punished for trying something new if it didn't work? In the event that your teaching evaluations are good, someone might ask if it's because the course (read: grading) is *easy*. There is evidence of a significant positive correlation between course grades and teaching evaluations (Gilbuagh 1982; Marsh 1987; Rice 1988).[186,187,188] It is, however, possible for many students to earn high grades while participating in a challenging course. But, you need evidence to demonstrate this.

Obtaining respectable student evaluation scores are very important but attaining high scores is not entirely under the control of the instructor. So, what is a faculty member to do? Fortunately, there are mechanisms for both improving those scores (by improving teaching) and offering alternative or additional evidence in support of teaching excellence.

Teaching portfolios are the tool that is often used at the time of promotion and tenure to evaluate someone's teaching. Traditional teaching portfolios are simply an accumulation of course materials, such as syllabi, assignments and exams. While valuable for demonstrating the work someone has done in preparing their course, teaching portfolios do not provide evidence of teaching effectiveness or student learning. Another viable option for demonstrating teaching effectiveness and student learning is the course portfolio.

In this chapter, I will discuss:
1. What a course portfolio is and how it differs from a teaching portfolio
2. How to prepare a course portfolio, with specific guidelines for developing and structuring a benchmark portfolio
3. How to prepare an inquiry portfolio and the value of peer interaction and review during the process of portfolio development
4. How to leverage the data collected for the portfolio into developing pedagogical publications

1. What Is It?

Course portfolios (www.courseportfolio.org) provide a mechanism for documenting the scholarly work of teaching. Each course portfolio is focused on one particular course. By preparing a portfolio, the instructor can investigate student learning and gather evidence to actually demonstrate it. Further, a course portfolio provides an opportunity to make teaching more public. With many universities moving in a direction where the teaching evaluations alone are not sufficient to demonstrate teaching excellence, course portfolios provide another means of demonstrating teaching excellence or at least awareness and improvement. Let me first explain what a course portfolio is.

A course portfolio differs from a teaching portfolio in three important ways:

i.   The course portfolio focuses on one course. In contrast, a teaching portfolio can be thought of as an accumulation of the syllabi and other teaching materials for all of the courses one has taught.

ii.   The course portfolio focuses on student learning, while the teaching portfolio focuses on teaching and delivery of materials.

iii. The course portfolio is a scholarly investigation of the relationship between teaching and student learning. The teaching portfolio does not include such an investigation.

There are a number of reasons for preparing course portfolios:

i.   From a professional perspective, course portfolios can be used as an alternative or a complement to traditional student evaluations of teaching. There are a number of courses in any particular domain that are deemed as challenges—those courses that no matter how good a teacher is, the nature of the course or types of students who take it renders it difficult to obtain high teaching ratings. The course portfolio can be used to provide evidence of student learning, regardless of student feelings toward the course or instructor.

ii.   Because the course portfolio requires a scholarly investigation of student learning, one by-product can be pedagogical publications. Many fields have specific outlets for research of this kind.

iii. From a personal perspective, a course portfolio can help answer the question, "is what I'm doing in the classroom working?" In addition, the evidence that is gathered can point out areas where teaching can be improved or help to highlight specific problems that students are having with the material.

iv.   Course portfolios can be used to train doctoral students or new faculty members. The details that are provided in a course portfolio provide a syllabus, learning outcomes and sample course assignments. These can be valuable for people who are just beginning to teach.

There are two types of course portfolios: benchmark and inquiry. The benchmark portfolio provides documentation of a course, including the syllabus, teaching materials and teaching methods. Included in a benchmark portfolio are illustrations of student work or other bits of evidence that allow a reader to assess student learning. In addition, the benchmark portfolio should include a reflection on the student learning as documented in the course portfolio. An outcome of a benchmark portfolio might be the identification of some aspect of a course that could benefit from a change or an intervention. The inquiry portfolio focuses on evaluating that change or intervention.

2. Preparing A Course Portfolio

In a perfect world, the process of creating a course portfolio would happen in a group setting. This way, you can receive feedback on the various elements of your portfolio. If this cannot happen, I suggest you find a colleague, at your school or another school, who is willing to read and comment on your documents. Having fresh eyes read your course syllabus, for instance, can help ensure that you are saying what you mean to say and that your learning objectives are clear and focus on what students should learn. Think about the course portfolio as a research project. You need to have a good, clear introduction, followed by the appropriate literature and convincing evidence to support your claims. Along the way, you might share it with peers to get feedback on the various aspects, just like you would with a research paper. One goal of course portfolios is to make teaching—and learning—more visible.

There are three key steps to beginning the portfolio:
i.   Select a course
ii. Develop the course goals
iii. Determine the type of portfolio you want to develop

i. Select A Course
The first step of creating a course portfolio is to select a course. For your first course portfolio, I recommend you use a course with which you are comfortable. Focus on a course you have taught and developed materials for so that you can begin making the connection between the course goals and the teaching materials.

ii. Develop The Course Goals
Once you have selected the course, take a step back and look at the syllabus. One thing that is very important in the creation of a course portfolio is to make sure that the goals for the course are clearly specified and measurable. If you have spent time on your learning outcomes, this step is already completed. In crafting the goals, think about where this course fits in the broader curriculum. For example, if this is the first course in the major, it is likely that students will learn something in this class that they will need later in their academic career. If it is the last course in the major, it might represent an opportunity to re-assess learning that should have occurred earlier in their academic program. If it's a class that all students have to take, what is the level of knowledge that students should acquire? In any event, both the instructor and the students need to understand where this course fits in the curriculum, and what the students should be bringing to the course and what they should be taking away.

iii. What Type Of Portfolio?
The next important question is to determine what type of portfolio you want to develop. If you have never created a course portfolio before, I recommend beginning with a benchmark portfolio. It provides a mechanism for truly understanding where the course is today and identifying things that might need to be changed in the future. If, however, you know there is

something wrong with an aspect of your course such that there is a negative impact on student learning, then an inquiry portfolio may be more appropriate.

3. Preparing The Benchmark Portfolio

Assuming you have spent good quality time making sure that the learning outcomes are well-articulated, you have a foundation upon which to build. The next step is to reflect on your teaching methods. This is where having a teaching philosophy statement is valuable. With the philosophy in mind, you should be able to think about the techniques you use in class and why you use them.

Consider the following questions as you reflect on your teaching:
i.   What methods are you using in and out of the classroom?
ii.   Why have you chosen these methods?
iii. What assignments are you having students do?
iv.   What is the purpose of each assignment?
v.   How is the larger curriculum influencing your choices?

As you answer each of these questions, you should be making connections between the methods and assignments in your course and the learning outcomes. This might lead you to rethink the course learning outcomes, but that is just fine—it's part of the process. Your answers to these questions will be used in developing the course portfolio. As you think about a specific method you use in your class and the rationale for using it, you should consider how it helps you achieve one or more learning outcomes. When you consider the assignments you have students do, think about the learning outcomes they address. The student assignments and the evaluation of them can provide documentation of student learning.

Once you have reflected on the syllabus and the teaching methods, it's time to determine what evidence you need to demonstrate student learning. How will you know if students have learned the material? This fundamental question is at the core of the assessment movement. It's important to acknowledge that there are many ways to determine whether or not students have learned key concepts. Certainly, exam questions are one valuable way to do this. However, there are many others. For example, in courses that have projects, some (or all) aspects of the project can be used to demonstrate that students have learned the material. As you work to connect the learning outcomes to the course assignments, this will become clearer. Another important element of providing evidence of student learning is the degree to which the assessment documents are able to differentiate across students. While it might be tempting to leverage assessments that demonstrate *all* students are learning at an extremely high level, it is unlikely to be an accurate reflection of reality.

There are two very important things to keep in mind as you are working on a benchmark portfolio. First, data collection could go on forever. You have a captive audience of subjects and their data will be valuable to you. However, you must have a stopping rule! The ideal scenario would be to collect the documents and evidence in one semester. For a benchmark portfolio, one semester should be sufficient to capture the snapshot of where the class is today. If your learning outcomes were not stated properly or you didn't have a good data collection plan laid out at the beginning of the semester, then it could flow over to a second semester. But, do not let this drag on for years! When I was creating a portfolio, there was a group of us that met regularly to develop our portfolios. One of the people in the group had been collecting data for three years. He had an entire binder filled with data and different analyses. You do not need that much information for the benchmark portfolio. Set a timeframe and when the time is up, be done! Second, I encourage you to approach this like a research project. Apply the same level of rigor in your data collection and analysis as you would for a research paper. This helps to make the connection between teaching and research. In addition, it increases the chances that the evidence you collect will be publishable in a pedagogical outlet.[189]

4. Structuring The Portfolio

Now that you have compiled all of the paperwork and gathered all of the evidence, it's time to prepare the course portfolio. Once again, I encourage you to think about this as a research project. Your portfolio will need to have an introduction, objectives, rationale, method, evidence, analysis and a discussion, though they have different headings:

i.   Overview of the portfolio
ii. Overview of the course
iii. Course goals
iv. Instructional practices
v.   Evidence of student learning
vi. Discussion

I elaborate on each of these sections so you know exactly what content goes into each of them. Below each description is an example of that section of the document.

i.   Overview Of The Portfolio

The first section of your portfolio should provide an overview. In this section, you should discuss the type of portfolio—benchmark or inquiry—and the purpose it serves. You should also outline the structure of the course portfolio to guide the reader. The overview provides a roadmap for the portfolio by highlighting the key components contained within it. Keep the focus in the portfolio overview at a fairly high level. In the sections that follow, you will drill down into increasingly more detail. Table 16-1 shows an illustration of the overview of a portfolio.

Table 16-1. Portfolio Overview

This benchmark course portfolio is intended to document the activities involved in designing and delivering a course in data management. The portfolio provides an overview of the course and its goals, a discussion of teaching techniques used to achieve those goals, and an assessment of the course and student learning. The portfolio concludes with a discussion of future directions for this course and my teaching of it.

ii. Overview Of The Course

The second section should provide a brief (one paragraph) overview of the course. Discuss the course, how many credits it is, who is taking the course and where it fits in the overall curriculum. Think about the courses that are pre- or co-requisites to this course as well as the courses that are next in sequence (if any). This is important information for thinking about what students should know coming into the class and what they need to learn for other classes. The same class positioned differently in the curriculum might have very different goals. Table 16-2 shows the overview of the course.

Table 16-2. Course Overview

S307: Data Management is a 3-credit, junior-level course that introduces students to the essential concepts in designing and implementing databases. The course is required for all students in the computer information systems (CIS) major and an elective for other majors. A course in visual programming (S205) is a pre-requisite to this course. A course in management of information systems (S302) is a co-requisite. S307 is on the critical path to graduation with a CIS major as it is a pre-requisite to S310 (Systems Analysis and Design), a required course for CIS majors, and S420 (Object-Oriented Design and Development), an elective course of CIS majors.

iii. Course Goals

The third section should identify the course goals. "Course goals" are more formally called "course objectives" in your syllabus. Earlier in chapter 15, I had highlighted the importance of writing good course objectives and explained how best to write objectives that focus on outcomes. This section of the portfolio is where the learning objectives or outcomes of the course take center stage. In this section, they should be listed and explained. Why are these the important learning outcomes? This can be explained from a curriculum perspective, such as what is needed by later classes. This can also be addressed through a professional perspective, such as what is needed to be a practitioner in this field. Remember that the course portfolio is designed to communicate to a broad audience (e.g., campus promotion committees), so being clear about how the course fits in the broader disciple is valuable. Table 16-3 shows the course goals.

Table 16-3. Course Goals

At the completion of S307, students should be able to:

i. Draw a picture, or conceptual model, of the data requirements for a particular business problem and translate that picture, through a process called normalization, into a set of statements that can be used to actually create the database

ii. Write statements, using structured query language (SQL), that create, modify, and query the data in the database

iii. Use and understand terminology associated with databases

These objectives are stated in the course syllabus under the heading *Course Objectives* (see previous chapter). These objectives are presented in the same order in which we cover them in the course. The logic of this order is that the first three objectives are reflective of the actual database design and implementation process that takes place in organizations. Specifically, the conceptual model precedes the normalization, which precedes the database creation and querying. While portions of the fourth objective are addressed throughout the course, additional terminology associated with database technologies and trends (e.g., data warehousing) is presented at the end of the course.

Meeting these objectives not only prepares students for follow-on courses in the computer information systems (CIS) curriculum, but also provides the necessary knowledge for their future employment. Systems Analysis and Design (S310) incorporates a significant data modeling and normalization component, while Object-Oriented Design and Programming (S420) relies on the SQL knowledge. Further, many recruiters and former students comment on the value of the concepts and skills that are learned in S307.

In deciding between depth and breadth, I focused on depth for the first two objectives, and breadth for the third objective. Students are thus deeply exposed to the core concepts in database management and are given ample opportunity to develop those skills through in-class activities and the course project. The third objective focuses on exposing students to a wide variety of topics and terminology in order to help them know the database-related opportunities that exist in organizations. These topics tend to be associated with database administration, data warehousing and data mining—issues that could be covered in entire courses by themselves and topics that are relevant to people specifically pursuing these as career options.

It is important to frame the learning goals articulated above within my overall approach to teaching. Two fundamental beliefs drive my teaching: people learn more when they are having fun and they have fun when they feel safe. Fun should not be confused with easy—rather, fun provides an environment in which students want to learn and engage with the material. Safety is not so much physical safety as it is emotional and social safety.

iv. Instructional Practices

The fourth section should tie the instructional practices to objectives. In my portfolio, I began this section with a discussion of my overall approach to teaching. This helps the reader to understand why you have made certain choices. This overview should be closely related to your teaching philosophy. The benefit of making that connection here is that it also provides a connection that can be used in your teaching statement for promotion and tenure evaluation. In the remainder of this section, you will discuss each learning outcome and what instructional practices you use to achieve them. I provide an example in Table 16-4. You will see that I also included a discussion of synthesizing course objectives. In my case, the project serves as a way to tie everything together. If you have something in your course that does this, it's definitely worth mentioning.

Table 16-4. Instructional Practices In Achieving Objectives

Overall

My primary approach to teaching this material is to actively engage the students in *doing*. I use four general approaches to engage students:

i. Fill-in-the blank class notes
ii. Active learning exercises
iii. Cooperative groups
iv. Board work

My class notes are fill-in-the blank to encourage students to attend class and to engage with the material rather than being passive recipients of it. For some of the blanks, I provide the material and students take notes; for other blanks, we engage in a discussion of the material and the students provide the answers. The material in this class is best understood through practice. The active learning exercises engage the students in actively thinking about how to apply the concepts. We spend classes *doing* data modeling, *doing* normalization and *doing* SQL.

Objective 1: Conceptual Modeling

The in-class activities are particularly essential for the conceptual, or data, modeling component of the course. Many students struggle with this material because, while there are guidelines, there are very few rules. I have found that the best way for students to truly understand data modeling is to do it *and* to see other peoples' models—right and wrong. In fact, when students are exposed to errors in data models, it helps them to avoid those errors. For data modeling, we start with very small (two-entity) data models and progress to more complex models—each time adding a layer of complexity and demonstrating one additional concept. This approach sets the stage for the rest of the course, both in terms of the interactive nature of instruction and in terms of the process of starting small and continually adding one new concept. Below is an example of an exercise for this objective.

Table 16-4 *Continued*. Instructional Practices In Achieving Objectives

Data Modeling Exercises:

A very basic, two-entity model:

Kisha, against the advice of her friends, was simultaneously studying data management and Shakespearian drama. She thought the two subjects would be an interesting contrast. However, the classes are very demanding and often enter her dreams. Last night, she dreamt that William Shakespeare wanted her to draw a data model. He explained, before she woke up in a cold sweat, that a play had many characters, but the same character never appeared in more than one play. "Methinks," he said, "the same name may have appeareth more than the once, but twas always a person of a different ilk." He then, she hazily recollects, went on to spout about the quality of data dropping like gentle rain… Draw a model to keep old Bill quiet and help Kisha get some sleep.

Also, a two-entity model, but with attributes associated with the relationship:

The Marathoner, a monthly magazine, regularly reports the performance of *professional* marathon runners. It has asked you to design a database to record details about the professional runners for all major marathons (e.g., Boston, London, Paris). Professional marathon runners compete in several races each year. A race may have thousands of competitors but only about 200 or so are professional runners, i.e., the ones *The Marathoner* tracks. For each race, the magazine reports a runner's time and finishing position and some personal details, such as name, gender and age.

To introduce weak entities and derived attributes:

Donald Trump has acquired so many hotels and casinos that he is now in need of a database to organize it all for him. He really needs to track the building information (name, location, number of rooms) as well as information about the various rooms in each building (type, resident, square feet). Finally, because they are all managed by different companies, he needs to know who is managing each building (company name, contact info, etc.) and how long they've been the building managers. Can you help "The Donald" get this straightened out?

To pull it together and to introduce subtypes:

The American Kennel Association is trying to create a database of AKC registered dogs—prior to their sale. They are preparing a prototype in Indiana. For each puppy, they want to retain the puppy's number (AKC registration code) and the puppy's official name. They also need to know if the puppy is show quality or pet quality (these are the only characterizations—and all puppies must fall into one of these groups). If a puppy is show quality, then they want to retain the date of last show and the place the puppy finished. If it is pet quality, they want to know the "defect" and if the puppy likes children. Each puppy lives in a kennel. Each kennel has a code, a name and a location. Most kennels house quite a few puppies. The kennel association also wants to keep track

Table 16-4 *Continued.* **Instructional Practices In Achieving Objectives**

of the tricks each dog can do. A trick can have an id code and a name. Some puppies can't do any tricks, while others can do many tricks. It's also important to know when a puppy learned a certain trick. Note that this context appears again in normalization and SQL.

Finally, a slightly different perspective—using documents to elicit data needs (this one requires some assumptions, which gives me the opportunity to discuss how assumptions turn into questions when you have a "live" client):

ORDER:	12498		DATE:	1/3/2001
CUSTOMER:	522		SALES REP:	12
	Mary Nelson			Miguel Diaz
	108 Pine, Ada, MI 49441			

Part Number	Part Description	Number Ordered	Unit Price	Total
AZ52	Dartboard	2	12.95	25.90
BA74	Basketball	4	29.95	119.80
			ORDER TOTAL	$145.70

Objective 2: Normalization

In moving from conceptual modeling to normalization, students tend to experience increased comfort due to the introduction of *some* rules. To help students truly understand the rules and how they all fit together, I use a cooperative learning exercise. In this exercise, students are put in groups and given three problems to work through. They are told that they will be evaluated *as a group* and, therefore, they should make sure that everyone in the group not only knows what the answer is, but also why it is what it is. As the groups work through the problems, I walk around the room and observe how they are addressing the questions. When a group is done with a problem, I look at their collective answer and then select one person in the group to explain the answer to me. I try to find the person who seems least sure of what is going on (either by their demeanor or earlier work in class). I ask some direct questions that help me know if the person and, therefore, the group understands the material. This exercise is particularly well-suited for normalization. Below is an example of this exercise, as well as, empirical data regarding the effectiveness of this technique.

Cooperative Learning Exercise for Normalization

i. Determine the normal form the relation is in, explain why, and fix it so it is in 3NF.

Worker (<u>WorkerID</u>, WorkerName, SkillType, BonusRate)

FD: SkillType --> BonusRate

ii. Transform the ER Diagram into a set of relations in at least 3NF. Be sure to include the foreign key constraints.

Table 16-4 *Continued*. Instructional Practices In Achieving Objectives

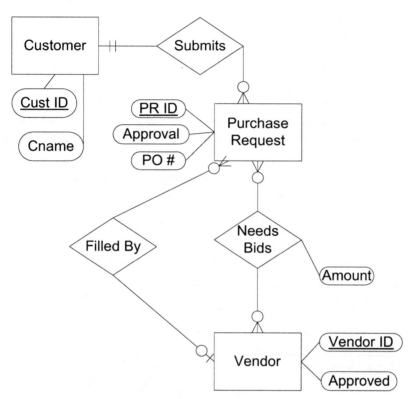

iii. Someone who obviously never took a database (or systems analysis) course, implemented the following table in Access. You need to identify one insertion anomaly, one deletion anomaly and one modification anomaly, and write the set of relations that SHOULD have been used to implement this stuff!

CustID	CustName	PartID	PartName	DateLastOrder
1235	Andersen, LLP	128	Lightbulbs - 50 Watts	4/5/98
1235	Andersen, LLP	521	Desk Chair - Black	4/5/98
1289	Lites R Us	128	Lightbulbs - 50 Watts	3/15/98
2345	Kraft Foods	431	Flour	1/5/98
2345	Kraft Foods	455	Milk	1/25/98

Analysis of Cooperative Learning Exercise
The students are placed into groups, given an assignment (for which the group can receive homework credit) and told that everyone in the group must understand the answer;

Table 16-4 *Continued*. Instructional Practices In Achieving Objectives

students are held accountable for each other's learning. When the group is ready to answer, I select the "explainer"—if the person can explain the answer, the whole group gets credit—if not, I go away while the group again tries to learn this concept. In order to understand if the students were really benefiting from this exercise, I administered a brief questionnaire. Students were asked to indicate how comfortable they felt with the material, both before and after the exercise, and they were asked to evaluate their learning directly related to the exercise. The results are presented in Table 1. For nearly every item, there was a significant improvement. I followed up with the students on the two items that did not show improvement. Based on their responses, I have a good idea of how to change the exercise in the future to specifically address those items.

Table 1: Analysis of Survey Results for Cooperative Learning Exercise

	Pre-exercise Mean	Post-exercise Mean	Significant?
I believe I could identify and fix:			
1. Modification anomaly	5.1364	6.1111	Yes *
2. Insertion anomaly	5.0455	6.1111	Yes **
3. Deletion anomaly	5.1364	6.1111	Yes **
4. Partial functional dependency	5.5000	6.6667	Yes ***
5. Transitive dependency	5.5000	6.6667	Yes ***
I can determine if a relation is in:			
6. First normal form	5.5000	6.3333	Yes *
7. Second normal form	5.3182	6.3333	Yes *
8. Third normal form	5.1364	6.2222	Yes *
9. BCNF	4.5000	5.6667	Yes *
I feel comfortable applying:			
10. Foreign key constraint	5.3636	5.8889	No
11. Translation rules	4.5455	5.6667	Yes **
I would have no trouble explaining:			
12. Referential integrity	4.1818	5.1111	Yes *

Table 16-4 *Continued*. Instructional Practices In Achieving Objectives

13. Entity integrity	4.3636	5.3333	Yes *
14. The null option	5.2727	6.0000	No
15. On delete options	5.0000	6.0000	Yes *
Overall, the cooperative learning group activity increased my understanding of normalization concepts.		6.3333	

Notes: All items were measured on a 7-point Likert scale, where 1=strongly disagree and 7=strongly agree; * $p \leq .05$, ** $p \leq .01$, *** $p \leq .001$

Objective 3: SQL

Finally, I use board work to get students moving. This is typically used for SQL, where students work at their desks on a particular query and other students put the answer on the board. In this way, students can participate "anonymously" to the extent that others are not watching them put their answers on the board and they do not later claim their answers. To me, this provides a safe mechanism for the more quiet students to participate. Participation is about contributing to the class—by putting their answers out there for us to discuss, they contribute a great deal. I strongly encourage students to take risks and put up wrong answers—again, hoping that when the students see what is wrong, it will help them to know what is right and why. Once all the answers have been put on the board, we go through the queries and the students tell me if they are right or wrong. This gives me the opportunity to pose additional "what if" questions to gauge the degree to which the students are putting it all together. Below is an example of an exercise for this learning objective.

SQL In-class Examples
Use the following database schema to express the queries in SQL:
CUSTOMER (<u>CUSTID</u>, CUSTNAME, ANNUALREVENUE, CUSTTYPE)
SHIPMENT (<u>SHIPMENT#</u>, ***<u>CUSTID</u>***, WEIGHT, ***TRUCK#, CITYNAME***, SHIPDATE)
TRUCK (<u>TRUCK#</u>, DRIVERNAME)
CITY (<u>CITYNAME</u>, POPULATION)

Simple Queries:
- What cities have we shipped to?
- Give IDs for customers who have sent shipments to Tucson or Baltimore (be sure to list each customer only once).
- Give names and annual revenue of customers that are not retailers.
  Create a list of retail customers who have at least $15 million in annual revenue. The list should be presented in order of annual revenue—from highest to lowest.
- How many different customers have sent shipments to cities with names starting with 'B'?

Table 16-4 *Continued*. Instructional Practices In Achieving Objectives

- What is the average weight of all shipments we have recorded?
- Give the shipment number, truck number and weight of all shipments for the past 90 days.
- Give names and <u>monthly</u> revenue of customers having annual revenue exceeding $10 million but less than $15 million.

Joins:
- To what destinations have customers with revenue less than $30 million sent packages?
- What are the names and populations of cities that have received shipments weighing over 100 pounds?
- Who are the drivers who have delivered shipments for customers with annual revenue over $20 million to cities with populations over 1 million?

Subqueries:
- Provide details for the shipment(s) that weigh the most.
- In terms of annual revenue, list the name of our smallest customer(s)?
- Which customers (provide names) have not yet shipped anything?

Objective 4: Terminology
In the "talk the talk" portion of the class, students are exposed to a great deal of terminology from a variety of contexts. Much of the time is spent putting the right words together with the right concepts. Because this is an area in which I am pursuing a strategy of breadth, we move fairly quickly through a large number of ideas. To help students keep all the terminology of the course straight, I create crossword puzzles. This allows me to reinforce the terms that are important and also point the students to topics in the book that we may not have discussed in class. The next page provides an example of an exercise for this learning objective.

Objective 5: Synthesizing Course Objectives
Everything up to this point has focused on examining the pieces of database design and development. What the students need is a means of pulling it all together so that they can see how data modeling feeds into normalization, which feeds into database development, which facilitates database querying. I believe that this class has limited value to the students unless it incorporates a semester-long project. The projects in this class have evolved significantly, primarily to build on the pre-requisite structure and to incorporate more SQL. The projects are structured such that students have three interim due dates prior to the final project submission. A subset of the student teams presents on each of those interim due dates so that the students learn from each other. Through these presentations, the students learn that the same information might be modeled in different ways, depending on your assumptions. At the end of the semester, the students are required to prepare a fairly extensive write-up of everything in the project, including the data modeling, normalization, SQL and some issues from "talk the talk." In addition, I require that the students discuss two issues: what did they learn about technology

Table 16-4 *Continued*. Instructional Practices In Achieving Objectives

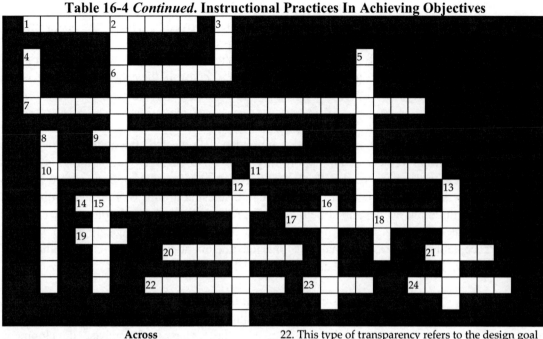

Across

1. This is used when data are highly sensitive and/or must be transmitted internationally

6. This "logic" typically refers to data storage and retrieval.

7. This is used to recover from inaccurate data entry

9. If you slice your tables by rows or columns in order to distribute the data, you are using this approach to data distribution

10. When you have a copy of your database distributed to a number of locations, you are using this approach to distribution

11. One of four characteristics of data in a data warehouse.

14. An issue that must be addressed when multiple users access the same data

17. This is the data modeling formalism used with data warehouses

19. This is the term used when there is a great deal of processing done on the client

20. The recovery technique used when a transaction aborts

21. Tools that allow users to analyze multidimensional data

22. This type of transparency refers to the design goal that users need not know where, exactly data are located

23. SQL processes this statement first

24. The pessimistic approach to concurrency control

Down

2. This "logic" typically refers to the GUI

3. The most common locking level (also thought of as a "chunk" of data)

4. The middleware used in a Windows environment to connect client and server relational databases

5. This problem occurs when there are inadequate controls in place in a multi-user database environment

8. The optimistic approach to concurrency control

12. The process of getting data ready to enter into a data warehouse

13. When two transactions are waiting for each other to release data, this occurs

15. Second on the worldwide database market

16. This type of transparency refers to the design goal that either all portions of a transaction are completed or none of them are

18. This is a table in Oracle that contains the names of all of your tables

Table 16-4 *Continued*. Instructional Practices In Achieving Objectives

(i.e., Visual Basic and Oracle) and what did they learn overall. These "lessons learned" components require the students to reflect on the entire project and discuss mistakes they made, what they would do differently next time and what they would do the same. Much of the project weight is on the write-up because that is how I know if they "get it." Below is an example of an exercise for this learning objective.

S307 - Group Project

The group project allows you to demonstrate that you have synthesized the materials covered in the course. The group project is an opportunity for you to design, build, implement and document a working database system. In order to give each group the opportunity to present their solution to the class (and not bore us all to tears), selected groups will present "solutions" for each of the three phases described below. Each group will present only once. After seeing the presentations (or giving your own), your group may decide to change direction. This is perfectly acceptable—all I ask is that you provide documentation of the change and your reasons for it. Do NOT blindly accept another model!!!

Specific Project Requirements:

Your project will begin with conceptual data modeling and conclude with the implementation of a database using Oracle and Visual Basic. The three phases of database development included in the project are: (1) conceptual data modeling; (2) logical database design; and (3) database implementation. This document describes work included in each phase of the project. You should refer to the syllabus for the due dates.

A. Conceptual Data Modeling

i.   Read the case description and associated material, and generate a list of questions that you need answered.
ii. Either submit these questions to me via email or set up a time to come talk with me about them (as though you were talking with an actual client).
iii. Create an entity-relationship diagram showing the conceptual data model for your system. You should prepare both the preliminary—and the implementation-oriented model.

B. Logical Database Design

i.   Normalize the relations to at least third normal form.
ii. Identify the primary and foreign keys for each relation (using appropriate notation).
iii. Identify and describe any indexes needed for nonkey attributes—justify your decision.
iv. Identify and describe referential integrity constraints needed to guarantee the integrity of your database—explain your choices.
v.   Consider whether you should denormalize some of your relations in order to reduce the time needed to retrieve data from your database. Present the justification for your denormalization decision. **If you decide to denormalize some of your relations, present**

Table 16-4 *Continued*. Instructional Practices In Achieving Objectives

---

a new set of relations for your database.

C. Preliminary Database Implementation

i.   Implement the database.
    a.   Define your database.
    b.   Create the tables needed to implement your database.
    c.   Define keys and indexes.
    d.   Define the relationships among your tables.
    e.   Define any necessary referential integrity constraints between your tables.
ii. Add sample data to the database tables.
iii. Design and implement the user interface needed to input data to your database and to access data from your database (e.g., to run queries). Consider user needs in both your selection and design of the forms.
iv. Write (and include) the SQL code necessary to produce answers to the questions posed.
v.   Produce documentation explaining how to use your database. **Consider the audience of the documentation to be the actual users of your system. Assume they are familiar with how to use a computer—but they are not familiar with your particular database.**
    a.   Discuss the organizational and people issues associated with implementing this system, including BUT NOT LIMITED TO expansion, data integrity and security (don't be constrained by this list!).

D. The Final System

See the next page for the detailed description of what to turn in on the project due dates (see syllabus for due dates).

Project Deliverables:

You will document your work by turning in many items and by giving an oral presentation. Details follow.

A. Presentation (10% of project grade)

The class presentation should highlight those aspects of the system likely to be of greatest interest to the class. The class presentations should be focused on the particular phase being presented. During the presentations, your class-mates will assume many roles (e.g., client, IS team member)—you should design your presentation accordingly. Your group will be the class experts for the portion of the project you present. For example, if you are presenting the conceptual model, you should be extremely familiar with ER diagramming. Please prepare and deliver professional presentations (note: **business casual attire**). Your grade for the presentation will be based on professionalism, clarity, fluency and accuracy. Of course, extra points will be available for pizzazz. Please refer to the course grading criteria for a generic description of what constitutes A, B, C, D, and F level work.

Table 16-4 *Continued*. Instructional Practices In Achieving Objectives

---

B. Interim Papers (Due on each presentation day)

On each of the presentation days, you will turn in a piece of the project. One format you might choose for these papers is a project folder or notebook. Use a folder to organize and record the information that is due for a given day. Another format would be, for example, an entity-relationship diagram, together with its supporting documentation (e.g., questions asked and answered, or in-group disagreements and how they were resolved). In any event, the interim papers should be used as your "working document"—they provide the documentation of what you've done along the way—they should NOT be included in the final written paper. ***Failure to turn in one of the papers on the due date will result in a full letter grade reduction for the group project.***

C. Database (30% of project grade)

You should turn in all files (tables, forms and reports) or URL needed to run your database system.

D. Written Paper (Due with final system) (60% of project grade)

Your final project paper should include (at a minimum) the items listed below. Essentially, you will have created nearly all of the necessary pieces throughout the project. For the final paper, you need to put them together in a more formal manner. You may present some of this information in appendices to your paper. Use your judgment about what should be in the body of the paper and what should be in the appendices. Your paper should provide an **interesting** description of what you have done and why. Be sure to organize your paper in a way that meets this objective. It is not a good idea to simply include each of the items listed here in the order given. Give some thought about how to best structure your paper. **You will also probably want to include transitions to tie all of these together.** For example, you might discuss how decisions you made during the logical design of your systems constrained your final implementation. You should also include material on the relationships between the components of your paper (e.g., how is what you learned through interviews and presentations reflected in the relationship diagram). The written paper provides evidence of your understanding of course concepts. As such, it receives a significant amount of weight in the final project grade.

Minimum Requirements for the Paper:

i. A summary of any questions asked, answers obtained and assumptions made (though there should be few assumptions by this time).
ii. Entity-relationship diagrams showing both the preliminary and implementation models for your database.
iii. The set of normalized relations for your database (including primary and foreign keys) and any discussion.
iv. A discussion of any indexes needed for nonkey attributes.
v. A discussion of any referential integrity constraints needed to guarantee the integrity of your database.

Table 16-4 *Continued*. Instructional Practices In Achieving Objectives
vi. A discussion of your justification for your denormalization decision (yes OR no). If you decide to denormalize some of your relations, include your new set of partial denormalized relations for your database.
vii. A diagram showing the structure of your **implemented** database. How is it different from the diagram in #1?
viii. A description of the properties of each field in the tables of your implemented database (i.e., a data dictionary).
ix. A depiction and description of the user interface that facilitates access to your database (input and output).
x. The SQL code needed to answer the questions posed.
xi. The user documentation for your database.
xii. Implementation issues and suggestions for addressing them.
xiii. Technology issues (strengths and limitations) that you discovered during the project.
xiv. Lessons learned (this is really important!!).

v. Evidence Of Student Learning

The fifth section is the data collection and analysis section of the portfolio. Assessment has recently become more important in higher education. This can be the most challenging part of the course portfolio. Think about multiple ways in which you can demonstrate learning. Exam questions provide one common mechanism for this. Key questions can be used to demonstrate learning associated with the objectives. Another way to think about exams is to demonstrate that they test the material proportionally to how much time was spent on the topic. Personally, I like Bloom's Taxonomy (1956)[190] as a way of making sure that students are tested across the cognitive levels. By analyzing your exams, you provide evidence that they are valid and reliable. Then, if you choose certain questions to demonstrate learning, you have built a solid foundation upon which to make that claim. Think about each of the activities that you use in your class and consider how they demonstrate student learning. The evidence might not be completely quantitative. In my portfolio, you will see that I used a portion of the group project to determine student learning with respect to indexes. I used the student write-ups to assess the degree to which each team truly understood and could apply what they learned about indexes. You will see that there are differences across the team write-ups that are included in the portfolio. Some other instructors have used journals, minute papers, case write-ups and other techniques that rely on qualitative assessment of student work. If using this kind of evidence in support of a tenure packet, I recommend that you have a colleague assess the work you have selected as evidence. Just as you would establish inter-rater reliability in a research paper, it is important to get a second opinion for this as well. Below are three samples of student work using the indexing example. I chose to examine indexing because it provides an excellent context to examine definition, application and justification. Table 16-5 shows samples of student work.

Table 16-5. Samples Of Student Work

Sample 1
Non-key Indexed Attributes

Attributes that are commonly accessed in a database should be given an index value so the DBMS can create a table to easily locate the rows. This speeds the processing time for finding those attributes in the database and also uses some processing power just to create the indexes, meaning that only frequently used attributes should have an index. All primary keys get an index value automatically and the designer can then create indexes for any attribute that they anticipate will get queried often. Here is our list of non-key attributes that we indexed and an explanation for why we indexed them.

Description

If a customer does not know the product ID code for a product they are ordering, our customer representative must search the database for the product by another means. Since the customer should know what the product is, this will be the most used search term and would benefit from an index.

Class & Type

Reports to determine what products are being ordered most and least often will be created, including ones that are grouped by product and/or class. Having these indexed, along with *description* will allow for product information to be easily queried at any time.

CustLname

The situation with a customer's last name is similar to product description. If they do not know their ID number, they can be found by their last name and we anticipate that this will happen often. Since last names do not change often, they are a good attribute to index.

Vname

Many reports concerning the vendors of Playball will be created on a daily basis concerning how vendors are performing and who supplied a returned item. In most cases, the name of the vendor should be included on the report.

EMPDOB

Since a report is run each month to determine who has a birthday, we added an index for this attribute. This information will seldom change so there will be less processing power used to create this index than other attributes.

nice choice

EMPphonenum

Employee current phone number reports are also generated regularly and do not change often, so an index will speed up the database overall.

Table 16-5 *Continued*. Samples Of Student Work

Sample 2

- Index is used to speed up searching on the table
- Index works better if there is great uniqueness in the data of the chosen attribute
- Data of the chosen indexes should not change often over time

drawbacks?

Here are the indexes created:
i.   Customer Last Name
This is used to pull out customer records if the customer/sales representatives do not know the customer# or invoice#.

SQL> **Create index** Clname_indx **on** Customer (Cust_lname);

ii.   Product Description
This is used when sales representative do not know the product code. A keyword search can be done.

SQL> **Create index** Pdesc_indx **on** Product(Prod_desc);

iii.   Vendor Name
This is used to search a vendor record when the Vendor# is not known.

SQL> **Create index** Vname_indx **on** Vendor(vendor_name);

iv.   Seller Name
This is used to search a seller record when the Seller# is not known.

SQL> **Create index** Sname_indx **on** Seller(Seller_lname);

Why these? It sounds as though I can't search these things w/out an index — is that true?!

Sample 3

Indexes are created in PlayBall's latest system to provide rapid random and sequential access to base-table data. Indexes are used primarily for data retrievals for applications such as PlayBall's. Indexes will improve query performance, however, each index consumes extra storage space and requires overhead maintenance time whenever indexed data change value. Therefore, we had to be selective in choosing appropriate keys.

Table 16-5 *Continued*. Samples Of Student Work

We have chosen to index the following fields:

- CustLastName
- OrderDate
- ReturnDate
- ProdClass
- ProdType
- ProdCategory

Why these?

Why not others?

We have chosen to include ProdClass, ProdType and ProdCategory to facilitate speedier searches in each of those fields and criteria.

more detail is needed here!   *what about the others?*

vi. Discussion

Finally, your course portfolio should have discussion and conclusion sections. What did you learn from preparing this course portfolio? This is where you should summarize what's going well and what could use improvement. Think about what you want to fix, how you might fix it and how you will know if it is fixed. This section can help to set up the topics for an inquiry portfolio, discussed next. Table 16-6 shows directions for future and a summary of the portfolio.

Table 16-6. Directions For Future And Summary

While students are achieving the first three learning objectives very well and the fourth objective reasonably well, there are some problems with the delivery mechanism of the fourth objective. After 12 weeks of leading a highly interactive course, I resort to lectures to cover the material in the terminology section. The students sense the change and have commented about it in my course evaluations. Additionally, grades on the final exam are lower than grades on the midterm. I believe this is due to students not processing the terminology and trends as deeply as they have processed the data modeling, normalization and SQL. To use a popular phrase, the end of the course is the "weakest link." In thinking about future changes, I would like to explore the use of cases, guest speakers, jigsaw techniques or student presentations for this section of the course. Assessment will take the form of evaluating final exam grades, potentially incorporating a terminology or trend question in the final project and assessing those answers, and doing one-minute papers at the end of the class sessions to quickly gauge student understanding.

The purpose of this portfolio was to document the activities associated with designing and

---
Table 16-6 *Continued*. Directions For Future And Summary
---
delivering a course in data management. Much as having students list their lessons learned makes their learning explicit, the process of creating this portfolio has helped me to make explicit the rationale for my pedagogical choices. It has also caused me to question some choices. Finally, and most importantly, the portfolio has helped me to identify areas for improvement in the data management course.
---

5. Inquiry Portfolio

An inquiry portfolio is aimed at addressing a specific issue. If you have identified something you want to correct in the benchmark portfolio, that is where you start the inquiry portfolio. Again, you should have an overview and a description of the course. In the inquiry portfolio, you will identify a particular issue or problem that you want to address. Following good research methodology, you will determine your intervention, identify the data you need to assess the intervention and run the "experiment." Once you have collected the data, you will need to analyze it and determine whether or not the intervention mattered. If the data show a positive outcome, that is great! It's also possible that even with a positive outcome, the data might give you a glimpse into other issues you hadn't seen before. This could help you launch another inquiry. If the data do not show a positive outcome, perhaps this process has highlighted a different issue or a new issue that you can investigate going forward. Perhaps the data have given you insights into what else won't work but some ideas about what might.

A caution here is that the inquiry portfolio can become a never-ending project where you go from one intervention to another. Unless you find yourself making headway toward a solution to your issue, here too, I recommend a stopping rule. If you have tried three interventions and you are not getting the results you expect, you are probably focusing on the wrong problem. I would encourage you to step back and ask yourself whether this issue is having a significant, negative impact on student learning. If it is, then by all means, continue looking for a solution. But, if students are learning the course material and you are simply looking for a more palatable way to present it, it's probably time to move on to something else.

6. Peer Interaction And Review

One of the most significant benefits of developing a course portfolio comes from the peer interaction and review process. While you might not be fortunate enough to participate in a formalized portfolio project, it is possible for a group of 3-5 faculty members to work together to do this. The University of Nebraska, Lincoln Peer Review of Teaching Projects website (www.courseportfolio.org) has excellent suggestions for how to do this in your institution. The benefit of working in a group on the course portfolio is that you can get and give feedback to one another. Through this process, you get to learn about how other people approach teaching and it might lead you to try some new things. In addition, having the collaborative commitment can help to keep the course portfolio on the priority list.

The peer review aspect of course portfolios is similar to peer review in research. Someone, who may or may not know the author (i.e., the instructor), reviews the course portfolio in terms of the course's intellectual content, the quality of teaching practices, the quality of student understanding, and the evidence of reflection and development. The external review can provide suggestions regarding your course as well as a perspective of your course in relation to the larger discipline.

7. From Course Portfolio To Pedagogical Publication

After collecting data for your benchmark or inquiry portfolio, you might consider its appropriateness for a pedagogical outlet. For example, in my class, I use cooperative learning activities to teach certain topics. Following Johnson et al.'s (1991)[191] guidelines, the activity is designed to have teams take responsibility for each other's learning. This activity involved putting students in teams and me going around to each team to ask them questions about their answers. If I asked a question and the person I asked did not understand the answer, the team did not get credit for the answer. Knowing the answer is not enough—students must also be able to explain why it's the answer. This activity is difficult to do as the class size increases so I wanted evidence that what I was doing was worth it to the students. The data provided evidence that it was a valuable exercise and the results were reported in Brown and Klein (2006).[192]

Do not underestimate the value of pedagogical research in writing your teaching philosophy or in your actual teaching. There is a wealth of literature on how to be a good teacher. If you can center your beliefs, goals and techniques in that literature, it provides an important connection between teaching and research. It surprises me how little we rely on the research by our colleagues in education. The reality is that we do not have to re-invent the wheel. We can leverage that research, adapt it to our discipline and the classes we teach.

Another way to use course materials (with or without direct evidence) is to develop a teaching tip. Think about something that you are doing in your class that is different. For example, Massey et al. (2005)[193] discusses some fun things that I have used in my classes. One approach was to use a crossword puzzle to reinforce terminology. Other fun things have been adaptations of game shows, like jeopardy, that are used to help students review for the final exam.

Concluding Thoughts

Teaching has been one of the most rewarding aspects of my career as a faculty member. I can name students who have had an impact on me and I believe I had an impact on a few of them. Seeing students put the pieces together and learn the material in a class is extremely rewarding to me. When I discovered course portfolios, it all came together. I could use what I knew about research to improve my teaching. I truly hope that everyone who enters the profession can be excited by all aspects of it—research, service and most of all, teaching. I hope this chapter helps you to create and leverage a course portfolio to become a more effective teacher.

Key Takeaways

1. Documenting teaching effectiveness is necessary to make you a better teacher, for promotion and tenure, and for accreditation purposes, thus making it particularly important
2. Course portfolios provide a mechanism for documenting the scholarly work of teaching (see www.courseportfolio.org)
3. Course portfolios are different from teaching portfolios in three ways:
   i. Course portfolios focus on one course, whereas teaching portfolios focus on all the courses one has taught
   ii. Course portfolios focus on student learning, whereas teaching portfolios focus on teaching and delivery methods
   iii. Course portfolios represent a scholarly investigation of the relationship between teaching and student learning, whereas teaching portfolios do not include such an investigation
4. Advantages of preparing a course portfolio include:
   i. Can be used as an alternative or complement to traditional student evaluations—this is particularly useful when the course taught is one that traditionally engenders lower evaluations because of the topic or because of the types of students who take the course
   ii. May result in pedagogical publications
   iii. Can tell you if your teaching approaches are effective
   iv. Can be used to train doctoral students or new faculty members
5. There are two types of course portfolios:
   i. Benchmark portfolios provide documentation of a course, including the syllabus, teaching materials, teaching methods, illustrations of student work or other evidence that helps assess student learning
   ii. Inquiry portfolios focus on evaluating change or interventions implemented as a result of a benchmark portfolio
6. Three steps to preparing a course portfolio are:
   i. Select a course
   ii. Develop the course goals
   iii. Determine the type of portfolio you want to develop
7. The benchmark portfolio is composed of 6 sections that are similar to a research paper (examples of these sections are provided in the chapter) and contains:
   i. Overview of the portfolio—This section discusses the type of portfolio and the purpose it serves, as well as, an outline of the portfolio
   ii. Overview of the course—This section describes the course, how many credits it is, who is taking it and how it fits into the curriculum

      iii. Course goals—This section is where the learning outcomes of the course are listed. Remember to phrase these in terms of action verbs
      iv. Instructional practices—In this section, describe your approach to teaching (drawing from your teaching philosophy), and discuss each learning outcome and what practices you use to achieve them
      v. Evidence of teaching effectiveness—This section describes the data collection and analysis methods you've used to assess learning (exams, key questions, student write-ups, etc.)
      vi. Discussion—In this section, a discussion and conclusions that reflect on what works and what doesn't work for your course

8. The inquiry portfolio is aimed at addressing a specific issue identified through your benchmark portfolio—it is structured similar to the benchmark portfolio, but is focused on one issue
9. As with research, peer interaction and reviews of your portfolio will help you to improve your teaching effectiveness
10. Consider converting the evidence you gather in support of different aspects of your teaching (if applicable) into a pedagogical publication

CHAPTER 17

REVIEWING

Reviewing is an important yet mostly, though definitely not completely, thankless task that we have to do as academics. The goal of this chapter is to shed light on some of the benefits of reviewing. This chapter is not about how to do a review. Several good sources exist that describe how to write a good review. Some of these are: Lee (1995),[194] Miller (2006),[195] Saunders (2005),[196] Schminke (2002),[197] Agarwal et al. (2006),[198] Bergh (2006),[199] Seibert (2006)[200] and Feldman (2004).[201]

During my term as an assistant professor, I rarely said no to review requests. Although I sometimes gave consideration to the quality of the journal, I said yes to requests to review a paper. Reviewing takes time. It can take a day or longer depending on how close to your area a paper is. Sometimes, it took me a lot longer as I had to read several other papers that I had never read before in order to fully understand and evaluate a paper. In any case, I see four good reasons to review papers:

1. Networking
2. Learning about hot issues within your topic area
3. Learning from other reviews
4. Learning from editor reports

1. Networking

The first and most obvious reason to do reviews is to build your network. You are usually asked to review papers by editors who typically tend to be more senior members of the field. As a junior member of the field, building a network is important so as to develop sympathetic ears to your ideas, papers and promotion case. I, for one, find it very annoying when I find someone not willing to do a review when, in fact, they have submitted a paper for review to the same journal. As Carol Saunders noted in her editorial in 2005[202] in *MIS Quarterly,* authors are obliged to review papers. Good and constructive reviews become the first step toward impressing editors that your work could have the same features. Good reviews and good scholarship (over time) also leads to editorial board appointments—a factor that can be important in promotion and tenure evaluations. Finally, editors are senior scholars and are frequently called upon to write evaluation letters for promotion, thus making them an important group to impress.

2. Learning About Hot Issues Within Your Topic Area

One of the benefits of doing reviews is to see what work is being conducted in your area of research. A window into others' thinking on a topic is always beneficial. Sometimes, reading papers in the review process can spark new ideas that will be worth pursuing or angles within data sets that you already have that can be converted into a paper. As I will elaborate more in the next three points, you can learn a lot from reading a paper to see what aspects or issues within your topic area are exciting to other researchers in this area (authors of the paper, other reviewers and editors). This is valuable information that can drive your research questions and, perhaps, more importantly, can help you learn how to frame your paper so that it is most appealing to others.

Something a bit more specific as a benefit is learning about general hot button issues. These are issues that could irritate or stimulate the thinking of reviewers. As I conducted research on gender differences, I knew there were certain ways of making a point (how ever innocent and unintentional) that would be viewed very negatively by a reviewer and a different phrasing would be received with open arms. I am not going to delve into the specifics of this for fear of further offending someone but suffice to say that in most every topic, there are hot button issues. Again, I must emphasize that these hot button issues can be those that lead to positive or negative reactions. A non-controversial example is the measurement of behavior in conjunction with an intention model—some reviewers will simply not tolerate it if behavior is not measured. On the positive side, some reviewers are very excited when they see the measurement of behavior (say objectively) in the study as it appeals to the importance they place on predictive validity, common method bias, distal dependent variables and multiple sources of data collection. Hot button issues and dealing with them in your own work will help you avoid instant rejection (in the minds of some reviewers) and potentially create instant favorable reactions (in the minds of some reviewers). Over time, learning from reviews and learning about hot button issues may or may not help you write the best paper possible but it will certainly help you write the paper most likely to be successful in the review process.

3. Learning From Other Reviews

Most of the time, reviewers simply set aside a review packet that comes back to them. They will pick it up only if the paper comes back for review as a revision. Reviews by others are educational in their own right and you should take full advantage of them. If and when papers do come back for a 2nd and/or 3rd round of review, there is a lot that can be learned from closely observing the review packet, the paper and the response document. Some of the revisions of papers you review will be successful, some will not. You can learn about what works and what does not work. For example, I learned that a polite tone in the response document is helpful. I also learned that you are more likely to succeed with a revision that addresses the concerns of reviewers in earnest rather than one that tries to explain why changes do not have to be or cannot be made. You will also learn about acceptable and unacceptable practices (theory, method, analysis, etc.) in the context of your topic area as you examine original submissions or revised submissions. As an assistant professor, a key benefit I derived from reviewing was learning from the reviews of other members of the panel. Seeing how other people think and react to a paper was most educational. In fact, whenever I have pointed this out to junior colleagues as a valuable part of the experience and when they have closely examined a review packet (of a paper other than their own) in conjunction with the paper, they have also noted that they learned a lot. This is particularly of value if the paper is directly in your area of research as is often the case when you are a reviewer.

4. Learning From Editor Reports

While the reviews and reviewers are mostly anonymous (with a few exceptions), some journals publish reviewers' names associated with specific papers (if the reviewers agree). When you are a reviewer, you will always know the identity of the editor(s) involved. This is quite helpful as the same person may serve as the editor on your paper as well. Given the non-anonymous nature of the interaction with the editor, this is one of the strongest bonds that you can form— not only in terms of networking, but also in terms of having someone who may be willing to look at your papers in the future and give comments. Much like the situation of being able to learn a lot from the reviews, the same thing applies to editor reports as well. The additional benefit in the case of editor reports is that you learn the thought processes and hot button issues non-anonymously. You can always engage in email exchanges with the editor on points he or she makes in a report and get reactions to alternative solutions (that you may have in mind). Such an approach will allow you to understand how the particular editor will see the same issue in the future (say in the context of your own paper).

Concluding Thoughts

Reviewing is a very important activity for junior scholars. It offers several benefits, not only to one's own research but also from a networking perspective. Beyond just the reviewing activity itself, benefits accrue from studying the review packet to see how others think and react to the same paper. Finally, reviewing revisions of papers provides great insights into how to manage the revision process for your papers.

Key Takeaways

1. Several good sources exist that describe how to write a good review, including: Lee (1995), Miller (2006), Saunders (2005), Schminke (2002), Agarwal et al. (2006), Bergh (2006), Seibert (2006) and Feldman (2004)
2. Try not to say no to review requests as an assistant professor—benefits include networking, learning about hot issues in your area, learning from other reviewers, and learning from editor reports
3. Networking
   i. Editors tend to be more senior members of the field—as a junior faculty member, it is important to build a network of such sympathetic ears to your ideas, papers and external evaluators of your promotion case
   ii. Junior faculty members should review papers for the journals to which they submit their work

      iii. Good and constructive reviews are the first step toward impressing editors that your work could have the same features

4. Learning about the hot issues within your topic area
      i. You can learn a lot from reading a paper to see what aspects or issues within your topic area are exciting to other researchers in this area (authors of the paper, other reviewers and editors)
      ii. Reading papers in the review process can spark new ideas that will be worth pursuing or angles within data sets that you already have that can be converted into a paper
      iii. These are issues that could irritate or stimulate the thinking of reviewers (for example, gender-related issues in technology use)
      iv. Being aware of hot button issues and dealing with them in your own work will help you avoid instant rejection (in the minds of some reviewers) and potentially create instant favorable reactions (in the minds of some reviewers)

5. Learning from other reviewers
      i. Seeing how other people think and react to a paper is very educational—this is particularly valuable if the paper is directly in your area of research as is often is the case when you are a reviewer
      ii. If and when papers do come back for a 2nd and/or 3rd round of review, there is a lot that can be learned from closely observing revisions
      iii. A polite tone in the response document is important
      iv. You are more likely to succeed with a revision that addresses the concerns of reviewers in earnest rather than one that tries to explain why changes do not have to be or cannot be made
      v. You will learn about acceptable and unacceptable practices (theory, method, analysis, etc.) in the context of your topic area as you examine original submissions or revised submissions

6. Learning from editor reports
      i. Reviews and reviewers are mostly anonymous
      ii. When you are a reviewer, you will always know who the editor is (editors are)
      iii. This is quite helpful as the same person may serve as the editor on your paper
      iv. Given the non-anonymous nature of the interaction with the editor, this is one of the strongest bonds that you can form—not only in terms of networking, but also in terms of having someone who may be willing to look at your papers and give comments
      v. In the case of editor reports, you can learn the thought process and hot button issues non-anonymously—such an approach will allow you to understand how the particular editor will see the same issue in the future (say in the context of your paper)

CHAPTER 18

KEYWORDS AND PHRASES I WORK BY
Andrew Burton-Jones

Assistant Professor
Sauder School of Business
University of British Columbia
Vancouver, Canada
andrew.burton-jones@sauder.ubc.ca

Growing up in Australia, I was far more interested in sports than work. As a teenager, the idea that I would become an academic would have sounded a little ridiculous to me. I didn't know any academics and from what little I had heard (mainly negative stereotypes), they didn't work in the "real world" or have "real world" skills. Since then, I have learned that academia offers a wonderful life and that many of the qualities I was learning at that time in sports, such as discipline, fair play and team work, would be very beneficial to me in my academic career. Another thing I learned in sports was to have a few keywords and phrases to help motivate and streamline my thinking. For example, I played a lot of competitive tennis between the ages of 10 and 20 and I found that during matches, simple phrases, such as "move your feet," "hit through the ball" and "out in front," would help me much more than focusing on all the details. The game is simply too complex to analyze it fully, especially in the moment. Over the years, I built up a collection of these phrases that I found helpful. I usually picked them up from things my Dad or my coaches said to me, or from other players I looked up to. If I was in a difficult situation in a match or having trouble with a shot, I would start saying the appropriate word or phrase to myself to provide the focus and energy I needed.

When I was asked to write this chapter, I found it useful to reflect on this idea of keywords and phrases. I began my PhD in 2001, so I have had a decade in this profession. Much as in my prior life, I have found a number of keywords or phrases useful to me. The particular phrases I have used might not be the most useful for everyone, but I think the idea of having keywords or phrases is a useful one and I use mine simply as a case study in what has worked for me. Moreover, they may give readers who are in the early stages of their academic career a taste for what lies ahead, or at least, what lay ahead for me and my way to keep myself focused. Table 18-1 presents an overview of the keywords and phrases that I will discuss.

Table 18-1. Keywords And Phrases I Work By

To stop me: Juggling
To focus: The light is an oncoming train; Keep it real; 15 seconds
For dealing with rejections: If life is subjective, pick a happy one

Table 18-1 *Continued*. Keywords And Phrases I Work By

For reviewing: Suspend disbelief; People's lives
For planning research: Who needs data? Engaged scholarship; Do something brilliant
For appreciating: A many-spired tent; Celebrate good times, come on!

1. Keyword To Stop Me

i. Juggling

In my early days in the doctoral program at Georgia State University (GSU), a professor mentioned that life as an academic was like juggling balls. In the beginning, they give you just one, then two, then three, then four and so on. The idea was that through your academic career you just keep getting more balls and you have to work out a way to keep going without dropping them. This idea is a bit depressing but I have often found it useful. In particular, when I started out, I thought that more balls were better. I said "yes" to any request asked of me and I began work on many different ventures. In my fourth year of my doctoral program, the problem with this strategy became evident. I was simply unable to do all the work I had promised to do. I remember telling my wife that I felt like I was in a pin-ball machine: I was just bouncing from one research meeting to another with little or nothing new to report except my apologies for such little progress. I had become a poor co-author and colleague, and it took me a long time to recover. In fact, I *still* have papers and projects from that time that I have not been able to finish because it has taken so long to finish other projects that I have since started and are of great interest to me. I still have the tendency to say yes to things, and to be excited by new projects and ideas. As a result, when I see myself being attracted by such prospects, I try to remind myself of the juggling metaphor. This helps me remember all the balls I have in the air and all the ones on the ground that I have dropped that then make me less eager to add a new ball to the mix.

2. Key Phrases To Focus

i. The Light Is An Oncoming Train

When I began my doctoral program, I read several books on life as a doctoral student and an assistant professor. I recall reading one chapter in which the doctoral student, who was nearing the end of her program, confided to a professor she admired that she was relieved that she could see the light at the end of the tunnel. The professor replied that the light was an oncoming train![203,204] Much like the metaphor of juggling, this metaphor is a bit depressing. However, again, I have found it useful. There is a great deal of randomness in academic life (much like other aspects of life) and I was fortunate to receive much more good luck than bad in my doctoral program and my early years as an assistant professor. Knowing that the "light is an oncoming train," however, has kept me focused on my work, rather than easing up to savor the fruits of my labor (or luck, as it may be). Each day at work, I walk down the corridor past Izak Benbasat's office on the way upstairs to get some coffee. Izak has long been among the most prolific researchers in his field (information systems) and he hasn't slowed down. Whenever I go past his office, he is almost always either in a research meeting or working on a paper at his computer. The continued commitment that he demonstrates always reminds me that I can't rely on past successes. I need to focus my attention on the possible train ahead and the need to keep working.

ii. Keep It Real

Now that I've mentioned Izak, I am reminded of another phrase that has helped me. After having arrived at the University of British Columbia, he and Yair Wand, two senior professors in the division, told me that I should write a couple of grant applications. This was definitely the last thing I wanted to do (see "juggling" discussed earlier)! However, I took their advice and wrote the applications. Izak offered to review my application. He highlighted the first paragraph of my application and wrote in the comments "KEEP IT REAL." That hit me hard. I thought that paragraph was very scholarly and nicely summed up all the research I had done in the last few years as a doctoral student. He felt, in contrast, that it was so abstract and academic that it didn't engage the reader at all. Reading his work, I am often reminded that although he is a true academic, he always tries to "keep it real." He tries to examine issues that are relevant in practice, and he invests a lot of time and attention in designing research and writing it up in a way that will speak to a broad readership. When authors focus on keeping their research and writing "real," their papers are more likely to resonate with readers, and achieving such a connection with readers is vital as, after all, we are in the business of communicating with people and asking them to accept our ideas.

iii. 15 Seconds

Veda Storey taught one of our doctoral seminars at GSU. Being a very successful professor with seven children, she is the best multitasker I have ever met. During a conversation in our doctoral seminar, it quickly became apparent why she is so good. The conversation was about what length of time you need to work on research. At the time, I used to like several days to work on a research idea. This would give me time to read everything related to it and analyze it fully, without distraction. Some other students, the better ones, would require a day, maybe a few hours. The best one said that he could do good work on a research idea if he had an hour to dedicate to it. Veda was quite unimpressed. She said, "what about 15 seconds?" She then described how she might be helping her kids at home with something and then, in a 15-second gap between helping one or another of them, do a bit more on the paper she was writing. I can safely say that I will never achieve that level of productivity and focus. However, the idea is helpful to me. I often think of it when I come back from teaching class. I often have a short window of time—it can vary from 10-30 minutes—between finishing class and having another meeting. In that short window, I can either choose to do nothing much or I can try to dedicate myself to my research. I have found that even 10 minutes can be beneficial. Sometimes, 10 minutes is all it takes to edit a key paragraph in a revision to get the argument "right," write a response to one more comment in a review packet or run a new analysis on a data set. I may never get to 15 seconds but it is good to have an ideal.

3. Key Phrase For Dealing With Rejections

i.   If Life Is Subjective, Pick A Happy One

I spent much of 2000 deciding whether or not to do a PhD. I would spend nights randomly looking at academics' websites, trying to glean something about the profession. Were these academics happy? Did I want to be one? One day, I came across Mary Lacity's website at the University of Missouri, St. Louis. I have never met Mary and her website no longer has this phrase (as I was sorry to discover!) but at the time it had the following phrase: "If life is subjective, pick a happy one." I had long been impressed with Mary's research on outsourcing and when I read the phrase on her website, I remember being very impressed with the approach to life that the phrase implied. Since then, I have often used the phrase when I felt down about one thing or another, especially rejections I receive from journals. My wife and I also use it when we want to cheer each other up about something. I have learned that it is a surprisingly powerful phrase, for while much of life is objective, the way we look at it is truly up to us.

4. Key Phrases For Reviewing

i.   Suspend Disbelief

I once read a presentation on reviewing. I don't remember any of the details except one phrase: "suspend disbelief." This phrase seemed to capture so fully the challenges I felt when reviewing papers at that time. As my career has progressed, I have been asked to do an increasingly large number of reviews. In the past, I would start reading a paper and my first emotional reaction was "why on earth would they study this?" I have since learned that this is a common question in low- or weak-paradigm fields—i.e., fields in which there is little consensus on the core questions of interest and the best ways to study them.[205] The idea of suspending disbelief has been useful to me because it has prevented me from anchoring too quickly on a particular judgment, especially when the authors have taken a different approach to what I would have done in that context. Saying the phrase to myself helps me to read the paper a little more from the authors' own eyes. After doing so, I often feel much more positive about the paper and more willing and able to give it a fair review. I also often gain new insights about my own research that I would not have if I had not kept this phrase in mind.

ii. Peoples' Lives

I had my first exposure to research in general, and information systems research in particular, when I was an undergraduate honors student at the University of Queensland. I had the good fortune of having Ron Weber as my advisor. Not surprisingly, many of my views about research stem from my interactions with Ron during that time. I recall Ron saying that we have to take the review process seriously because otherwise we are "playing with people's lives." This is perhaps the objective counterpart to my earlier phrase "If life is subjective." Ron's point was that the lives of researchers, especially those early in their careers, can be greatly affected by just one publication in a top journal. I wasn't aware then exactly how true this was but I have since heard and seen several cases where "just one paper" made all the difference to a job offer or tenure case. As a result, I try to keep this in mind when reviewing papers, especially for top journals. I am a slow reviewer and towards the end of a review, I often feel quite frustrated that it is taking so long. I feel worried that my other work is backing up and I feel tempted to just conclude the review and leave the hard decision to the editor. In these moments, I repeat Ron's phrase to myself. If someone has spent several years of their life working on this paper and could be affected for several more years if the paper is rejected, surely I can spend a few more hours on it and give the authors a little more help.

5. Key Phrases For Planning Research

i. Who Needs Data?

This is another phrase that came from my doctoral program at GSU. A group of us asked Dan Robey if he could give us some guidance on writing conceptual papers. Much to our good fortune, he decided to give a course on the topic. The opening paper of the course was his paper "Who Needs Data?" This phrase was useful to me because it motivated me to write conceptual papers. The fact that such papers could be written was nothing original. But the idea that *I* could write one struck me instantly. Dan's phrase has been particularly helpful in the last 12 months. Because it takes a long time to get papers published, I spent the first few years of my career at UBC trying to finish old papers rather than start new ones. Although this helped me get some publications, it meant that I hadn't gathered a good data set in a while. Writing conceptual papers—papers with no data—provided me with a buffer, allowing me to get papers out while planning a good empirical study. It also helped me develop my theoretical ideas more completely, allowing me to identify additional data that I should collect that I would not have thought of without this conceptual work. Finally, writing conceptual papers has allowed me to tackle problems that interest me for which data would be difficult to collect. When I talk with doctoral students about interesting issues, they sometimes say "Well, we can't study that because the data would be too hard to get." Thanks to Dan, my response is "Who needs data?"

ii. Engaged Scholarship

This is a relatively new one. I have long admired Andy Van de Ven's research so I would occasionally visit his website to see new papers he had published. One day, I stumbled across his book "Engaged Scholarship."[206] I found that it nicely summed up what had been missing in much of my research. Early in my doctoral program, I learned that you need to publish to make a contribution. Looking back, I realize that I pursued that aim to the detriment of real engagement with practitioners. I even remember making a derogatory comment at one research workshop about the lack of rigor in practitioner-oriented research. I wish I could go back in time to that workshop and give myself a slap. I am still in the early stages of correcting this aspect of my research. I recently started an Executive Advisory Board here at UBC in the hope that it could help other faculty members (and me!) to improve links between our research and industry. I greatly admire those researchers in our field who combine their academic achievements while still engaging with industry. Arun Rai and Lars Mathiassen at GSU are great examples of this. Although they have very different research styles (Arun specializes in quantitative research while Lars specializes in qualitative action research), both have demonstrated an ability to produce excellent scholarship that has real value to organizations and to build institutional mechanisms that can make this work over time (reflected, for example, in GSU's Center for Process Innovation). I hope I can emulate what people like Arun and Lars have accomplished, and I plan to keep this phrase in mind as much as possible from now on.

iii. Do Something Brilliant

I owe this one to Mike Gallivan. In the early stages of a paper we began during my doctoral program, Mike said to me "do something brilliant." I looked up to Mike a lot. Because he had studied at the very top universities in the US (Harvard, Berkeley and MIT), I was sure that *he* could do something brilliant but the idea that someone like him thought that someone like *me* could do so was so uplifting. I do not think I ever came close to achieving it but I know I tried with all my might. I distinctly remember trying to work on a "higher plane" and felt inspired to do a great job. In my day-to-day work, I rarely think about Mike's phrase. But occasionally, when I am presented with a difficult revision on a paper, a hard class to teach or a new research project, it comes back to me and inspires me to do my best. It has also helped me in my work as an advisor to graduate students. Rather than assume that I have to come up with all the brilliant ideas, I feel confident that I can ask them to do so. And, they do!

6. Key Phrases For Appreciating

i. A Many-spired Tent

Many of the phrases I have discussed are a little negative—emphasizing what I should aim for, even if I cannot do it or have not done it, to date. This one is more positive. Near the end of Karl Weick's excellent book on sensemaking, there is a poem by Mary Van Sell on her impressions on attending her first Academy meeting.[207] She ends the poem likening the Academy to a "jazz band of questioners" in a "many-spired tent." I liked her analogy very much. Like good jazz, our work can be fun and uplifting. We don't need a conductor. We can play our own tune while working creatively with other people's tunes to create broader melodies that shift and change. Moreover, our jazz band is large. In fact, we have many different jazz bands all under one roof, with players and bands moving and mixing and the different melodies, harmonies and beats moving and mixing with them. Because there are multiple spires to this tent, there are multiple "centers of action" rather than just one. It is an inspiring image! Perhaps because of the time in my life when I read it (shortly after travelling to the US to do my PhD, full of energy and expectation), I always remember this analogy fondly. Amidst all the difficulties and randomness of academic life, it is certainly a wonderful and blessed life. Like many academic fields, the information systems discipline, of which I am a part, has people doing research on all manner of topics, at different levels of analysis, and from many different countries, philosophies and traditions. Because information systems is a low- or weak-paradigm field, the variety in this field is even greater than in some others. Variety, creativity and open-mindedness are characteristics of almost all academic fields. In short, life as a scholar is incredibly rich and stimulating, and I am very lucky to be part of it.

When I am confronted by the difficulties that I face in academic life, I enjoy remembering Mary Van Sell's poem and the positive images that it evokes.

ii. Celebrate Good Times, Come On!

I was very fortunate to have Detmar Straub as my doctoral thesis advisor. One word that conveys Detmar's energy and influence on me is "celebrate." This word appeared on the last slide of a presentation he gave on publishing when I was a doctoral student. His point was that the publication process is so long, you must take time to celebrate when a paper finally "hits." However, I use the word more broadly here to reflect an eagerness to celebrate others' achievements. Much of our work is "serious" and we don't get much time to celebrate. Moreover, in the competitive world of academia, it is perhaps natural to envy those doing well and rue lost chances of one's own. More than anyone I know, Detmar avoids these sins and looks for reasons to celebrate others' achievements. I recall several times when I (or other people) had suggested to Detmar that such-and-such a paper was published even though it was mediocre or that so-and-so had been awfully lucky to get some paper accepted. On these occasions, Detmar was always quick to retort that the paper is excellent and that the person did terrific work. Likewise, when working on review teams in which Detmar is the editor, I have seen him champion papers through to acceptance because he wanted to celebrate rather than criticize the authors' ideas. His positive nature is reflected well in an *MIS Quarterly* editorial he co-authored with Varun Grover and Pamela Galluch on positive thinking in our field.[208] Thanks to Kool & the Gang, I can even put his idea to music, as many people know their tune: "Celebrate good times, come on!" After working with Detmar for some time, I have learned that it is not only better to celebrate than to criticize, but also more enjoyable.

Concluding Thoughts

I presented an overview of my keywords and phrases in Table 18-1. Having never written them down before, doing so was surprisingly therapeutic. I feel enthusiastic about the class I am going to teach soon and the short amount of time before it in which I will do some research. At the same time, looking over the list gives me some grief as an academic. I did not compile the list based on any research. I have also not categorized them well. There seems to be some overlap amongst them and I am sure they could be more complete. Nevertheless, I am at ease with it. I am sure that some of these phrases will become less important to me over time, while others will grow in importance and new ones will be added to the mix. But for now, analyzing them too much would miss the whole point of the phrases: to provide me with focus, energy and clarity "in the moment." In short, they combine emotional and cognitive elements. Over-analyzing them would take out the emotional aspects that are critical for their effectiveness.

The source of the words and phrases in my list are much the same as the source of the list I developed as a teenager: most of them are from coaches, mentors and people I look up to. This is interesting because these people said many things to me but what seemed to stick was just a word here or a phrase there. Moreover, I do not recall any of them sitting me down and prefacing their remarks with something like "Now, remember what I am about to tell you...." Instead, they were just fragments of discussions, suggestions or statements that somehow struck me and stuck with me. It is timely for me to reflect on this because in my roles as a research advisor, teacher and father, I now often have to give advice. It is humbling to think that much of my advice, even those things I think should be remembered, will never be remembered by those I advise. Likewise, statements I make off the cuff may be remembered by others for years on their road to success. Writing this chapter has helped me realize that I do not have as much control as I thought over what parts of my advice will resonate and what will not, what will be useful and what will not. I somehow have to be at ease with this. To all my research advisees, students and my two lovely daughters, all I can say is that I will try my best. And with that, I will finish with one of my eldest daughter's favorite phrases when talking to me: All done!

Key Takeaways

1. Having a few keywords and phrases can help motivate and streamline one's thinking—over the years, it can be helpful to build up a collection of these keywords and phrases that provide you with focus, energy and clarity "in the moment"
2. To stop me...
   i. Juggling: Academic life is like juggling balls—as you go through your academic career, you just keep getting more balls and you have to work out a way to keep going without dropping them, which also means you should stop and think about whether you can juggle yet another "ball" before accepting new projects or assignments
3. To focus...
   i. The light is an oncoming train: The light at the end of the tunnel is an oncoming train—focus your attention on the possible train ahead and keep working
   ii. Keep it real: Keep your writing and your research "real"
   iii. 15 seconds: Even in a short window of time, you can do research—even 10 minutes (for some, 15 seconds!) can be beneficial
4. For dealing with rejections...
   i. If life is subjective, pick a happy one: Much of life is objective but the way we look at it is up to us
5. For reviewing...
   i. Suspend disbelief: Avoid anchoring too quickly on a particular judgment about a paper, especially when authors have taken a different approach to what you would do in that context
   ii. People's lives: If someone has spent several years of their life working on a paper and their life could be affected for several more years if the paper is rejected, surely you can spend a few more hours on it and give the authors a little more help
6. For planning research...
   i. Who needs data? Writing a conceptual paper—i.e., a paper with no data—can provide you with a buffer to allow you to get papers out while planning or conducting a good

empirical study

   ii. Engaged scholarship: You need to publish to make a contribution but make sure you don't pursue this aim at the detriment of real engagement with practitioners

  iii. Do something brilliant: You may not ever achieve it but try with all your might

7. For appreciating…

   i. A many-spired tent: Academia in general provides an incredibly rich and stimulating environment in which to live and work

  ii. Celebrate good times, come on—celebrate when a paper finally "hits" and celebrate others' achievements

CHAPTER 19

ACHIEVING BALANCE IN YOUR LIFE (HOW TO BE A PRODUCTIVE ACADEMIC AND ALSO HAVE A PERSONAL LIFE)

Gordon B. Davis

Honeywell Professor of Management Information Systems, Emeritus
Carlson School of Management
University of Minnesota
Minneapolis, MN
gdavis@umn.edu

There are some inherent difficulties in being a productive academic, both as a teacher and a researcher, and having a balanced life that includes non-academic interests, such as spouse, family, friends, community and hobbies. This chapter is framed in terms of an academic career but the issues and principles apply to a broad range of largely self-managed knowledge work positions and activities. Some people have good intuition (natural understanding) relative to a balance in life, while some others have no clue about it. The purpose of this chapter is to help those who already have good intuition to be even better in their balance and to help those who have poor intuition to achieve satisfactory balance.

The way to be productive and also have a full life is deceptively simple. The solution is to make balance an explicit goal in your life and adopt explicit methods to achieve it. However, it is not usually effective merely to decide to set boundaries and dedicate part of your time to the non-academic activities that will balance your life. It usually requires some rethinking of priorities and changing some behaviors that will otherwise lead you to consume all your time with your academic work and leave no time and energy for vital, personal activities.

There is a balance problem because the natural tendencies of an academic life are against achieving a full, balanced life. To offset this tendency, you should be proactive in managing your life. With modest effort, you can get the best of both worlds—the rewards from an academic career and the rewards of a personal life. This chapter explains the tendencies that lead to neglect of personal life, and it suggests methods and behaviors to overcome them.

Warning! Most of us avoid even the simple planning and goal setting I describe. I don't think we avoid it because it is too hard. Rather, there seems to be a common feeling that plans and goals constrain us. They reduce our freedom. However, this is one of those cases where our intuition is wrong. Doing simple planning and goal setting frees us because we allocate time to important things and do not spend valuable time achieving things that have little importance.

Overview Of How To Achieve Balance In Your Life As A Knowledge Worker

Achieving balance is a life-long process. It consists of both understanding the forces related to achieving balance and taking actions to achieve it. *Understanding* means to ponder deeply so that you appreciate the power of the forces against balance. *Taking action* means to internalize and make operational in your life the thinking and the actions to achieve balance. Five key things related to *understanding* and *taking action* are:

1. Understand and keep in mind throughout your life the dynamics of an academic career (or any other largely self-managed knowledge work career) that prevent balance. These dynamics are not necessarily obvious to many of us. We need to understand the forces that work against the easy achievement of our balance objective.

2. Develop clarity in your goals, values and talents. Doing this will help you be mindful of what is important for you if you are to live a full, productive and satisfied life. Knowing what is important to you will help you to protect important non-work goals and values from being pushed out by the demands of your academic work.

3. Understand and apply methods of knowledge work planning and schedule-discipline to your life so that you achieve your most important work goals and also achieve your most important personal goals. You want both and there are ways to achieve both.

4. Understand and apply ways that work for you to balance personal life and the demands of your academic career. Achieving the balance you want means you have to manage both your work and your personal times. It is not sufficient to say that you will clearly define and protect dedicated, set-aside times for the non-work activities that are important to you. Making this a goal is vital but making it work requires activities to manage your academic activities so that you have enough time and energy for non-work activities. You need to apply some planning and management activities to achieve the results that are most important and minimize the effort devoted to the less important.

5. Don't get over planned and over scheduled. In your planning and schedule-discipline activities, take time periodically to review your goals. Also, allow for the unplanned and unexpected. If you have clarity in your broad objectives and know what is important, you can re-plan and re-schedule when unexpected events change the dynamics of your life or when unexpected opportunities arise. You will be able to assess whether an opportunity (such as teaching, research and service) that you did not expect to be available to you will be good for you in achieving your important life goals.

Source Of My Analysis And Advice

The ideas and recommendations in this paper are not the result of systematic data collection and analysis. They come from personal observation of hundreds of faculty members and doctoral students. They reflect some "aha moments" in my own life (moments when understanding or solutions become clear) or "aha" observations of others. These moments surfaced the fact that there are large differences in the ability of bright people to deal with some common problems in academic work or other self-managed knowledge work careers. My advice is consistent with books and articles from many advice-givers. I have given many talks and written articles that explain my advice. For this chapter, I have reused some ideas presented in my "Last Lecture" given at the Americas Conference on Information Systems in San Francisco August 7 of 2009. It has also been published in the *Communications of the Association for Information Systems.*[209]

The value I can add to other advice-givers is that my advice comes from the academic world. I have observed many successes and failures. I have personally had both successes and failures. I have pondered these events, and I have extracted some principles and best practices. Typically, the advice has come about because I was puzzled by what happened with me or I was puzzled by the actions of others. As a result of observations, thinking about what I observed, thinking about explanations and relating the situations to theories of individual behavior, I formulated advice that has proved remarkably robust when colleagues and doctoral students apply it. Four examples illustrate the kinds of moments that motivated my search for good advice:

1. Understanding the problem but not understanding there is a solution. A doctoral student that I thought had great promise came to me to tell me he was dropping out of the doctoral program. He explained that he was overwhelmed with the workload in becoming a scholar, and that his wife and he had decided they couldn't have a satisfying life if he became an academic. In pondering the incident and my lack of a well-reasoned solution to his concern, I realized the issue of a balanced life was very important, but I did not have a well-formulated answer to help students understand that it was possible to deal with the overwhelming amount of things to know and do, and still have a life. This chapter is what I should have told the student who was overwhelmed.

2. The effect of achieving clarity and focus for a goal-achieving activity. I have told this story many times and it has been repeated by many others. When I was a doctoral student, I was doing library research and developing concepts. I was enthralled with reading and thinking. One day my wife asked, "how many pages did you write today?" This question underscored a vital goal-achieving activity. The goal was to write the dissertation. The goal-achieving activity was writing some pages every day. The incident changed my behavior in finishing the dissertation. The full import of this incident and the effect of goal clarity emerged as I counseled many doctoral students who couldn't seem to make progress on the dissertation. I worked to change their goal from vague ideas related to thinking to a schedule of manageable activities and events to produce vital results on a timely basis.

3. Structure and guidelines makes a difference. Most doctoral students are bright yet many do not get their PhD because they do not complete the dissertation. They have learned the content of the academic field and the practice of research, but many of them do not know how to structure and manage the dissertation project. I wrote a short book (*Writing the Doctoral Dissertation*)[210] that has been used by more than 60,000 doctoral students. This little book has elicited more "thank you" notes than anything else I have written. I believe it had such an impact because it laid out a simple approach that provided structure, explained the main elements of a solution, and provided some guidelines for planning and managing a project that, for many students, seemed to be completely unstructured.

4. Having clarity of goals and necessary processes makes a difference. I was talking casually with a faculty member who was approaching a tenure decision. He was not going to get tenure. He understood it. He mentioned to me that "perhaps I should have done things differently." I thought, "of course, why didn't you know it?!" The incident illustrated how bright people can have a vague goal but may not intuitively do the simplest planning and activity management to achieve it.

An Underlying Premise: Individual Differences In Ability To Manage Work

I have observed very large individual differences among my colleagues and students in managing their work. For each activity involved in a project, some of them seem to be able to plan it and to do it easily—sometimes intuitively, with little thought. Others who are equally bright struggle with accomplishing activities leading to progress even though they may believe the activities are vital. For the purposes of thinking about the issue, assume a normal distribution of ability to accomplish important activities by intuitively applying adequate planning and schedule-discipline. The problem is that only a small percentage of us can achieve good results using only our intuitive ability. For most of us (say 95% of us), our intuitive ability by itself is not sufficient to yield good results. This does not mean that only a few can achieve planning and schedule-discipline to succeed—it means that most of us need to add explicit methods to our intuitive ability in order to do well. This means that some of you will have to be more explicit than others to achieve planning and schedule-discipline to accomplish your important activities, but I believe it is possible for everyone to do reasonably well. Also, even those who have high intuitive skills at planning and schedule-discipline will improve their performance with the simple explicit methods I outline.

The idea that there are large individual differences in ability to manage individual knowledge work is fundamental to my reasoning. It means that some people can manage their knowledge work with little explicit effort, but others are at a complete loss unless they use explicit methods. Virtually everyone will do better with explicit methods. Using explicit methods does not abolish individual differences but it does reduce the impact of the differences on success.

A personal example will illustrate the point about a distribution of intuitive abilities. A very important knowledge work task is estimating the time to complete an assignment, such as writing a paper, reviewing a paper or preparing a lecture. Over time, I have observed that if I make an intuitive estimate of the duration to complete, I consistently and significantly underestimate the time required. When I break the project into a few smaller tasks and explicitly estimate each of these, I do reasonably well in estimating the duration for completion that works for me. I have colleagues who can intuitively estimate very accurately, but I cannot. If I am asked, "can you write a two-page commentary on a news item within your area of expertise?" My intuitive belief is that this is easy and my answer (because I am probably at the 20th percentile for native schedule estimating ability) may be an hour. If I explicitly examine the task and its component activities, I will make a more reasonable estimate (for example three to four hours). Note that if I keep making intuitive estimates that are far too low, I will tend to make delivery commitments that I cannot keep unless I use vital non-work personal time for them. In other words, because I make poor intuitive estimates of time required, I must do explicit estimating in order to keep my commitments in line with the time I have available.

Let me emphasize the vital lesson that comes from this concept. It is that most of us do not intuitively do what we need to do to have a productive, interesting and balanced academic career. Fortunately, by being explicit in our objectives and following simple rules for productivity, most or perhaps all of us can achieve results that are very satisfactory and satisfying to us.

Most of the time, these principles and best practices will help you be more productive, help you to not commit to more than you can really handle and help you have a happier personal life. Of course, they may not work perfectly for you but, in all cases, they should help you think more clearly about your life and your choices. They will help you figure out a solution that works for you.

Can everyone follow the recommendations in this article? In general, yes. However, as a counterpoint, I had a very bright, interesting student on his way to a productive career who said "I can't do it" when I suggested some knowledge work management procedures. He managed without doing what I suggested but I believe he would have been more productive in his career if he had adopted my advice. In the remainder of the article, I will explain my five recommendations in more detail.

1. Understand And Keep In Mind Throughout Your Life The Dynamics Of An Academic Career That Prevent Balance

Generally, the problem is not that we are lazy. Faculty members work hard and spend long hours working. The average faculty work week is more than 50 hours and many hard workers average much more. However, the problem is not due to failure to work hard; it is in the failure to set boundaries and limits to work projects. The nature of knowledge work that academics do is that natural limits to work that are found in many production or clerical work or manual activities do not apply. This means that natural boundaries between work life and personal life are weak or not found in academic work and similar knowledge work. Consider some of the dynamics:

i.   There is no limit to the amount of relevant knowledge a knowledge worker can acquire. Think of any academic field. There is no limit to the journal articles to be read, related fields to study, etc.

ii. There are almost no natural limits on the amount of work that can be done (and that seems worthwhile to do) for a task or project. There are no natural limits (except deadlines) to the amount of work you can do for a knowledge work project. Consider a simple example: suppose you are asked to do an analysis of summer employment of college students by a set of local companies. If you were given one week, the report would focus on numbers of students hired, company supervisor experiences and recommendations. If you were given two years, you could expand your report to examine student motives, reactions of co-workers during the student work time, effects on productivity, effectiveness of recruiting, etc. Many non-knowledge work tasks have clear natural limits—e.g., digging a ditch, delivering newspapers—and are finished when the physical task is complete but most knowledge work projects do not have such clear limits. There is no limit except the time that is available and often there is no externally imposed time. The time available is not a good measure of how much time you should use (and can profitably use). If you are going to manage your academic work life so that you have appropriate time and energy for non-work life, you will need to learn to set limits on the amount of time you will spend for your knowledge work activities and projects.

iii. Academics do most of their own scheduling and task management. This applies to many other knowledge workers. The amount of employer specification and scheduling may differ for knowledge workers but typically, knowledge workers, such as academics, have much of the responsibility for managing their knowledge work projects—including scheduling, deadlines, scope and stopping rules. This means that an academic with poor work management skills relative to scheduling and poor skills at time management will have many re-occurring crises that require the use of time that should be part of his or her personal life. You don't have to be a whiz at scheduling and task management to achieve satisfactory results for your life, but you do need to apply some simple, explicit planning and scheduling processes so as to not rely on intuition alone.

iv. Another difficulty with academics and many other knowledge workers is that there are no natural physical boundaries to the work day—between work and non-work. Work is not defined by the time spent at the office. Knowledge work can be done almost any time and any place. There is no location, such as an office, that sets a boundary between knowledge work and personal life. Technology (Internet, e-mail, ubiquitous computing and the portability of knowledge work materials) has severely weakened boundaries between work and non-work. There is nothing inherently wrong with working from your home office or your portable devices. However, it means that you need to manage this work time so that it does not crowd out important non-work activities.

v. In general, knowledge work has more structure than personal activities. It is more compelling because of the cognitive rewards and deadlines (actual or implied). Structured activities tend to impinge on, or crowd out, unstructured activities. Therefore, professional activities will tend to crowd out personal activities. It is important to understand how the structure and the nature of knowledge work rewards can affect your ability to maintain balance.

The important lesson from these points is that the characteristics of knowledge work remove or weaken boundaries between work life and personal life, and there are work life tendencies that lead to neglect of personal life unless explicit actions are taken to create appropriate boundaries and protection for personal life.

2. Develop Clarity In Your Goals, Values And Talents

Goals, values and talents help you keep in mind what is important if you are to live a full, productive and satisfied life. These will help you keep in mind the important non-work goals and values that you need to protect from being pushed out by the demands of your work.

A common thread through all the "success" literature is the need to set explicit goals and priorities for your life. In a life with many competing interests and demands, it is vital to allocate your time and talents wisely so you achieve the outcomes that are most important to you. These goals and priorities can be simple and straightforward. I suggest focusing on two important issues in developing clarity in your goals, values and talents:

i.   Figure out your talents and gifts and decide how to maximize and take advantage of your best talents and compensate for your worst ones.
ii. Because there is usually more than one important goal, learn how to divide your time, talents and energy among your most important goals (academic and personal).

It helps to know your natural talents and gifts, and things at which you are not particularly good. There is, at least conceptually, a portfolio of skills to be a good academic and to live a productive life. However, it is not likely you will be equally good at all of them. You may be outstanding in some, good in others and likely with effort passable in the rest. By understanding your talents, you can take advantage of your best talents and compensate for your weakest ones. If you are intuitively a very good teacher, take advantage of this natural ability and work to become an outstanding teacher. If you have poor natural ability as a teacher, learn how to be an acceptable teacher and apply yourself to compensate for your weakness by being excellent at something else. The concept applies broadly to the important activities in being an academic and in being a productive person.

How do you discover your talents and your gifts as an academic? You can observe yourself and notice those activities and interactions where you seem to do very well and also observe those where you do not do so well. You should observe patterns of ability. A few examples of talents and gifts that are important in your academic life are: ability to formulate clear concepts, ability to explain facts and concepts simply and clearly in writing, ability to explain facts and concepts simply and clearly in lectures or exchanges with students and other audiences, ability to generate lots of ideas (ideaphoria), ability to see patterns in observations and in data, ability to relate to students and other audiences, and ability to see value in alternative methods and views. There could, of course, be other talents and just about no one has all of them.

When you understand your gifts and talents and understand that they allow you to naturally perform some activities better than most of your colleagues, you can develop them and emphasize them. When you understand that you have some poorly developed talents, you can work to improve them to an acceptable level.

Example: I found out very early I was quite good at explaining things and writing explanations. I also have high ideaphoria (I can generate lots of interesting ideas). I was also good at seeing the existence of systems (or lack of systems) in organizations. I had a competitive advantage in conceptualizing and thinking of solutions or alternative explanations for problems. However, I could plan and schedule only moderately well, and I didn't do it instinctively. I had to work at it. I was not good at analytical modeling and numerical analysis. One of the factors in success in my career has been the fact that I have tended to take advantage of and apply my best skills and talents.

Example: One of the exercises I have used with new doctoral students is to have them make a 10-year research plan. They look at me as if I was crazy because they have a hard time planning for the next term. I point out that a 10-year plan will take them through a doctoral program and to the tenure decision. Once they see this, they can formulate a simple, rough plan that is helpful to them. The plan gets changed but changes are easier to make, compared to thinking and creating a new one.

Example: Be realistic. Early in my advising, I encouraged a doctoral student to learn everything I wished I had learned and do everything I wished I could have done. I loaded him up with unrealistic expectations and he got so discouraged that he dropped out. I learned from that advising failure to help doctoral students focus rather than trying to know everything and do everything.

Because you will have more than one important goal, it is important to not focus on one and lose sight of other important goals. You may want to be a great researcher, a great teacher, a great advisor/mentor, a great husband/wife and a great parent. Dividing your time and talents among these goals will require you to set priorities and limits. I will talk more about this later.

> *Example:* Develop clarity of goals for your personal life. Marriage and family are vital goals for most people, and they should be explicitly considered. A faculty member can get so caught up in becoming a great scholar that he or she forgets to find a great companion to marry or to nurture a marriage or to have a great family relationship. For most of us, the search for a companion and the nurturing of a marriage and a family are worthy goals to include in our top priorities.

3. Understand And Apply Methods Of Knowledge Work Planning And Schedule-discipline To Your Life So That You Achieve Your Most Important Work Goals And Also Achieve Your Most Important Personal Goals

The first two points—(i) understanding academic life; and (ii) developing clarity about your goals and talents—deal with preparation. The third point deals with getting your academic work done. Because there is not enough time to do everything, your task is to develop and apply a reasonable level of planning and schedule-discipline. This sounds constraining and harsh but when you learn to do it reasonably well, you will be freer and less harried than the person who does not learn this. Being successful in setting goals and achieving them creates energy. Success breeds success.

By the time you start your degree program or start your academic career as an assistant professor, you should be able to examine your behavior and evaluate your natural ability for planning and schedule-discipline. As I mentioned earlier, I believe there is a normal curve for such ability. Some people have very high intuitive ability and others are almost devoid. Your intuitive ability to plan and schedule is a starting point. For most people, the intuitive ability at that point is insufficient. Fortunately, planning and schedule-discipline can be learned and your normal, intuitive ability can be dramatically increased by explicit attention to doing it.

> *Example:* I started out when I was a doctoral student somewhat below the middle of the normal curve for intuitive planning and schedule-discipline. I had been able to meet course requirements but these were doable in short periods of concentration. They did not require long-term planning and schedule-discipline. I have improved in planning and schedule-discipline but I still have to work at it. If I stray from the principles of planning and scheduling, and if I meander when working on a project, my performance deteriorates. I see the effect when I don't apply planning and schedule-discipline.

> *Example:* Working with colleagues or staff who exhibit good planning and schedule-discipline can be helpful to you. You can learn from them. However, there is a danger

if you exhibit poor discipline when working with colleagues and delay the completion of a project, you may find you will not have opportunities to work with those colleagues again. If you are willing to accept the help and example of those who have schedule-discipline, you will benefit. I have worked with colleagues who were very good at completion and they helped me to be productive because I was motivated to meet the deadlines we set.

Example: It took me a while after I started my academic career to appreciate and think about the severe problem some people had in completing doctoral dissertations (because I had not experienced it). The problem was especially severe when they accepted faculty positions before completing their dissertations. In several cases, they could not complete the dissertation while doing the full-time work of a faculty member. In order to complete it, they left home and closeted themselves in an apartment in the city of the university granting the degree. Only by this drastic measure were they able to complete their dissertations. They were all bright. They were all motivated. Something was missing. It appeared that they did not understand the dynamics of planning, scheduling and motivating themselves to complete daily knowledge work required to complete an independent dissertation.

In order to get you going in your quest to understand how to plan, manage and complete your work (schedule-discipline), I suggest five things you can do:

i.   Know how long it takes YOU to do knowledge work tasks. Develop some explicit estimators for planning.

ii. Set time and effort limits on each knowledge work project (or major parts if it is a large project).

iii. Plan for motivating yourself. Define short-term deliverables to *measure* your progress and *motivate* you (I call this the M&M approach). This is very important.

iv. Schedule your activities to match your productivity patterns during a day or other periods of time.

v.   Schedule hard things for uninterrupted times when you can concentrate and schedule things requiring little concentration (and that can be interrupted) for what I term as rest times or tired times.

You must have some rough but explicit estimators for doing activities in a knowledge work project. Why explicit? Because many (or perhaps most) of us intuitively underestimate the time it takes to do knowledge work activities. My observation is that we tend to underestimate worse if we estimate the total time than if we estimate the different parts of the knowledge work project. Some people are good at intuitively estimating the time it takes to complete a project. I am not and many of my colleagues are not. Don't be fooled into believing you are an accurate intuitive estimator unless you have lots of evidence.

Example: I estimate that it takes 2 hours per double-spaced page to organize and put on paper ideas that I already know well and have talked about. It takes up to 5 hours per page for fuzzy ideas that I have to formulate into coherent content. This means a 10-page write-up of things I know well will take 20 hours; my intuitive estimate without applying the page estimate algorithm is likely to be 5 or 6 hours.

Example: I estimate it takes me an average of 3 to 4 hours to prepare properly for a one-hour course lecture and class discussion. Again, my intuitive estimate will tend to be very optimistic. I say to myself, "I know the subject so I will be ready in an hour" and this intuitive feeling is wrong.

The next idea for planning and schedule-discipline is to set time and effort limits for a knowledge work project. If there are no time and effort limits, knowledge work will expand to take all the time and effort that are available. The adage was articulated as Parkinson's Law by a British humorist, Cyril Northcote Parkinson, as the first sentence of a humorous essay published in November 1955 in *The Economist*[211] and in a subsequent book. This humorous adage turns out to be a serious, important principle. You can spend whatever time you are allowed. This principle was demonstrated in early information system development projects that tended to go on and on without being completed. Only by breaking projects down into short projects with deliverables (sometimes natural deliverables but sometimes artificial deliverables that demonstrated progress) were we able to get development projects done on time.

Example: It is possible to spend almost unlimited time on a research project. It is also possible to over-prepare for teaching. Without a plan for a class session with appropriate goals and objectives, an instructor may accumulate too much material, add irrelevant stories and examples, and bore the students.

The third idea is to plan and schedule in a way that helps your motivation. It is hard to maintain motivation for a goal that is ill-defined or distant. Short-term deliverables help with motivation. Each deliverable or milestone is motivating. Remember the psychology experiments with rats where they gave a rat that did a task a reward (a food pellet) to motivate them. We tend to need a reward for completion. Each completion gives us a motivating reward—a psychological candy (think of an M&M). It gives us success-energy and helps us to continue on to the next part of the project. Therefore, you need to identify and focus on short-term deliverables that motivate you. Just don't make them too long. Create short ones that lead you to accomplish the big result you want. Rather than thinking of writing an article as a single knowledge work task, break it into shorter deliverables that can be done in a day, a few days or a week.

Example: Short-term task deliverables typically required for an article are an abstract (write it first), an outline, a description of the problem, explanation of significance, etc. Short deliverables for teaching a course may be the outline of learning objectives, the outline of course topics organized by day of delivery, detailed notes for a single lecture, etc.

When you finish a milestone, the completion will give you an M&M. It will motivate you to proceed. In some cases, you may want to have an explicit reward to celebrate a significant completion. Examples of rewards might be as simple as a short recreational activity (e.g., a movie, a ball game, reading a book, watching a television program). It can be for you alone or it can involve your spouse and/or children (given that they have waited for you to finish).

Example: My personal style is to write an abstract first. If I can't write an abstract describing what I expect the article to say, I have a hard time writing the article. The next task is a list of the headings for the article (sort of a table of contents with a short description of the expected contents). The same concept applies to a book or a dissertation. I can then set a schedule and time limits for each part. If I need to do some research, look up references or any other preparatory work, I can define them as deliverables and estimate the time I expect them to take.

Example: Deliverables from activities to help you be a better teacher—seminars on teaching improvement, feedback from faculty members you invite to listen to your class as a mentor (you can do this for others) and feedback from students. You can teach the same class more than once to develop your lectures and teaching style.

The fourth idea for planning and schedule-discipline is to take advantage of your individual productivity patterns. Most of us have distinct productivity patterns during a day or during a week. Some people are most productive early in the morning. That is true of me. Some work best late at night. It is important to schedule difficult tasks during high productivity times and easy tasks at less productive times. Because some things can be done in the midst of interruptions, you should schedule interruptible tasks during rest times or tired times. Not everybody is the same, so figure out what works for you and then plan and schedule the way it works best for you. Remember that every completion gives you an M&M so using valuable high productivity time for things that do not require concentration and attention means you have wasted the time. You will get M&Ms but you won't have used your time resources wisely—your M&Ms per day will be lower!

Example: If your best time for productivity is early in the morning, then don't start by answering email or doing other things that can be done during low productivity times. Email entices you to read it instead of focusing on tasks that require concentration (because you get a stream of M&Ms by completing a stream of short tasks). Learn to control the interruptions of email and texting, and the associated enticement to avoid important work.

Example: Editing and proofreading are easy for me to do during rest or tired times. I try not to use high productivity, concentration times for it.

4. Understand And Apply Ways That Work For You To Balance Personal Life And The Demands Of Your Academic Career

Because the nature of academic life does not set natural boundaries and natural times for personal life, you must do it explicitly. The most important method is dedicated time. You set aside times for personal and family non-work activities. You protect the dedicated, set-aside times from the demands of work. Work impinging on dedicated, set-aside personal and family times can, of course, happen, but it should be very infrequent. You may even want to have a rule that you will compensate for such events with special dedicated times.

The idea for dedicated time is that a time boundary is set and professional activities must stop and the personal or family activity begins. Knowledge workers faced with this problem have developed different strategies and one size does not necessarily fit all. The point is to make sure you have a boundary strategy that works for you. In my experience and observation, the dedicated time concept works best if there are some important personal and family activities that are scheduled for these dedicated times. Some examples that I have experienced, seen or heard about:

i.   Family night each week with children
ii. Special time for personal interaction with each child
iii. Time set aside each week with spouse (a date night) or for courtship if you want a spouse
iv. Time for developing and maintaining friendships
v.   Time for hobbies, service, religion, etc.

Example: It is easy for spouse and family to get the idea that you have important work to do and that you probably will not have time for them (or that they will not have any priority). The solution is to be proactive and put dedicated times on the calendar—time in which your spouse and family will be first.

5. Don't Get Over Planned And Over Scheduled

If you have clarity in your broad objectives and know what is important, you can re-plan and re-schedule when unexpected events change the dynamics of your life or there are unexpected opportunities. You will be able to assess whether an opportunity (such as teaching, research or service) that you did not expect to be available to you will be good for you in achieving your important life goals. Of course, you also need to think about personal and family considerations when opportunities arise.

226

Example: Sabbaticals or leaves without pay provide the opportunity to work at another university or with another organization, such as a government agency or a consulting firm. I have observed some of these that were great for the faculty member and for their family. I have seen others that didn't turn out so well. I had three leaves without pay—one with a professional organization in New York, one with an Institute in Brussels working with European doctoral students in management and one at the National University of Singapore. One reason that the leaves were successful was not only careful consideration of the impacts on my career, but also thoughtful consideration with my wife and children of the effects on them, and a discussion of actions to make the leaves personally interesting for them and me.

Even though you should have some ideas about your talents and have thought through goals and a plan to guide your life and developed schedule-discipline to help you be productive and have tough boundaries to keep a happy, balanced life, you should always be open to interesting opportunities. They can come at unlikely times and disturb your plans—but don't reject them without serious and thoughtful consideration. In general, opportunities come because you do things that elicit them. Four thoughts illustrate how you can increase the likelihood of interesting opportunities:

i.   Be open to interaction with colleagues and students with diverse backgrounds and interests. Be interested and helpful. These are likely to be sources of opportunities.

ii. Be open to great opportunities that are likely to employ and expand your natural talents. Ponder about them carefully and be willing to change your plans to accept them.

iii. Be open to unlikely research opportunities. Problems you experience, observe or hear about (even small ones) can be the basis for great research. Consider partnering with colleagues who can augment your research skills for a research project.

iv. Be open to leaves and sabbaticals (mine were great!). Consider leaves in industry or government. Leaves can be for a quarter, a half year, a year or longer. They can be close by so that you don't have to relocate or they can be in far and away places. It is a good idea to talk through the advantages and disadvantages with your spouse and children if the decision will impact them. The discussion may surface interesting implications and interesting opportunities for them as well as for you.

Reality Check: I Have Had Failures Along The Way Because I Didn't Always Follow My Own Advice

I believe the advice I have given will help my colleagues to be more productive and happier in their lives. However, it may be helpful to disclose that I didn't always follow my own advice. I label these failures as a "persistence failure," a "leaning too far in the future failure," and a "project selection failure." Each of these illustrates some things for which you should watch out. A "persistence failure" occurred when I became discouraged and dropped a project that might have succeeded with some more effort. "Leaning too far in the future failure" is when I had some ideas that were premature, given the poor state of principles and research data available to support my tentative ideas. A "project selection failure" occurred in my life when I had many projects from which to choose and I chose the easiest rather than the one with the most long-run impact and, therefore, never did do the most important.

What If You Have Not Followed My Advice: Looking Forward And Not Backward

If the advice in this paper is clear and compelling, why do many of us fail to follow it? I understand the natural tendency to "go with the flow" and not plan and, therefore, not make choices among the alternatives that become evident when doing some planning. I understand it because I have done it at times in my life. The good thing about the advice in the chapter is that you can start with better planning and schedule-discipline at any point in your life. Time spent on regrets is time wasted unless it helps you to look forward.

At any point in your life, you can look forward. You can evaluate what you have done and ponder the talents and gifts you appear to possess. You can evaluate potential opportunities you expect and those you would like to have. You can evaluate your intuitive ability to plan and schedule your time and effort and begin applying explicit methods to improve your productivity and performance in your work and improve your allocation of time and effort to your personal life. If you have not accomplished something in your work or personal life that is important to you and it is feasible, you can make explicit plans and take explicit actions to achieve it. Of course, it is always easier said than done but not trying can often be the worst course of action.

Concluding Thoughts

My advice is based on observations of many academics, including myself. It provides a starting point for an academic to manage his or her life so that there is balance with both academic and personal life receiving appropriate attention and energy. I believe that, for most of us, a key step to achieving greater balance is to use explicit methods to plan and manage our time and effort. We tend to believe that we have intuitive ability sufficient for planning and schedule-discipline. My experience and observations suggest that virtually all of us will do much better with planning and schedule-discipline if we are explicit in how we plan and manage.

Being an academic is challenging and rewarding. The danger is that you may not divide your time properly and thus not achieve good balance. My challenge is for you to find the right way for you. My hope is that my suggestions will provide a good start for you.

Key Takeaways

1. The way to be productive and also have a full life is deceptively simple—the solution is to make balance an explicit goal in your life and adopt explicit methods to achieve it
2. It is not usually effective merely to decide to set boundaries and dedicate part of your time to the non-academic activities that will balance your life—it usually requires some rethinking of priorities and changing some behaviors that will otherwise lead you to consume all your time with your academic work and leave no time and energy for vital personal activities
3. Understand and keep in mind throughout your life the dynamics of an academic career that work against balance—to offset this tendency, you should be proactive in managing your life and overcoming the tendencies against balance
4. Overview of how to achieve balance in your life as a knowledge worker
    i. The dynamics of an academic career that work against balance are not necessarily obvious to many of us—we need to understand the forces that work against the easy achievement of our balance objective
    ii. Develop clarity in your goals, values and talents
    iii. Understand and apply methods of knowledge work planning and schedule-discipline to your life so that you achieve your most important work goals and also achieve your most important personal goals
    iv. Understand and apply ways that work for you to balance personal life and the demands of your academic career—apply some planning and management activities to achieve the results that are most important and minimize the effort devoted to the less important
    v. Don't get over planned and over scheduled. If you have clarity in your broad objectives and know what is important, you can re-plan and re-schedule when unexpected events change the dynamics of your life or there are unexpected opportunities
5. Source of my analysis and advice
    i. The advice given in this chapter comes from the academic world, and from observing both successes and failures—four issues illustrate the kinds of moments that motivate a search for good advice about achieving balance in work and life:
        a. Understanding the problem (no balance in your life) but not the solution (how to achieve balance)
        b. Having vague ideas about goals (spending too much time reading and thinking) but not having clarity about goal-achieving activities (writing the dissertation)
        c. Structure and guidelines makes a difference, especially when it comes to the dissertation
        d. Having clarity of goals and necessary processes make a difference. Bright people can have a vague goal but may not intuitively do the simplest planning and activity management to achieve it
6. An underlying premise: Individual differences in ability to manage work
    i. Some people can manage their knowledge work with very little explicit effort; others

are at a complete loss unless they use explicit methods; virtually everyone will do better with explicit methods

7. Reality check
   i. I have had failures along the way because I didn't always follow my own advice Beware of:
      a. Persistence failure—becoming discouraged and dropping a project that might have succeeded with some more effort
      b. Leaning too far in the future failure—you have some ideas that are premature, given the poor state of principles and research data available to support your tentative ideas
      c. Project selection failure—you have many projects to choose from and you choose the easiest rather than the one with the most long-run impact

8. What if you have not followed my advice: Looking forward and not backward
   i. You can start with better planning and schedule-discipline at any point in your life. Time spent on regrets is time wasted unless it helps you to look forward
   ii. If you have not accomplished something in your work or personal life that is important to you and is feasible, you can make explicit plans and take explicit actions to achieve it

CHAPTER 20

CONCLUSIONS

Writing this book has been an absolute delight. It gave me an opportunity to share the lessons learned from my many experiences and observations in academia over the past two decades. I hope that you have benefited from reading this book, whether in your capacity as a PhD student or a junior faculty member or a senior faculty member. The aim of the book was to provide advice and tools to successfully navigate the various phases and aspects of academic life. The specific aspects discussed, as noted at the outset, pertained to:

1. Building and sustaining a research program
2. Writing a paper
3. Responding to reviews
4. Planning and monitoring through various stages of the PhD program
5. Becoming an effective teacher
6. Achieving work-life balance

I would like to close on a somewhat personal note by sharing my top-10 list of things that worked for me across the various pieces of advice shared in my chapters. Then, I pick two pieces of advice from each of the guest contributions.

So, from my chapters, my top-10 list of things that have most helped me...

1. Focus on a research project, not a research study (chapter 2). Focusing on a research project means you will collect more data than is necessary for just one paper. The additional data you collect should delve laterally into concepts and constructs, and, whenever possible, collect data related to competing and complementary theories.

2. Time management is crucial to success (chapter 2). Time management deserves attention at various level of abstraction. You should have papers in various stages of the research process. You should manage your days, weeks and months so as to devote time to papers in various stages—for instance, reserve your best times of day for the papers in the most intellectually demanding state (for me, this was writing).

3. The outlining tool in chapter 4 helps me stay on point and helps ensure that I put the right content in the right place of the paper. Daryl Bem's paper on writing an empirical journal article also has been very helpful to me. When I write a paper, I have these two "crutches" by my side at all times.

4. Revising a paper requires a systematic approach. I use punch lists to help me in the process (chapter 5). Create the outline for the new paper and write the new paper. Don't just edit the previous submission.

5. Teaching doesn't interfere with research like it is often made out to be (chapter 6). Teaching, like research, involves delivery of content to those who aren't as familiar with the material as you are. Understanding your strengths and weaknesses as a teacher will help you become a better researcher given the overlapping skill set.

6. Collaboration is vital to success in today's academic world but it should be done for the right reasons—i.e., effectiveness and efficiency gains (chapter 7). What has particularly worked to achieve these goals for me is mixing business and pleasure by collaborating with my best friends in the field.

7. The planning document (chapter 8) is vital to success in a PhD program. I found this immensely helpful both when I was a student and as an advisor. One of the critical elements of using the planning document over time is ensuring that a PhD student builds the entire set of skills required for success in the program and beyond.

8. Beware! Here comes the most unstructured time of your life: the dissertation! Manage it carefully so as to complete it successfully (chapter 9).

9. Managing your life as an assistant professor is easy (chapters 12 and 13): put your head down and work within your two or three research streams. As you get closer to the promotion and tenure evaluation, don't try to start new papers (they will seldom make it into the top journals in a short timeframe) but rather, move papers to closure. Ultimately, research is the most mobile currency you can have—work to building it up!

10. Reviewing is tremendously valuable (chapter 17). Not only does it provide you the opportunity to network, but also it gives the opportunity to learn from the reports of other reviewers and editors (and this will help your research).

The guest contributors have provided a great many pieces of advice and distilling them into two per contributor was not easy. As I said at the outset, this is more of a personal list—it's what appealed to me the most and it reflects varying levels of abstraction.

Dr. Maruping's chapter (chapter 3) provided a very useful perspective on building and sustaining a healthy pipeline of papers. It relates to my chapter 2. The two things that appealed to me most were:
- "Time" is of the essence. The chapter provided a great deal of insights into the time many things (e.g., papers) take and how best to manage your activities to be sensitive to that in various stages of your career, be it as a PhD student or an assistant professor.
- I think the "loner" strategy is infeasible, the "opportunist" strategy is inadvisable and the "managed program" strategy embodies the spirit of what can help build a successful research portfolio.

Dr. Sykes' chapter (chapter 10) had a very personal touch to it. It is rich with advice—of that, two things that stood out to me were:

- Work with organizations—it helps you collect good data. More importantly, you never know where in your rolodex your next data set may be hidden!
- The perfectionism-procrastination paradox is a big challenge not just for Tracy. On the one hand, you don't want to hand off garbage (be it to your advisor or your co-authors). On the other hand, you don't want to seek perfection (it cannot be achieved). Striking the right balance is crucial to success.

Dr. Grover's chapter (chapter 11) is filled with loads of advice that will help both PhD students and advisors alike in ensuring the success of students. Two specific golden nuggets to me were:

- The checklist (essay 3) is a terrific diagnostic tool that helps monitor progress and effect course corrections.
- Networking is crucial to success—do it well but do it right. Essay 4 offers enormous amount of advice on how to achieve this.

Dr. Brown's three chapters (chapters 14, 15 and 16) on teaching can transform a mediocre teacher into a thoughtful and effective teacher. Two key things that I know will help me as I continue my journey as a teacher are:

- The syllabus is a key document and writing a good syllabus is not easy. Chapter 15 provides many useful suggestions to produce a good syllabus.
- There are different types of course portfolios, each with a different purpose. Chapter 16 contains a lot of good advice on how to set up each different type of portfolio and what you can hope to get out of each one.

Dr. Burton-Jones' chapter (chapter 18) was appealing to me because of the way in which he was able to simplify—to transform complex advice into simple phrases. The phrases that stood out to me:

- 15 seconds! I never thought I could do research in 15 seconds! Like he says, I too may never achieve the ideal of 15 seconds but chunking tasks into small bits so they can be squeezed into small windows of time is something I aspire to do more.
- Suspend disbelief (and people's lives)—i.e., doing good by others and their research is key to the nobility of the profession and the creation of new knowledge.

Dr. Davis' chapter (chapter 19) contains valuable advice on how to make academic life work with your life in general. Two things in particular that struck me were:

- The lifestyle of an academic interferes with achieving balance. Make balance an explicit goal and follow the many pieces of advice offered in this chapter to achieve balance.
- Look forward! Even Gordon has, at times, failed to follow his advice.

Good luck on your journey down the road of success!

ENDNOTES

[1] As a critical part of the promotion and tenure evaluation process that is typically conducted during the sixth year as an assistant professor, most universities require letters from leading scholars in the field to assess the contributions and future potential of the person being evaluated for promotion and tenure.

[2] Acronym for the widely employed research model called the *Technology Acceptance Model.*

[3] Venkatesh, V., Morris, M. G., Davis, G. B., & Davis, F. D. (2003). User acceptance of information technology: Toward a unified view. *MIS Quarterly, 27*(3), 425–478.

[4] Venkatesh, V., Morris, M. G., Davis, G. B., & Davis, F. D. (2003). User acceptance of information technology: Toward a unified view. *MIS Quarterly, 27*(3), 425–478.

[5] Venkatesh, V. (2000). Determinants of perceived ease of use: Integrating control, intrinsic motivation, and emotion into the technology acceptance model. *Information Systems Research, 11*(4), 342–365.

[6] Venkatesh, V., & Davis, F. D. (2000). A theoretical extension of the technology acceptance model: Four longitudinal field studies. *Management Science, 46*(2), 186–204.

[7] Venkatesh, V., Morris, M. G., Davis, G. B., & Davis, F. D. (2003). User acceptance of information technology: Toward a unified view. *MIS Quarterly, 27*(3), 425–478.

[8] Venkatesh, V., Morris, M. G., Davis, G. B., & Davis, F. D. (2003). User acceptance of information technology: Toward a unified view. *MIS Quarterly, 27*(3), 425–478.

[9] Venkatesh, V., & Morris, M. G. (2000). Why don't men ever stop to ask for directions? Gender, social influence, and their role in technology acceptance and usage behavior. *MIS Quarterly, 24*(1), 115–139.

[10] Venkatesh, V., Morris, M. G., & Ackerman, P. L. (2000). A longitudinal field investigation of gender differences in individual technology adoption decision making processes. *Organizational Behavior and Human Decision Processes, 83*(1), 33–60.

[11] Morris, M. G., & Venkatesh, V. (2000). Age differences in technology adoption decisions: Implications for a changing workforce. *Personnel Psychology, 53*(2), 375–403.

[12] Venkatesh, V. (1999). Creation of favorable user perceptions: Exploring the role of intrinsic motivation. *MIS Quarterly, 23*(2), 239–260.

[13] Sykes, T. A., Venkatesh, V., & Gosain, S. (2009). Model of acceptance with peer support: A social network perspective to understand employees' system use. *MIS Quarterly, 33*(2), 371–393.

[14] Venkatesh, V., & Speier, C. (1999). Computer technology training in the workplace: A longitudinal investigation of the effect of mood. *Organizational Behavior and Human Decision Processes, 79*(1), 1–28.

[15] Venkatesh, V., & Johnson, P. (2002). Telecommuting technology implementations: A within- and between-subjects longitudinal field study. *Personnel Psychology, 55*(3), 661–688.

[16] Morris, M. G., & Venkatesh, V. (2010). Job characteristics and job satisfaction:

Understanding the role of enterprise resource planning system implementation. *MIS Quarterly, 34*(1), 143–161.

[17] Venkatesh, V., & Brown, S. A. (2001). A longitudinal investigation of personal computers in homes: Adoption determinants and emerging challenges. *MIS Quarterly, 25*(1), 71–102.

[18] This pertains to several of the papers shown in the table:

Venkatesh, V., & Davis, F. D. (2000). A theoretical extension of the technology acceptance model: Four longitudinal field studies. *Management Science, 46*(2), 186–204.

Venkatesh, V. (2000). Determinants of perceived ease of use: Integrating control, intrinsic motivation, and emotion into the technology acceptance model. *Information Systems Research, 11*(4), 342–365.

Venkatesh, V., & Davis, F. D. (1996). A model of the antecedents of perceived ease of use: Development and test. *Decision Sciences, 27*(3), 451–481.

Davis, F. D., & Venkatesh, V. (1996). A critical assessment of potential measurement biases in the technology acceptance model: Three experiments. *International Journal of Human-Computer Studies, 45*(1), 19–45.

Carswell, A. D., & Venkatesh, V. (2002). Learner outcomes in an asynchronous distance education environment. *International Journal of Human-Computer Studies, 56*(5), 475–494.

Venkatesh, V., Morris, M. G., Davis, G. B., & Davis, F. D. (2003). User acceptance of information technology: Toward a unified view. *MIS Quarterly, 27*(3), 425–478.

Venkatesh, V. (1999). Creation of favorable user perceptions: Exploring the role of intrinsic motivation. *MIS Quarterly, 23*(2), 239–260.

Venkatesh, V., & Speier, C. (2000). Creating an effective training environment for enhancing telework. *International Journal of Human-Computer Studies, 52*(6), 991–1005.

Venkatesh, V., & Speier, C. (1999). Computer technology training in the workplace: A longitudinal investigation of the effect of mood. *Organizational Behavior and Human Decision Processes, 79*(1), 1–28.

Venkatesh, V., & Morris, M. G. (2000). Why don't men ever stop to ask for directions? Gender, social influence, and their role in technology acceptance and usage behavior. *MIS Quarterly, 24*(1), 115–139.

Venkatesh, V., Morris, M. G., & Ackerman, P. L. (2000). A longitudinal field investigation of gender differences in individual technology adoption decision making processes. *Organizational Behavior and Human Decision Processes, 83*(1), 33–60.

Morris, M. G., & Venkatesh, V. (2000). Age differences in technology adoption decisions: Implications for a changing workforce. *Personnel Psychology, 53*(2), 375–403.

Venkatesh, V., & Johnson, P. (2002). Telecommuting technology implementations: A within- and between-subjects longitudinal field study. *Personnel Psychology, 55*(3), 661–688.

Venkatesh, V., Speier, C., & Morris, M. G. (2002). User acceptance enablers in individual decision-making about technology: Toward an integrated model. *Decision Sciences, 33*(2), 297–316.

Speier, C., & Venkatesh, V. (2002). The hidden minefields in the adoption of sales force automation technologies. *Journal of Marketing, 66*(3), 98–111.

Venkatesh, V., & Brown, S. A. (2001). A longitudinal investigation of personal computers in homes: Adoption determinants and emerging challenges. *MIS Quarterly, 25*(1), 71–102.

Brown, S. A., & Venkatesh, V. (2003). Bringing non-adopters along: The challenge facing the PC industry. *Communications of the ACM, 46*(3), 76–80.

Agarwal, R., & Venkatesh, V. (2002). Assessing a firm's web presence: A heuristic evaluation procedure for the measurement of usability. *Information Systems Research, 13*(2), 168–186.

Venkatesh, V., Ramesh, V., & Massey, A. (2003). Understanding usability in mobile commerce and ramifications for wireless design: 'e' ≠ 'm'. *Communications of the ACM, 46*(12), 53–56.

[19] Venkatesh, V. (2000). Determinants of perceived ease of use: Integrating control, intrinsic motivation, and emotion into the technology acceptance model. *Information Systems Research, 11*(4), 342–365.

[20] Such sole-authored papers are only possible if the advisor's role has been minimal in various aspects of the particular paper.

[21] Venkatesh, V. (1999). Creation of favorable user perceptions: Exploring the role of intrinsic motivation. *MIS Quarterly, 23*(2), 239–260.

[22] Venkatesh, V. (2000). Determinants of perceived ease of use: Integrating control, intrinsic motivation, and emotion into the technology acceptance model. *Information Systems Research, 11*(4), 342–365.

[23] Of course, as mentioned earlier, other research beyond the dissertation was also crucial to get tenure.

[24] Venkatesh, V. (1999). Creation of favorable user perceptions: Exploring the role of intrinsic motivation. *MIS Quarterly, 23*(2), 239–260.

[25] Venkatesh, V., & Johnson, P. (2002). Telecommuting technology implementations: A within- and between-subjects longitudinal field study. *Personnel Psychology, 55*(3), 661–688.

[26] Venkatesh, V., & Morris, M. G. (2000). Why don't men ever stop to ask for directions? Gender, social influence, and their role in technology acceptance and usage behavior. *MIS Quarterly, 24*(1), 115–139.

[27] Venkatesh, V., Morris, M. G., & Ackerman, P. L. (2000). A longitudinal field investigation of gender differences in individual technology adoption decision making processes. *Organizational Behavior and Human Decision Processes, 83*(1), 33–60.

[28] Morris, M. G., & Venkatesh, V. (2000). Age differences in technology adoption decisions: Implications for a changing workforce. *Personnel Psychology, 53*(2), 375–403.

[29] Venkatesh, V., Morris, M. G., Sykes, T. A., & Ackerman, P. L. (2004). Individual reactions to new technologies in the workplace: The role of gender as a psychological construct. *Journal of Applied Social Psychology, 34*(3), 445–467.

[30] Morris, M. G., Venkatesh, V., & Ackerman, P. L. (2005). Gender and age differences in employee decisions about new technology: An extension to the theory of planned behavior. *IEEE Transactions on Engineering Management, 52*(1), 69–84.

[31] Agarwal, R., & Venkatesh, V. (2002). Assessing a firm's web presence: A heuristic evaluation procedure for the measurement of usability. *Information Systems Research, 13*(2), 168–186.

[32] Venkatesh, V., & Agarwal, R. (2006). From visitors into customers: A usability-centric perspective on purchase behavior in electronic channels. *Management Science, 52*(3), 367–382.

[33] Venkatesh, V., & Ramesh, V. (2006). Web and wireless site usability: Understanding differences and modeling use. *MIS Quarterly, 30*(1), 181–206.

[34] Straub, D. W. (2008). Why do top journals reject good papers? *MIS Quarterly, 32*(3), iii-viii.

[35] Maruping, L. M., & Agarwal, R. (2004). Managing team interpersonal processes through technology: A task-technology fit perspective. *Journal of Applied Psychology, 89*(6), 975–990.

[36] Cao, Q., Maruping, L. M., & Takeuchi, R. (2006). Disentangling the effects of CEO turnover and succession on organizational capabilities: A social network perspective. *Organization Science, 17*(5), 563–576.

[37] Venkatesh, V., Maruping, L. M., & Brown, S. A. (2006). Role of time in self-prediction of behavior. *Organizational Behavior and Human Decision Processes, 100*(2), 160–176.

[38] Stewart, K. J., Ammeter, A. P., & Maruping, L. M. (2006). Impacts of license choice and organizational sponsorship on user interest and development activity in open source software projects. *Information Systems Research, 17*(2), 126–144.

[39] Bem, D. J. (2003). Writing the empirical journal article. In J. M. Darley, M. P. Zanna, & H. L. Roediger III (Eds.), *The compleat academic: A practical guide for the beginning social scientist* (pp. 185–219). Washington DC: American Psychological Association.

[40] Bergh, D. D. (2003). From the editors: Thinking strategically about contributions. *Academy of Management Journal, 46*(2), 135–136.

[41] Feldman, D. C. (2004). The devil is in the details: Converting good research into publishable articles. *Journal of Management, 30*(1), 1–6.

[42] Rynes, S. L. (2002). From the editors: Some reflection on contribution. *Academy of Management Journal, 45*(2), 311–313.

[43] Schminke, M. (2004). From the editors: Raising the bamboo curtain. *Academy of Management Journal, 47*(3), 310–314.

[44] Starbuck, W. H. (1999). *Why I hate passive verbs and love my word processor.* Retrieved from http://www.stern.nyu.edu/~wstarbuc/Writing/Fussy.htm

[45] Weber, R. (2003). Editor's comment: Theoretically speaking, *MIS Quarterly, 27*(3), iii–xii.

[46] Whetten, D. A. (1989). What constitutes a theoretical contribution? *Academy of Management Review, 14*(4), 490–495.

[47] Perceived usefulness is defined as the degree to which an individual believes that using the system will help him or her to attain gains in job performance (Davis et al. 1989). Perceived ease of use is defined as the degree to which a person believes that using an IT will be free of effort (Davis et al. 1989). Intention to use technology is defined as the degree to which a person has formulated conscious plans to use or not use a technology in the future (Venkatesh et al. 2006).

[48] Davis, F. D., Bagozzi, R. P., & Warshaw, P. R. (1989). User acceptance of computer technology: A comparison of two theoretical models. *Management Science, 35*(8), 980–1002.

[49] Venkatesh, V., Maruping, L. M., & Brown, S. A. (2006). Role of time in self-prediction of behavior. *Organizational Behavior and Human Decision Processes, 100*(2), 160–176.

[50] Van der Heijden, H. (2004). User acceptance of hedonic information systems. *MIS Quarterly, 28*(4), 695–704.

[51] Venkatesh, V. (1999). Creation of favorable user perceptions: Exploring the role of intrinsic motivation. *MIS Quarterly, 23*(2), 239–260.

[52] Venkatesh, V., & Morris, M. G. (2000). Why don't men ever stop to ask for directions? Gender, social influence, and their role in technology acceptance and usage behavior. *MIS Quarterly, 24*(1), 115–139.

[53] Davis, F. D., Bagozzi, R. P., & Warshaw, P. R. (1989). User acceptance of computer technology: A comparison of two theoretical models. *Management Science, 35*(8), 980–1002.

[54] Venkatesh, V., & Davis, F. D. (2000). A theoretical extension of the technology acceptance model: Four longitudinal field studies. *Management Science, 46*(2), 186–204.

[55] Venkatesh, V. (2000). Determinants of perceived ease of use: Integrating control, intrinsic motivation, and emotion into the technology acceptance model. *Information Systems Research, 11*(4), 342–365.

[56] Bem, D. J. (2003). Writing the empirical journal article. In J. M. Darley, M. P. Zanna, & H. L. Roediger III (Eds.), *The compleat academic: A practical guide for the beginning social scientist* (pp. 185–219). Washington DC: American Psychological Association.

[57] Bem, D. J. (1995). Writing a review article for psychological bulletin. *Psychological Bulletin, 118*(2), 172–177.

[58] Bem, D. J. (2003). Writing the empirical journal article. In J. M. Darley, M. P. Zanna, & H. L. Roediger III (Eds.), *The compleat academic: A practical guide for the beginning social scientist* (pp. 185–219). Washington DC: American Psychological Association.

[59] Bem, D. J. (2003). Writing the empirical journal article. In J. M. Darley, M. P. Zanna, & H. L. Roediger III (Eds.), *The compleat academic: A practical guide for the beginning social scientist* (pp. 185–219). Washington DC: American Psychological Association.

[60] Boice, R. (1990). *Professors as writers.* New York, NY: New Forums Press.

[61] Bem, D. J. (2003). Writing the empirical journal article. In J. M. Darley, M. P. Zanna, & H. L. Roediger III (Eds.), *The compleat academic: A practical guide for the beginning social scientist* (pp. 185–219). Washington DC: American Psychological Association.

[62] Bem, D. J. (1995). Writing a review article for psychological bulletin. *Psychological Bulletin, 118*(2), 172–177.

[63] Venkatesh, V., Morris, M. G., & Ackerman, P. L. (2000). A longitudinal field investigation of gender differences in individual technology adoption decision making processes. *Organizational Behavior and Human Decision Processes, 83*(1), 33–60.

[64] Agarwal, R., & Venkatesh, V. (2002). Assessing a firm's web presence: A heuristic

evaluation procedure for the measurement of usability. *Information Systems Research, 13*(2), 168–186.

[65] Dennis, A. R., Valacich, J. S., Fuller, M. A., & Schneider, C. (2006). Research standards for promotion and tenure in information systems. *MIS Quarterly, 30*(1), 1–12.

[66] Saunders, C. (2005). From the trenches: Thoughts on developmental reviewing. *MIS Quarterly, 29*(2), iii–xii.

[67] Agarwal, R., Echambadi, R., Franco, A. M., & Sarkar, M. (2006). Reap rewards: Maximizing benefits from reviewer comments. *Academy of Management Journal, 49*(2), 191–196.

[68] Bergh, D. D. (2006). Editing the 2004 AMJ best article award winner. *Academy of Management Journal, 49*(2), 197–202.

[69] Daft, R. L. (1985). Why I recommended that your manuscript be rejected and what you can do about it. In L. L. Cummings, & P. J. Frost (Eds.), *Publishing in the organizational sciences* (pp. 193–209). Irwin, Homewood, IL: Sage Publications Inc.

[70] Lee, A. (1995). Reviewing a manuscript for publication. *Journal of Operations Management, 13*(1), 87–92.

[71] Rynes, S. L. (2006a). Making the most of the review process: Lessons from award winning authors. *Academy of Management Journal, 49*(2), 189–190.

[72] Rynes, S. L. (2006b). Observations on 'Anatomy of an R&R' and other reflections. *Academy of Management Journal, 49*(2), 208–214.

[73] Seibert, S. E. (2006). Anatomy of an R&R (or, reviewers are an author's best friends…). *Academy of Management Journal, 49*(2), 203–207.

[74] Bala, H., & Venkatesh, V. (2007). Assimilation of interorganizational business process standards. *Information Systems Research, 18*(3), 340–362.

[75] Dyer, J. H., & Singh, H. (1998). The relational view: Cooperative strategy and sources of interorganizational competitive advantages. *Academy of Management Review, 23*(4), 660–679.

[76] DiMaggio, P., & Powell, W. W. (1983). The iron cage revisited: Institutional isomorphism and collective rationality in organizational fields. *American Sociological Review, 48*(2), 147–160.

[77] Gilbert, C. G. (2005). Unbundling the structure of inertia: Resources versus routine rigidity. *Academy of Management Journal, 48*(5), 741–763.

[78] Yin, R. K. (2002). *Case study research, design and methods.* Newbury Park, CA: Sage Publications.

[79] Benbasat, I., Goldstein, D. K., & Mead, M. (1987). The case research strategy in studies of information systems. *MIS Quarterly, 11*(3), 369–386.

[80] Dubé, L., & Paré, G. (2003). Rigor in information systems positivist case research: Current practices, trends, and recommendations. *MIS Quarterly, 27*(4), 597–636.

[81] Lee, A. S. (1989). A scientific methodology for MIS case studies. *MIS Quarterly, 13*(1), 32–50.

[82] Sambamurthy, V., & Zmud, R. W. (1999). Arrangements for information technology governance: A theory of multiple contingencies. *MIS Quarterly, 23*(2), 261–290.

[83] Malhotra, A., Gosain, S., & El Sawy, O. A. (2005). Absorptive capacity configurations in supply chains: Gearing for partner-enabled market knowledge creation. *MIS Quarterly, 29*(1), 145–187.

[84] Dyer, J. H., & Singh, H. (1998). The relational view: Cooperative strategy and sources of interorganizational competitive advantages. *Academy of Management Review, 23*(4), 660–679.

[85] DiMaggio, P., & Powell, W. W. (1983). The iron cage revisited: Institutional isomorphism and collective rationality in organizational fields. *American Sociological Review, 48*(2), 147–160.

[86] Gilbert, C. G. (2005). Unbundling the structure of inertia: Resources versus routine rigidity. *Academy of Management Journal, 48*(5), 741–763.

[87] Yin, R. K. (2002). *Case study research, design and methods.* Newbury Park, CA: Sage Publications.

[88] Benbasat, I., Goldstein, D. K., & Mead, M. (1987). The case research strategy in studies of information systems. *MIS Quarterly, 11*(3), 369–386.

[89] Dubé, L., & Paré, G. (2003). Rigor in information systems positivist case research: Current practices, trends, and recommendations. *MIS Quarterly, 27*(4), 597–636.

[90] Lee, A. S. (1989). A scientific methodology for MIS case studies. *MIS Quarterly, 13*(1), 32–50.

[91] Sambamurthy, V., & Zmud, R. W. (1999). Arrangements for information technology governance: A theory of multiple contingencies. *MIS Quarterly, 23*(2), 261–290.

[92] Lavie, D. (2006). Capability reconfiguration: An analysis of incumbent responses to technological change. *Academy of Management Review, 31*(1), 153–174.

[93] Weitzel, T., Beimborn, D., & Koniga, W. forthcoming. Unified economic model of standard diffusion: The impact of standardization cost, network effects, and network topology. *MIS Quarterly.*

[94] Zhu, K., Kraemer, K. L., Gurbaxani, V., & Xu, S. forthcoming. Migration to open-standard interorganizational systems: Network effects, switching costs, and path dependency. *MIS Quarterly.*

[95] Benbasat, I., Goldstein, D. K., & Mead, M. (1987). The case research strategy in studies of information systems. *MIS Quarterly, 11*(3), 369–386.

[96] Dubé, L., & Paré, G. (2003). Rigor in information systems positivist case research: Current practices, trends, and recommendations. *MIS Quarterly, 27*(4), 597–636.

[97] Lapointe, L., & Rivard, S. (2005). A multilevel model of resistance to information technology implementation. *MIS Quarterly, 29*(3), 461–491.

[98] Lee, A. S. (1989). A scientific methodology for MIS case studies. *MIS Quarterly, 13*(1), 32–50.

[99] Sambamurthy, V., & Zmud, R. W. (1999). Arrangements for information technology governance: A theory of multiple contingencies. *MIS Quarterly, 23*(2), 261–290.

[100] Sherif, K., Zmud, R. W., & Brown, G. J. (2006). Managing peer-to-peer conflicts in disruptive information technology innovations: The case of software reuse. *MIS Quarterly, 30*(2), 339–356.

[101] Sambamurthy, V., & Zmud, R. W. (1999). Arrangements for information technology governance: A theory of multiple contingencies. *MIS Quarterly, 23*(2), 261–290.

[102] Sherif, K., Zmud, R. W., & Brown, G. J. (2006). Managing peer-to-peer conflicts in disruptive information technology innovations: The case of software reuse. *MIS Quarterly, 30*(2), 339–356.

[103] Bain, K. (2004). *What the best college teachers do.* Cambridge, MA: Harvard University Press.

[104] MaKeachie, W. J. (1999). *Teaching tips: Strategies, research, and theory for college and university teachers.* Boston, MA: Houghton Mifflin Company.

[105] Rotenberg, R. L. (2005). *The art and craft of college teaching: A guide for new professors and graduate students.* Chicago, IL: Active Learning Books.

[106] Provitera-McGlynn, A. (2001). *Successful beginnings for college teaching.* Madison, WI: Atwood Publications.

[107] Filene, P. (2006). *The joy of teaching: A practical guide for new college instructors.* Chapel Hill, NC: University of North Carolina Press.

[108] Please be mindful of your university's *Institutional Review Board* guidelines and rules.

[109] Agarwal, R., & Venkatesh, V. (2002). Assessing a firm's web presence: A heuristic evaluation procedure for the measurement of usability. *Information Systems Research, 13*(2), 168–186.

[110] Venkatesh, V., Ramesh, V., & Massey, A. (2003). Understanding usability in mobile commerce and ramifications for wireless design: 'e' ≠ 'm'. *Communications of the ACM, 46*(12), 53–56.

[111] Venkatesh, V., & Agarwal, R. (2006). Turning visitors into customers: A usability-centric perspective on purchase behavior in electronic channels. *Management Science, 52*(3), 367–382.

[112] Venkatesh, V., & Ramesh, V. (2006). Web and wireless site usability: Understanding differences and modeling use. *MIS Quarterly, 30*(1), 181–206.

[113] Venkatesh, V., & Johnson, P. (2002). Telecommuting technology Implementations: A within- and between-subjects longitudinal field study. *Personnel Psychology, 55*(3), 661–688.

[114] Venkatesh, V., Morris, M. G., & Ackerman, P. L. (2000). A longitudinal field investigation of gender differences in individual technology adoption decision making processes. *Organizational Behavior and Human Decision Processes, 83*(1), 33–60.

[115] Bacharach, S. B. (1989). Organizational theories: Some criteria for evaluation. *Academy of Management Review, 14*(4), 496–515.

[116] Dubin, R. (1976). Theory building in applied areas. In M. D. Dunnette (Ed.), *Handbook of industrial and organizational psychology* (pp. 17–40). Chicago, IL: Rand McNally.

[117] Eisenhardt, K. (1989). Building theories from case study research. *Academy of Management Review, 14*(4), 532–550.

[118] Feldman, D. C. (2004). What are we talking about when we talk about theory? *Journal of Management, 30*(5), 565–567.

[119] George, J. M., & Jones, G. R. (2000). The role of time in theory and theory building. *Journal of Management, 26*(4), 657–684.

[120] Langley, A. (1999). Strategies for theorizing from process data. *Academy of Management Review, 24*(4), 691–710.

[121] Poole, M. S., & Van de ven, A. H. (1989). Using paradox to build management and organization theories. *Academy of Management Review, 14*(4), 562–578.

[122] Sutton, R. I., & Staw, B. M. (1995). What theory is not. *Administrative Science Quarterly, 40*(3), 371–384.

[123] Weick, K. E. (1989). Theory construction as disciplined imagination. *Academy of Management Review, 14*(4), 516–531.

[124] Weick, K. E. (1995). What theory is not, theorizing is. *Administrative Science Quarterly, 40*(3), 385–390.

[125] Whetten, D. A. (1989). What constitutes a theoretical contribution. *Academy of Management Review, 14*(4), 490–495.

[126] Weber, R. (2003). Editor's comment: Theoretically speaking. *MIS Quarterly, 27*(3), iii–xii.

[127] Zmud, R. W. (1998). Editor's comments. *MIS Quarterly, 22*(2), xxix–xxxii.

[128] Weber, R. (2003). Editor's comment: Theoretically speaking. *MIS Quarterly, 27*(3), iii–xii.

[129] Whetten, D. A. (1989). What constitutes a theoretical contribution. *Academy of Management Review, 14*(4), 490–495.

[130] Weick, K. E. (1995). What theory is not, theorizing is. *Administrative Science Quarterly, 40*(3), 385–390.

[131] Whetten, D. A. (1989). What constitutes a theoretical contribution. *Academy of Management Review, 14*(4), 490–495.

[132] Weber, R. (2003). Editor's comment: Theoretically speaking. *MIS Quarterly, 27*(3), iii–xii.

[133] Johns, G. (2006). The essential impact of context on organizational behavior. *Academy of Management Review, 31*(2), 386–408.

[134] Alvesson, M., & Karreman, D. (2007). Constructing mystery: Empirical matters in theory development. *Academy of Management Review, 32*(4), 1265–1281.

[135] Sutton, R. I., & Staw, B. M. (1995). What theory is not. *Administrative Science Quarterly, 40*(3), 371–384.

[136] Sutton, R. I., & Staw, B. M. (1995). What theory is not. *Administrative Science Quarterly, 40*(3), 371–384.

[137] Weick, K. E. (1995). What theory is not, theorizing is. *Administrative Science Quarterly, 40*(3), 385–390.

[138] Benbasat, I., & Zmud, R. W. (1999). Empirical research in information systems: The practice of relevance. *MIS Quarterly, 23*(1), 3–16.

[139] Lee, A. (1999). Strategizing for compelling and significant research. *MIS Quarterly, 22*(2), xxv–xxviii.

[140] Zmud, R. W. (1996). On rigor and relevance. *MIS Quarterly, 20*(3), xxxivv–xxxix.

[141] Benbasat, I., & Zmud, R. W. (1999). Empirical research in information systems: The practice of relevance. *MIS Quarterly, 23*(1), 3–16.

[142] Sutton, R. I., & Staw, B. M. (1995). What theory is not. *Administrative Science Quarterly, 40*(3), 371–384.

[143] Weick, K. E. (1995). What theory is not, theorizing is. *Administrative Science Quarterly, 40*(3), 385–390.

[144] Weick, K. E. (1995). What theory is not, theorizing is. *Administrative Science Quarterly, 40*(3), 385–390.

[145] Runkel, P. J., & Runkel, J. (1984). *A guide to usage for writers and students in the social sciences.* Totowa, NJ: Rowman and Allanheld.

[146] Weick, K. E. (1995). What theory is not, theorizing is. *Administrative Science Quarterly, 40*(3), 385–390.

[147] Sutton, R. I., & Staw, B. M. (1995). What theory is not. *Administrative Science Quarterly, 40*(3), 371–384.

[148] Weick, K. E. (1995). What theory is not, theorizing is. *Administrative Science Quarterly, 40*(3), 385–390.

[149] Sutton, R. I., & Staw, B. M. (1995). What theory is not. *Administrative Science Quarterly, 40*(3), 371–384.

[150] Robey, D. (2001). Answers to doctoral students' frequently asked questions (FAQs). *Decision Line, 32*(2), 10–12.

[151] Schniederjans, M. J. (2001). A short bill of rights for Ph.D. students. *Decision Line, 32*(4), 11–12.

[152] Davis, G. B., & Parker, C. A. (1997). *Writing the doctoral dissertation.* New York: Barron's Educational Series, Inc.

[153] Gordon, P. J. (2003). Advising to avoid or to cope with dissertation hang-ups. *Academy of Management Learning & Education, 2*(2), 181–187.

[154] Davis, G. B. (2000). Writing a doctoral dissertation: A systematic approach. *Decision Line, 31*(2), 19–20.

[155] Aronson, J. E. (2001). Working on the doctoral dissertation. *Decision Line, 32*(5), 7–9.

[156] Grover, V., & Malhotra, M. K. (2003). Interaction between a doctoral student and advisor: Making it work! *Decision Line, 21*(4), 457–473.

[157] Robey, D. (2001). Answers to doctoral students' frequently asked questions (FAQs). *Decision Line, 32*(2), 10–12.

[158] Nahapiet, J, & Ghoshal, S. (1998). Social capital, intellectual capital, and the organizational advantage. *Academy of Management Review, 23*(2), 242–266.

[159] Attributed to W. Clement Stone

[160] Sykes, T. A., Venkatesh, V, & Johnson, J. (2007). Enterprise system implementation: Personality, system-related advice networks and job performance. *Proceedings of the International Conference for Information Systems.*

[161] Grover, V. (2004). A rough model for success in doctoral study. *Decision Line, 35*(5), 23–25.

[162] Grover, V., (2001). 10 mistakes doctoral students make in managing their program. *Decision Line, 32*(3), 11–13.

[163] Grover, V. (2006). How am I doing? Checklist for doctoral students at various stages of their program. *Decision Line, 37*(2), 24–26.

[164] Grover, V. (2010). "Hi, I'm me": Judicious networking for the doctoral student. *Decision Line, 41*(1), 10–12.

[165] Grover, V. (2004). A rough model for success in doctoral study. *Decision Line, 35*(5), 23–25.

[166] Azuma, R. T. (1997). *"So long, and thanks for the Ph.D.!" a.k.a. "Everything I wanted to know about C.S. graduate school at the beginning but didn't learn until later."* Retrieved from http://www.cs.unc.edu/~azuma/hitch4.html

[167] Grover, V., & Malhotra, M. K. (2003). Interaction between a doctoral student and advisor: Making it work! *Decision Line, 34*(1), 16–18.

[168] Dennis, A. R., Valacich, J. S., Fuller, M. A., & Schneider, C. (2006). Research standards for promotion and tenure in information systems. *MIS Quarterly, 30*(1), 1–12.

[169] Angelo, T. A., & Cross, K. P. (1993). *Classroom assessment techniques: A handbook for college teachers.* San Francisco, CA: Jossey-Bass Publishers.

[170] Johnson, D. W., Johnson, R. T., & Smith, K. A. (1991). *Active learning: Cooperation in the college classroom,* Edina, MN: Interaction Book Company.

[171] Huba, M. E., & Freed, J. E. (1999). *Learner-centered assessment on college campuses: Shifting the focus from teaching to learning,* Needham Heights, MA: Allyn and Bacon.

[172] Seldin, P., Miller, J. E., & Seldin, C.A. (2010). *The teaching portfolio: A practical guide to improved performance and promotion/tenure decisions,* Fourth Edition, San Francisco, CA: Jossey-Bass Publishers.

[173] Boice, R. (2000). *Advice for new faculty members.* Needham Heights, MA: Allyn & Bacon.

[174] Davis, B. G. (1993). *Tools for teaching,* San Francisco: Jossey-Bass Publishers.

[175] Fink, L. D. (2003). *Creating significant learning experiences: An integrated approach to designing college courses,* San Francisco, CA: Jossey-Bass Publishers.

[176] McKeachie, W. J. (2006). *McKeachie's teaching tips: Strategies, research, and theory for college and university teachers,* Twelfth Edition, Boston, MA: Houghton Mifflin.

[177] Walvoord, B. E., Anderson, V. J., & Angelo, T. A. (1998). *Effective grading: A tool for learning and assessment,* San Francisco, CA: Jossey-Bass Publishers.

[178] *New directions for teaching & learning,* Jossey-Bass, http://www.josseybass.com/WileyCDA/Section/id-290038.html

[179] Covey, S. R. (1990). *The 7 habits of highly effective people,* New York, NY: Free Press.

[180] Davis, B. G. (1993). *Tools for teaching,* San Francisco: Jossey-Bass Publishers.

[181] Huba, M. E., & Freed, J. E. (1999). *Learner-centered assessment on college campuses: Shifting the focus from teaching to learning,* Needham Heights, MA: Allyn and Bacon.

[182] Kulik, J. A., & McKeachie, W. J. (1975). The evaluation of teachers in higher education. In

E N. Kerlinger (ed.), *Review of research in education*. Itasca: Peacock.

[183] Marsh, H. W., & Dunkin, M. (1992). Students' evaluations of university teaching: A multidimensional perspective. In J.C. Smart (Ed.), *Higher education: Handbook on theory and research*, 8, 143–234. New York: Agathon Press.

[184] McKeachie, W. J. (1979). Student ratings of faculty: A reprise. *Academe, 6S* (6), 384–397.

[185] Anderson, K., & Miller, E. (1997). Gender and student evaluations of teaching. *Political Science and Politics*, 30(2), 216–219.

[186] Gilbaugh, J. W. (1982). Renner substantiate. *Phi Delta Kappan, 63*, 428.

[187] Marsh, H. W. (1987). Student evaluations of university teaching: Research findings, methodological issues, and directions for future research. *International Journal of Educational Research, 11*, 253–388.

[188] Rice, L. (1988). Student evaluation of teaching: Problems and prospects. *Teaching Philosophy, 11*, 329–344.

[189] Please note that there are rules governing the protection of human subjects in research. It is important to ensure all research that involves humans—including pedagogical research—complies with your institutional review board requirements, if you intend to use the data collected for the purpose of evaluating effectiveness and/or student learning in a pedagogical publication.

[190] Bloom, B. S. (1956). *Taxonomy of educational objectives, handbook I: The cognitive domain.* New York: David McKay Co. Inc.

[191] Johnson, D. W., Johnson, R. T., & Smith, K. A. (1991). *Active learning: Cooperation in the college classroom*, Edina, MN: Interaction Book Company.

[192] Brown, S. A., & Klein, B. (2006). Are cooperative learning techniques fragile in information systems: An examination in the context of a database management course. *Journal of Informatics Education Research*, 8(2), 15–36.

[193] Massey, A. P., Brown, S. A., & Johnston, J. D. (2005). Teaching tip: It's all fun and games … Until students learn. *Journal of Information Systems Education, 16*(1), 9–14.

[194] Lee, A. S. (1995). Reviewing a manuscript for publication. *Journal of Operations Management, 13*(1), 87–92.

[195] Miller, C. C. (2006). Peer review in the organizational and management sciences: Prevalence and effects of reviewer hostility, bias and dissensus. *Academy of Management Journal, 49*(3), 425–431.

[196] Saunders, C. (2005). From the trenches: Thoughts on developmental reviewing. *MIS Quarterly*, 29(2), iii–xii.

[197] Schminke, M. (2002). From the editors: Tensions. *Academy of Management Journal, 45*(3), 487–490.

[198] Agarwal, R., Echambadi, R., Fraco, A. M., & Sarkar, M. B. (2006). Reap rewards: Maximizing benefits from reviewer comments. *Academy of Management Journal, 49*(2), 191–196.

[199] Bergh, D. D. (2006). Editing the 2004 AMJ best article award winner. *Academy of Management Journal, 49*(2), 197–202.

[200] Seibert, S. E. (2006). Anatomy of an R&R (Or, reviewers are an author's best friends…). *Academy of Management Journal, 49*(2), 203–207.

[201] Feldman, D. C. (2004). Being a developmental reviewer: Easier said than done. *Journal of Management, 30*(2), 161–164.

[202] Saunders, C. (2005). From the trenches: Thoughts on developmental reviewing. *MIS Quarterly, 29*(2), iii–xii.

[203] During the final revision of this chapter, I found the chapter in which this is written (Gist 1996). I was surprised to find that the actual phrase is "…an oncoming locomotive!" Nonetheless, just as having keywords and phrases is useful, appropriating them is too, so I will stay with my version!

[204] Gist, M. E. (1996). Getting tenure. In P. J. Frost, & M. S. Taylor (Eds.), *Rhythms of academic life: Personal accounts of careers in academia.* Thousand Oaks, CA: Sage Publications Inc.

[205] Glick, W. H., Miller, C. C., & Cardinal, L. B. (2007). Making a life in the field of organization science. *Journal of Organizational Behavior, 28,* 817–835.

[206] Van de Ven, A. (2007). *Engaged scholarship: A guide for organizational and social research.* New York: Oxford University Press.

[207] Weick, K. E. (1995). *Sensemaking in organizations.* Thousand Oaks, CA: Sage Publications Inc.

[208] Grover, V., Straub, D., & Galluch, P. (2009). Turning the corner: The influence of positive thinking on the information systems field. *MIS Quarterly, 33*(1), iii-viii.

[209] Davis, G. B. (2009). Useful lessons from my career as an academic in information systems. *Communications of the Association for Information Systems, 25*(36), 437–449.

[210] Davis, G. B., & Parker, C. A. (1997). *Writing the doctoral dissertation.* New York: Barron's Educational Series, Inc.

[211] Parkinson, C. N. (1955, November). Parkinson's law. *The Economist.* Retrieved from http://www.economist.com/node/14116121?story_id=1411612.

Lightning Source UK Ltd.
Milton Keynes UK
UKOW02f2319071013
218630UK00003B/11/P